D0530114

Language Hub

PRE-INTERMEDIATE
Student's Book

DANIEL BRAYSHAW
JON HIRD

macmillan
education

B1

Contents

	LESSON · OBJECTIVES	GRAMMAR	VOCABULARY	PRONUNCIATION	READING · LISTENING	SPEAKING · WRITING
U7	**MIND**					
7.1	**Smile** (p62) Discuss what makes you happy	**articles**	feelings	/ə/ (schwa) in *a / an*	read an article about smiling	do a class survey about everyday things that make people happy
7.2	**The internet and the brain** (p64) Write an online comment about the effects of the internet	*used to*	shortened words	*used to*	read a blog about the effect of the internet on our brains	write a comment on a blog discuss the effects of the internet
7.3	**Intelligence** (p66) Talk about intelligence and achievements	**no article (*school*, *the school*)**	phrasal verbs	practising *the*: /ði:/ or /ðə/	listen to a podcast about a child prodigy **KEY SKILL** Listening for the order of events	**SPEAKING HUB** give a presentation about a child prodigy
7.4	**Café Hub** **Neena's dinner** (p68) Describe an object and say what you use it for		describe an object and say what you use it for	objects	▶ watch someone describing an object and saying what you use it for	talk about objects
	UNIT REVIEW p70	**WRITING** (p164) Write a survey report	**KEY SKILL** Using survey report language			
U8	**ART**					
8.1	**Musical taste** (p72) Talk about taste in music and your favourite songs	**reflexive pronouns**	music	consonant clusters in words	listen to a podcast about music read a short text about a radio programme	talk about types of music you like
8.2	**Unusual art** (p74) Talk about art and artists	**infinitive of purpose**	types of art	/ɪ/ and /i:/	read a blog about art	talk about art
8.3	**Telling stories** (p76) Describe films and books	**first conditional**	film and book genres; adjectives for describing films and books	word stress in longer words	listen to a podcast about films and books **KEY SKILL** Identifying contrasts	**SPEAKING HUB** recommend a film or book
8.4	**Café Hub** **First date** (p78) Show interest in a topic		show interest in a topic	intonation	▶ watch people showing interest in a topic	show interest
	UNIT REVIEW p80	**WRITING** (p165) Write a review	**KEY SKILL** Describing and recommending			
U9	**MONEY**					
9.1	**Spending money** (p82) Talk about attitudes to money and about spending money	**second conditional**	prepositions in money phrases	/ɑ:/, /ʌ/ and /æ/	read an article about whether spending money can buy you happiness	talk about spending money
9.2	**Getting and giving** (p84) Talk about philanthropy and charities	**defining relative clauses**	verbs connected with money	/s/ and /z/	listen to a lecture about philanthropists	discuss different charities and attitudes towards giving money to charity
9.3	**Who needs money?** (p86) Discuss your skills and how they could help others	**gerunds**	*make* and *do* expressions	/ʒ/ and /dʒ/	read an article about bartering **KEY SKILL** Using context to guess unknown words	**SPEAKING HUB** speak about exchanging skills and services
9.4	**Café Hub** **Difficult customer** (p88) Go shopping for clothes and ask for a refund		go shopping for clothes and ask for a refund	adding emphasis	▶ watch someone shopping for clothes and asking for a refund	roleplay buying and returning a gift
	UNIT REVIEW p90	**WRITING** (p166) Write a 'for sale' advert	**KEY SKILL** Describing a product			

Welcome

USEFUL PHRASES
Classroom

🔊 0.1 **A** Write the words in the correct order to make useful questions for the classroom. Listen and check.

1 repeat / please / that, / Can / you / ?
2 say / do / How / you / English / *trabajar* / in / ?
3 slowly, / Could / speak / more / please / you / ?
4 do / pronounce / How / you / that / ?
5 spell / do / that / you / How / ?
6 *brilliant* / What / mean / does / ?

Dates

B SPEAK Work in pairs. Answer the questions.

1 Which months have exactly 30 days?
2 What are the days of the week?
3 How do you say the ordinal numbers 1–20?
4 What date is it today?

PRONUNCIATION
Word stress

🔊 0.2 **A** Listen and underline the stressed syllables. Then listen again and repeat the words.

happy   polite   amazing   beautiful

The /ə/ sound

🔊 0.3 **B** Listen and underline the schwa /ə/ sound. Then listen again and repeat the words.

father   magazine   afternoon   actor

Third person -*s* endings and past simple regular endings

🔊 0.4 **C** How do you pronounce the underlined sounds? Listen and repeat. Choose the correct option.

1 work<u>s</u>   /s/ /z/ /ɪz/
2 ha<u>s</u>   /s/ /z/ /ɪz/
3 finish<u>es</u>   /s/ /z/ /ɪz/
4 play<u>ed</u>   /d/ /t/ /ɪd/
5 watch<u>ed</u>   /d/ /t/ /ɪd/
6 want<u>ed</u>   /d/ /t/ /ɪd/

GRAMMAR
Tenses, structures and auxiliary verbs

A Choose the correct words to complete the questions.

1 What *do / does / are* you do?
2 *Are / Is / Can* you cook?
3 *Were / Will / Are* you reading a good book at the moment?
4 What *is / am / are* your parents' names?
5 Where *do / does / is* your best friend live?
6 Can you *swimming / swim / to swim*?

B SPEAK Work in pairs. Ask and answer the questions in Exercise A.

VOCABULARY
Word sets

A Look at the word sets. Cross out the odd one out. Check your answers with a partner and explain your choices.

1 serious   ~~old~~   friendly   happy

2 at five o'clock   next to me   in the afternoon   on Tuesday

3 opposite the bank   four years ago   near the school   behind the library

4 egg   bottle   bag   tin

5 two years ago   in a month   last Friday   yesterday evening

6 banana   apple   bread   orange

Parts of speech

B Match the parts of speech in the box with the words in **bold**.

~~adjective~~   adverb   article   auxiliary   noun   preposition   verb

1 My **favourite** subject is English.   *adjective*
2 I **read** emails in English at work.   _____
3 There are 12 students **in** our class.   _____
4 **Do** you speak any other languages?   _____
5 We have **a** test today.   _____
6 This is my new English **book**.   _____
7 Please listen **carefully**.   _____

Question words

C Complete the questions with the words in the box.

How many   How much   ~~What~~   When   Where   Who   Why

1 ___*What*___ 's your name?
2 _____ are you from?
3 _____ is your birthday?
4 _____ brothers and sisters do you have?
5 _____ do you know in this class?
6 _____ are you studying English? Do you need it for work?
7 _____ time do you spend studying English each week?

D SPEAK Work in pairs. Ask and answer the questions in Exercise C.

> My best friend is the one who brings out the best in me.
> Henry Ford

Iñupiat friends play in the first of the winter snow, Nome, Alaska.

OBJECTIVES

- find out about someone new
- talk about different types of people
- describe someone's personality
- greet people and give personal information, make introductions
- write information about yourself

Work with a partner. Discuss the questions.

1 Who's your best friend?
2 Look at the picture. Who was your best friend when you were a child?
3 What qualities do you look for in a friend?

LISTENING

A Complete the definitions with the words in the box.

> conversation   relationship   successful   tip   topic

1 A private and informal talk between two people is a
_____.

2 A useful suggestion is a _____.

3 When you achieve the result you want, you are
_____.

4 A subject that you write or speak about is a
_____.

5 When two or more people or things are connected in
some way, they have a _____.

B SPEAK Work in groups. Discuss the questions.

1 What is happening in the photo at the top of the page?

2 Where do people often meet for the first time?

3 How do you usually start a conversation with someone
you have just met?

C LISTEN FOR KEY WORDS Listen to an interview with
1.1   psychologist Isabelle Ackerman.

1 What topic does she talk about?

2 What should you start a conversation with?

3 What are two safe topics of conversation to 'break
the ice'?

> **Glossary**
>
> **break the ice (phrase)** to do or say something that makes people feel
> less shy or nervous in a social situation
> **politics (n)** the activities of governments which control a country
> or area
> **psychology (n)** the study of the mind and how it affects behaviour
> **religion (n)** the belief in the existence of a god or gods
> **social life (n)** the time you spend enjoying yourself with friends

D LISTEN FOR DETAIL Listen again and complete each tip
1.1   with the correct verb.

> ask   discuss   feel   give   know   say

1 _____say_____ something positive about the place
or situation you are in, and then ask a question.

2 _____Ask_____ about other people.

3 Don't be negative about other people because you don't
know who they _____know_____.

4 Ask lots of questions and _____give_____ lots of
answers.

5 When you _____feel_____ more relaxed, ask some
personal questions.

6 Don't _____discuss_____ topics like religion or politics
with someone you don't know.

E SPEAK Work in groups. Discuss the questions.

1 What did you think of the tips in the podcast?

2 What other topics are easy to talk about with new people?

GRAMMAR
Question forms

A WORK IT OUT Complete the questions with the words
1.2   in the box. Listen again and check your answers.

> are   did (x2)   do (x2)   have   is (x2)   were

1 What ___do___ you say to a stranger at a party or a new
colleague at the office?

2 _____ it OK to talk about some topics, but not others?

3 _____ you ever met someone new and had no idea
what to talk about?

4 _____ you having fun?

5 What _____ your favourite band?

6 _____ you enjoy the ceremony?

7 _____ you at school together?

8 Where _____ you study?

9 _____ you have children?

B Look at the questions in Exercise A. What tense are they? Write *present simple*, *past simple*, *present continuous* or *present perfect* next to each one.

C Choose the correct words to complete the rules. Use Exercise B to help you.

> **Question forms**
>
> 1 We use the auxiliary verb (*do, does, did*) **before** / **after** the subject.
> 2 We use *be* (*am, is, are, was, were*) **before** / **after** the subject.
> 3 We use present perfect *have* **before** / **after** the subject.

D Go to the **Grammar Hub** on **page 122**.

E Rewrite the questions with the verb in brackets in the correct place.

1 why you studying English? (*are*)

_____

2 you have any brothers or sisters? (*do*)

_____

3 you ever met a famous person? (*have*)

_____

4 you do anything nice last weekend? (*did*)

_____

5 you like tea or coffee? (*do*)

_____

6 you a late-night or early-morning person? (*are*)

_____

7 who your funniest friend? (*is*)

_____

8 who the first person you talked to this morning? (*was*)

_____

9 you ever been to a wedding? (*have*)

_____

10 what the last good film you saw? (*was*)

_____

F **SPEAK** Work in pairs. Ask and answer the questions in Exercise E.

VOCABULARY
People

A Go to the **Vocabulary Hub** on **page 146**.

B **SPEAK** Work in pairs. Answer the questions.

1 How many relatives do you have? How often do you see them all?

2 How many of your colleagues or other students in your class are also your friends?

3 Do you find it easy to talk to strangers? Why/Why not?

PRONUNCIATION
The alphabet

 A Listen and repeat.
1.3

> a b c d e f g h i j k l m n o p q r s t u v w x y z
>
> A B C D E F G H I J K L M N O P Q R S T U V W X Y Z

B Work in pairs. Write the letters of the alphabet in the correct place. Listen and check.
1.3

/e/	/uː/	/ɑː/	/iː/	/aɪ/	/əʊ/	/eɪ/
f	u	r	e	i	o	a

C **SPEAK** Work in pairs. Look again at Vocabulary Exercise A on **page 146**. Take turns to spell the words.

SPEAKING

A Find out some information about your classmates. Write six questions using the ideas below to help you. Then write two more questions using your own ideas.

- ice breakers
  Hi, my name's _____. It's nice to meet you. So, …
- personal questions
- family and friends
  Do you come from a large family?
- interests and hobbies
- childhood and school
- work and study
- favourite things/places
- last weekend/holiday
  Where did you go for your last holiday?

B Work in pairs. Work with someone you do not know well and follow the instructions.

1 Stand up and meet the other people in the class. Take turns asking and answering the questions you wrote in Exercise A.

2 When you have broken the ice, sit down with your partner and tell him/her about the people you met. Was it easy to break the ice or do you need some more help?

〇— **Find out about someone new**

V— types of people **P**— using a dictionary **G**— frequency words and phrases

READING

A Work in groups. Discuss the questions.

1 Which websites do you visit most often and why?

2 Which blogs, vlogs (video blogs) or video channels do you know or follow?

3 What kind of topics do you enjoy reading about online?

B **READ FOR MAIN IDEA** Read *Three of the best* quickly. Which blog sounds most interesting to you and why?

C **READ FOR DETAIL** Read again. Complete each sentence with the name of a blogger, Emma, Maria or Mihaela.

1 _____ is interested in visiting people around the world.

2 _____ has children.

3 _____ writes about a variety of subjects.

4 _____ has a high number of readers.

5 _____ is interested in trying new things.

6 _____ wants people to understand that everyone is beautiful.

D **SPEAK** Work in pairs. Discuss the questions.

1 Is running a blog a difficult job?

2 Why do these people spend so much time on their blogging activities?

3 What topic would you blog about?

VOCABULARY
Types of people

A Work in pairs. Make a list of different types of people. You have one minute.

father of two, music fan, …

B Go to the **Vocabulary Hub** on **page 146**.

C **SPEAK** Work in pairs. Write down the names of three people you know and describe them to your partner. Say what type of person each one is. Ask questions about the people your partner describes.

PRONUNCIATION
Using a dictionary

Macmillan English Dictionary

www.macmillandictionary.com

The *Macmillan English Dictionary* gives clear, simple explanations and real life examples showing you how and when the word is used.

A Look at this entry from the *Macmillan English Dictionary*. Match the definitions (1–5) with the labels (a–e).

1 definition

2 part of speech

3 stressed syllable and pronunciation

4 different meaning

5 frequency rating

gorgeous – definition and synonyms ★[a]
[b]ADJECTIVE Pronunciation /ˈgɔː(r)dʒəs/[c]

[d]**1** very beautiful
Mandy was there, looking gorgeous as usual.

[e]**2** very enjoyable or pleasant
The weather was absolutely gorgeous.

B Look up the following words in the *Macmillan English Dictionary*. <u>Underline</u> the stressed syllable and write down the part of speech and one meaning for each word.

cloud   expedition   positive   rare

Three of the best
Blogs by *Calvin Norton*

With over 150 million blogs online, there is something for every type of person from the **animal lover** to the **gamer** to the **sports fan.** But, if you are looking for something a bit different, here are my top three blogs.

1 Brain Pickings

Maria Popova is a **book lover**, **music fan** and writer. Her blog *Brain Pickings* is a collection of articles about history, news, books and culture. Maria is keen on reading and spends hundreds of hours each month doing research for her blog. It's an extremely popular blog and many people enjoy Maria's interesting mix of articles.

2 The Atlas of Beauty

The Atlas of Beauty is a picture blog showing beauty in different cultures. Romanian photographer, **blogger** and **traveller** Mihaela Noro takes pictures of women of all ages, races and nationalities living their everyday lives. It's a wonderful collection which shows that beauty be found everywhere.

 For more interesting blogs, listen to Calv this week's **Emma Fry Show**

GRAMMAR
Frequency words and phrases

A Listen to an interview with Calvin Norton about another blog, *Humans of New York*, and answer the questions
1.5

1 What is the blog about?

2 What type of people does Brandon Stanton interview?

B Listen and complete each sentence from the radio show with one word.
1.5

1 _____ a week, we bring you reviews and recommendations from the wonderful world of the internet.

2 I'm _____ out in the real world.

3 I'm _____ at home, online in front of my laptop.

4 But luckily for us, you _____ escape.

5 Now and _____, a blog is so good that I just have to mention it again.

6 Stanton focuses on the lives of normal New Yorkers _____ of the time.

7 He includes someone well known _____ so often.

8 It's a very simple idea, but it _____ gets boring.

C **WORK IT OUT** Write the four frequency words in Exercise B in the correct place.

Frequency words

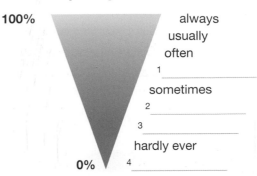

100%   always
usually
often
1 _____
sometimes
2 _____
3 _____
hardly ever
0%   4 _____

D Complete the frequency phrases in the table with words from Exercise B.

once		day
twice	1 _____	week
three times		month
		year

every 2 _____ often

3 _____ and again

most of the 4 _____

E Choose the correct words to complete the rules. Use Exercise B to help you.

Frequency words and phrases

1 We usually put frequency words *before / after* the main verb and *before / after* the verb *be*.

2 We use frequency phrases *at the beginning / in the middle* of a sentence.

3 We also use frequency phrases *in the middle / at the end* of a sentence.

F Go to the **Grammar Hub** on **page 122**.

G **SPEAK** Work in pairs. Discuss the questions.

1 Would you enjoy the blog *Humans of New York*?

2 Why do you think it is so popular?

---

3 *Emma's Bucket List*

After her father and step-father died, Emma Stewart Rigby decided to live a full and exciting life. Emma, a **mother of three**, made a list of 246 things to do before she dies and in her blog she writes about her experiences. Emma is a **people person** and gives lots of friendly advice on life. She's also a **foodie**, and her bucket list includes unusual foods or interesting restaurants she plans to try. A great blog for ideas on how to live life to the max!

Glossary

blog (n) a website containing short articles called posts that are changed regularly

blog (v) to write short articles for a website on your opinions, interests and experiences

culture (n) activities which involve music, books and other arts

subscriber (n) someone who joins and follows a blog

SPEAKING

A Interview each other about websites, blogs or vlogs you like. Make notes about:

• what they are about

• why you like them

• examples of interesting things on them

• what type of people would enjoy them and why

B Work in groups. Interview each other. Which ones sound most interesting?

○— **Talk about different types of people**

1.3 Personality

○– Describe someone's personality

G– indefinite pronouns   V– personality adjectives, adjective + preposition
P– word stress in multisyllable adjectives   S– previewing a text

READING

A SPEAK Work in pairs. Discuss the questions.

1 Which do you do more often: write by hand or use a keyboard?

2 Which do you find easier? Why?

3 What kind of things do you write by hand (e.g. shopping lists)?

B Preview the text, and then answer the questions. Use the information in the box to help you.

> **Previewing a text**
>
> Before you read a text, look quickly at the title and any headings, pictures or diagrams. Use this information to decide what kind of text it is, what it's about and why someone might want to read it. This will make the text easier to understand.

1 What is the text about?

2 Is it from a science paper or a popular magazine? How do you know?

3 What do you think you will learn from the text?

4 Can you trust the information in the article?

C READ FOR MAIN IDEA Read *What does your handwriting say about you?* Was your preview correct?

D READ FOR SPECIFIC INFORMATION Read again and answer the questions.

1 What is graphology a study of?

2 How do graphologists help in court cases?

3 Do all graphologists agree that there is a link between handwriting and personality?

E SPEAK Work in pairs. Discuss the questions.

1 Do you believe there is a connection between handwriting and personality? Why/Why not?

2 Is it important for children to learn to write by hand these days? Why/Why not?

What does your *handwriting* say about you?

Everybody has their own style of handwriting, but can someone's handwriting tell you what they are like? The study of handwriting is called graphology. Graphologists are often <u>involved in</u> legal cases. They are <u>responsible for</u> matching criminals to their handwriting or deciding if signatures are real.

Some graphologists think handwriting can show anything: what kind of job you will be <u>good at</u>, how healthy you are and even what kind of partner you might be <u>happy with</u>.

If you are <u>interested in</u> what your handwriting says about you, check out our information.

Letter size   Small: Medium: Large:

You're probably a **hard-working** person. People with small handwriting are rarely **lazy**.

The research says you're **sensible**; you think carefully about the decisions you make.

Big writing – big personality! People with large writing are usually keen on parties and social events and are rarely shy.

Letter shape

Rounded letters: Rounded letters suggest you are a **creative** person. Are you good at art or music?

Pointed letters: You are **curious**. Your favourite question is 'Why?'!

Dotting your i

Dot high over the i: The research says you have a good imagination.

Dot low over the i: You are a **well-organised** person. Are your desk and room tidy?

Spacing between words

Wide spacing: Narrow spacing:

You're an **independent** type and you are happy on your own.

You're very **sociable** and you need other people in your life.

Your signature

Difficult to read: You are a private person. Like your signature, you can be difficult to read.

Easy to read: Confident people often have signatures that are easy to read. You know what you are good at and you don't mind telling other people about it.

> **Glossary**
>
> **legal (adj)** relating to the law or lawyers
> **spacing (n)** the amount of space between things

Does your handwriting match your personality? Don't be disappointed with the results if not. Not every graphologist believes there is a connection.

GRAMMAR
Indefinite pronouns

A **WORK IT OUT** Look at the extract from the article and choose the correct words to complete the rules.

Everybody has their own style of handwriting, but can someone's handwriting tell you what they are like?

Indefinite pronouns

1 We use indefinite pronouns to talk about people or things *so we can say* / *without saying* who or what they are.

2 We use indefinite pronouns with *-body* and *-one* to talk about *people* / *things*.

3 After indefinite pronouns, we use *singular* / *plural* verbs.

4 We use *'s* with indefinite pronouns for *possessives* / *plural nouns*.

B **PRACTISE** Find and <u>underline</u> another example of an indefinite pronoun in the article.

C Go to the **Grammar Hub** on **page 122**.

VOCABULARY
Personality adjectives, adjective + preposition

A Match the personality adjectives in **bold** in *What does your handwriting say about you?* with the speakers below.

1 'I believe I can do anything if I try. I don't usually worry about things.' _____confident_____

2 'I love my job. I work a lot, but that's OK.' _____

3 'I can paint pictures, write stories and make music.' _____

4 'I plan my time carefully and I always know where to find my things.' _____

5 'I don't like work. I like doing nothing! My perfect day? Staying in bed with a pizza.' _____

6 'I like to think about things carefully before I do them.' _____

7 'I have lots of friends and we meet and go out all the time.' _____

8 'I like learning new things and I ask a lot of questions.' _____

9 'I like to do things myself.' _____

B Look at the <u>underlined</u> phrases in the article. Complete the questions with the correct preposition.

1 Are you involved _in_ any clubs, groups or teams? Which ones?

2 What are you good ____?

3 Who is responsible ____ doing the cooking in your home?

4 Are you happy ____ your mobile phone? Why/Why not?

5 What websites, magazines or TV shows are you interested ____?

6 Are you keen ____ books and reading?

C **SPEAK** Work in pairs. Ask and answer the questions in Exercise B.

PRONUNCIATION
Word stress in multisyllable adjectives

 A Listen and complete the table with the words in the box.
1.7

hard-working	independent	lazy	sensible

1 ●○	2 ●○○	3 ○●○	4 ●●○●
		hard-working	

 B Listen again and repeat the words.
1.7

 C Look again at the article. Find the other personality adjectives in **bold** and write them in the correct place in Exercise A. Listen and check and repeat.
1.8

D **SPEAK** Work in pairs. Practise saying the words. Listen and check your partner's pronunciation.

◯ SPEAKING HUB

A Work in pairs. You are going to study your classmates' handwriting. Follow the instructions.

1 Sign your name and write this sentence on a piece of paper.

The quick brown fox jumps over the lazy dog.

2 Swap papers and use the information in *What does your handwriting say about you?* to write five things about your partner's personality.

B **DISCUSS** Using your notes, tell your partner what their writing says about them.

◯─ **Describe someone's personality**

My name is Gaby. I'm originally from
¹_____, but now, London is
my home. I'm a ²_____,
I like travelling and I drink a lot of
³_____. I live in this
⁴_____ with Neena and Zac.

My name's Zac. I live with
⁵_____ and Neena. I'm
originally from ⁶_____.
I make ⁷_____ games.

My name's Sam. This is my café!
I'm ⁸_____. I like food.
I love ⁹_____. I live here
in ¹⁰_____.

I'm Milly. This is my clothes store.
I'm ¹¹_____. I watch
¹²_____, listen to music
and I read a lot. ¹³_____ a
good friend of mine.

Neena here. I live here in London
with my two friends, Gaby and
¹⁴_____. I'm a lawyer.
I work in ¹⁵_____.

COMPREHENSION

A ▶ 00:00–02:50 Watch the first part of the video.
Complete the paragraphs above.

B Write a question about each person in Exercise A.

Where is Gaby from? What does Zac do?

C **SPEAK** Work in pairs. Test your memory! Close your
books and ask each other your questions from Exercise B.

D ▶ 02:50–04:27 Watch the second part of the video and
<u>underline</u> the correct verb form to complete each sentence.

1 Neena *is / isn't* going to an interview.
2 Sam *is / isn't* good.
3 Zac *had / didn't have* a good holiday.
4 Zac *has / hasn't* asked Milly out.
5 Zac *invites / doesn't invite* Sam to the flat.
6 Sam *eats / doesn't eat* Zac's croissant.

FUNCTIONAL LANGUAGE
Greet people and give personal information, make introductions

A Complete the phrases with the words in the box.

> doing   going   hello   let's   long   meet (x2)   what

Greeting	Reply
Say hello	
¹_____	Hi there! / Hey!
Greet new people	
Nice/Good to ²_____ you.	Nice/Good to ³_____ you, too.
Greet friends	
How are you? How's it ⁴_____? How are you ⁵_____?	I'm good. How about you?
What's new?	Not much.
It's great to see you! ⁶_____ a nice surprise!	⁷_____ time, no see.
Say goodbye	
See you later. See you soon. I've gotta (got to) go.	⁸_____ do something soon.

B ▶ Watch the video again. Check your answers to Exercise A.

MILLY

SAM

NEENA

ZAC

GABY

USEFUL PHRASES

A Match the useful phrases (1–8) with the pictures (a–h).

1 Dream job! ____
2 I love it here! ____
3 Good luck! ____
4 What can I tell you? ____
5 Come with me. ____
6 What else? ____
7 Come over to the flat this weekend. / Will do. ____
8 Here we are. This is home. ____

B ▶ Watch the video again and check your answers to Exercise C.

C How do you say these phrases in your language?

PRONUNCIATION
Word stress and intonation

A ▶ 03:02–03:34 Watch part of the video. Read out the conversation at the same time as Sam and Zac. Copy the word stress and intonation.

> **Sam:** Hey <u>Zac</u>. It's <u>great</u> to <u>see</u> you. What a <u>nice</u> surprise.
>
> **Zac:** I <u>know</u>. Long <u>time</u>, no <u>see</u>.
>
> **Sam:** <u>Do</u> you want a <u>coffee</u>?
>
> **Zac:** <u>Sure</u>, and a <u>croissant</u>.
>
> **Zac:** So, <u>how</u> are you <u>doing</u>?
>
> **Sam:** I'm <u>good</u>. How about <u>you</u>? Did you have a nice <u>holiday</u>?
>
> **Zac:** <u>Yeah</u>. <u>Always</u> good to see <u>family</u>. What's <u>new</u> with <u>you</u>?
>
> **Sam:** Not <u>much</u>. Same, <u>same</u>.

B SPEAK Work in pairs. Practise the conversation. Listen and check your partner's pronunciation.

SPEAKING

A Walk around the class. Introduce yourself to everybody.

A: Hello, my name's Sven. Nice to meet you.
B: Hi, I'm Ahmed. Good to meet you.

B Walk around the class again. Greet the people you know.

A: Hi, Maria. How's it going?
B: Good, thanks. How about you? What's new with you?
A: Not much. I've gotta go. See you later.

C Prepare a 'selfie' presentation. Follow the instructions.

- Make notes about what you want to say. Use the sentence beginnings below to help you.
- Include at least two useful phrases.
- Record your presentation.

Hi! My name's …	I work in …
I'm from … / I'm originally from …	I like …
I'm a …	I watch / listen to …

D **SPEAK** Work in groups. Compare your presentations. Which is the best one?

◯– **Greet people and give personal information, make introductions**

➤ Turn to **page 158** to learn how to write information about yourself.

VOCABULARY

A Complete the words for types of people.

1 someone who likes animals
a _nimal_ l _over_

2 someone who likes spending time with others
p_____ p_____

3 someone who plays video games
g_____

4 someone who is very interested in food
f_____

5 a man who has two children
f_____ o_____ t_____

6 someone who listens to music regularly
m_____ f_____

B Complete the *About me* section of Emma's social media page with the personality adjectives in the box. There is one adjective you do not need.

> creative   curious   ~~hard-working~~   independent
> sensible   sociable   well organised

> Hi, I'm Emma and I'm a student nurse. I study
> and work a lot ¹(_hard-working_) and I make
> lists so I know what I am doing and when
> ²(_____). I always think carefully
> before I make decisions ³(_____).
> I feel it is important to ask a lot of questions
> ⁴(_____) in my social life and at work.
> I have a good imagination and in my free time
> I like to write songs ⁵(_____).
> I also have a great group of friends and I love
> spending time with them ⁶(_____).

C Choose the correct prepositions to complete the sentences.

1 In my family, we are all responsible *for / on / with* doing the housework.

2 I'm not keen *on / about / to* people who talk about themselves all the time.

3 As a child, I was involved *in / with / at* lots of after-school clubs and activities.

4 I'm happy *at / with / on* my job.

GRAMMAR

A Complete the questions with the correct form of *do, be* or *have*.

1 Do you _____ a pet?

2 _____ you from a large family?

3 _____ you have a party for your last birthday?

4 _____ you ever been to your country's capital city?

5 What _____ your favourite book or toy when you were a child?

B Complete the article with the missing words.

> ## Student Life Online
> ### Your university, your site
>
> **This week, we asked students what blogs they read. This is what they said.**
>
> Erica: Most ¹_____ the time, I read blogs about football.
>
> Jake: ²_____ so often, I read a cooking blog.
>
> Ammar: I ³_____ ever read blogs. I don't have time.
>
> Mark: Once a ⁴_____ , on Sunday mornings, I sit down and read my favourite travel blog.
>
> Tina: ⁵_____ and again, I read news blogs.
>
> Nazreen: I don't read blogs, but I do use Twitter. I check it at least ten ⁶_____ a day.
>
> **What are your favourite blogs? Leave your comments below.**

C Choose the word which is *not* possible in each sentence.

1 *Everybody / Somebody / Anybody* can have nice handwriting.

2 I don't agree with *everything / anything / nothing* that the graphologists say.

3 Everyone *use / uses / has* a keyboard these days.

4 Do you know *anybody / anyone / anything* that is sociable?

FUNCTIONAL LANGUAGE

Reorder the words in the boxes to complete the conversations.

> name's / Hi, / my / Erwin
> myself / me / Let / introduce
> meet / Nice / to / you

Erwin: ¹_____ _Hi, my name's Erwin._ _____

Laura: Oh, hi, Erwin.²_____.
I'm Laura, the office manager.

Erwin: ³_____.
I think you're going to be my boss!

> nice / What / surprise / a
> days / are / doing / What / you / these

Alan: Dan?

Dan: Alan! ⁴_____! How are you?

Alan: Oh, fine, thanks. ⁵_____?

Dan: I'm still teaching.

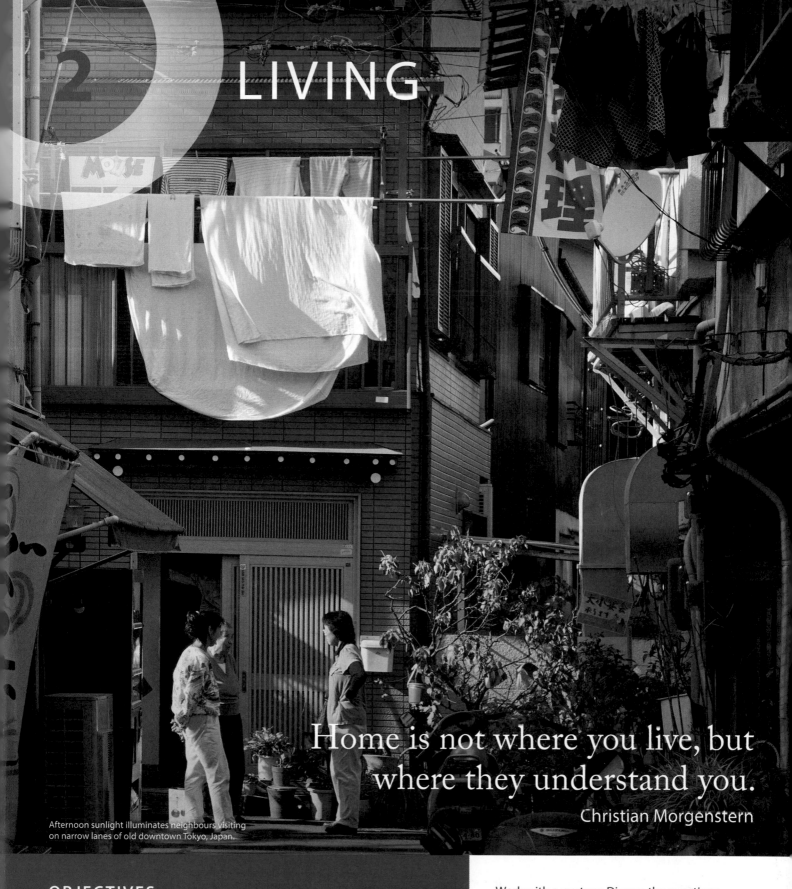

2 LIVING

> Home is not where you live, but where they understand you.
>
> Christian Morgenstern

Afternoon sunlight illuminates neighbours visiting on narrow lanes of old downtown Tokyo, Japan.

OBJECTIVES

- talk about your neighbourhood
- talk about your life and routine
- talk about life events
- ask for and give advice
- write an email of complaint

Work with a partner. Discuss the questions.

1 Read the quote. Where is 'home' for you?
2 Look at the picture. What do you think the people are talking about?
3 Do you know your neighbours?

READING

A Work in pairs. Discuss the questions.

  1 Do you love where you live? Why/Why not?

  2 Look at the pictures. What can you see?

  3 Look at the glossary. How can a building be environmentally friendly?

B **SCAN** Read *The forest in the sky* quickly and complete the sentences with the correct word or number from the text.

  1 Bosco Verticale is an Italian name that means 'vertical _____'.

  2 The apartment buildings are in the city of _____ in Italy.

  3 There are nearly _____ trees on the balconies of the buildings.

  4 The plants help make the noise from the _____ and people in the street quieter.

  5 The apartment buildings are close to the city's services and _____.

  6 The architects plan to build another forest city in _____ in the future.

C **READ FOR DETAIL** Read again and answer the questions.

  1 What are the four problems of life in central Milan that the writer mentions?

  2 How do the Bosco Verticale buildings solve these problems?

  3 What is the main problem with buildings like Bosco Verticale?

  4 Does the writer think forest cities are a good idea?

D **SPEAK** Work in pairs. Answer the questions.

  1 Do you want to see forest cities in your country? Why/Why not?

    Forest cities are a good idea because …

  2 Should we pay more to live in clean cities? Why/Why not?

    I don't think we should pay more to live in clean cities because …

THE FOREST IN THE SKY

Where in the world can you live on the top floor of a 111-metre high-rise building, near the centre of a **lively** city, but still have breakfast under a tree on your balcony? Sounds almost impossible! Well, not if you live in the Bosco Verticale (vertical forest) buildings in Milan, Italy. Architect Stefano Boeri has created a completely new approach to designing buildings.

Like many big cities, Milan is **noisy** and **polluted**. It's hot in the summer and in the city centre the green spaces are often quite **crowded**. But Boeri's team have found a very green answer to these problems.

Nearly 900 trees grow high above Milan on the balconies of **modern** buildings. The trees keep the apartments cool in summer and warm in winter. They also produce oxygen, which keeps the air **clean**. The buildings are so **quiet** because the trees and plants stop the noise from the people and traffic in the streets below.

Bosco Verticale is really **convenient** for the city's shops, services and transport, it's **attractive**, and it's environmentally friendly. So, will there be more buildings like this in the future? Well, possibly. The architects want to build a new forest city in China and the Netherlands, but there is one more problem to solve. Buildings like this are extremely expensive. At 65 million euros, Bosco Verticale cost 5 per cent more to build than a normal high-rise building. But if we want to live in cool, quiet cities with clean air, it will be worth the cost.

Glossary
architect (n) someone whose job is to design buildings
environmentally friendly (adj) something designed not to harm the natural environment
vertical (adj) standing, pointing or moving straight up

GRAMMAR
Adverbs of degree

A **WORK IT OUT** Complete the sentences from *The forest in the sky* with the correct adverbs of degree.

1 Sounds _____ impossible!

2 Stefano Boeri has created a _____ new approach to designing buildings.

3 Boeri's team have found a _____ green answer to these problems.

B Underline four more adverbs of degree in the article.

C Choose the correct words to complete the rules.

> **Adverbs of degree**
>
> 1 Adverbs of degree are usually used *before / after* the adjective that they modify.
>
> 2 We *use / don't use* adverbs of degree when we want to make something stronger or weaker.
>
> 3 We *can / can't* use adverbs of degree with adverbs and verbs:
> - *She is speaking very fast.*
> - *He almost finished the race.*

D Go to the **Grammar Hub** on **page 124**.

E **SPEAK** Work in pairs. Look at the pictures of unusual buildings and use adverbs of degree to describe them.

A: It's so different from a normal building.
B: It's very strange!

VOCABULARY
Describing places

A Read the sentences and look at the adjectives in **bold**. Then write the opposite adjectives.

1 The air in my city is quite **clean**. There aren't many factories. _____*dirty*_____

2 My neighbours are very **loud**. They often play music late at night. _____

3 It's quite an **inconvenient** place to live. Our house is far from the shops and transport. _____

4 The shopping centre is very **old-fashioned**. It looks like it's from the 1970s. _____

5 My flat is in an **ugly** high-rise building. I don't like living there. _____

6 The main streets are very **dirty**. People often drop litter. _____

7 My neighbourhood is very **peaceful**. I rarely hear cars or people in the street. _____

B Use the adjectives in Exercise A to write five sentences about your neighbourhood.

C **SPEAK** Work in pairs. Say an adjective. Your partner says the opposite. Take turns.

PRONUNCIATION
Stress in two-syllable adjectives

🔊 **A** Listen and underline the stressed syllable in each
2.1 adjective.

1	dirty	3	modern	5	noisy
2	quiet	4	peaceful		

🔊 **B** Listen again and repeat the words.
2.1

C Most two-syllable adjectives have the same stress pattern. Read the text below and underline the stressed syllable in all the two-syllable adjectives.

> The Chang (Elephant) Building is in Bangkok, Thailand. Some people think it is modern and interesting; some people think it is strange and funny. Other people think it is ugly and totally awful!

SPEAKING

A Tell your partner about your neighbourhood. Use these ideas to help you.

- Location – is it convenient? Close to public transport?
- Appearance – is the area clean, modern?
- People – who lives there? Families or young professionals?
- Environmentally friendly – are there local parks?

B Work in pairs. Take turns to ask and answer your questions.

○ **Talk about your neighbourhood**

V— verb + preposition **G**— present simple and present continuous **P**— consonant pairs at the beginning of words

LISTENING

A Work in pairs. Discuss the questions.

1 Why do people move out of their parents' home?
2 When do people usually leave home in your country?
3 Why do some adults continue to live at home?
4 What problems could this cause?

 B LISTEN FOR GIST Listen to the first part of *The boomerang generation* and answer the questions.

1 What does 'boomerang generation' mean?
2 How old is Richard?
3 Why is Richard living at home with his parents?
4 Does he enjoy living at home?

Glossary

boomerang (n) a curved stick that comes back to you when you throw it
generation (n) a group of people in society who are born and live around the same time
permanent (adj) happening or existing for a long time

 C Listen to all of *The boomerang generation* and match two questions with each speaker. Write Richard (R), Gordon (G), Alice (A) or Carla (C).

Who …

1 says their child can live at home for a long time? _C_
2 seems worried about their child? ___
3 isn't working at the moment? ___
4 plans to do something to thank their parents? ___
5 wants to make a change to their house? ___
6 likes living with their parents? ___
7 is happy they are not alone? ___
8 isn't happy with the house rules? ___

D SPEAK Work in pairs. What are the advantages and disadvantages of living with your parents as an adult?

VOCABULARY
Verb + preposition

 A Complete the sentences from the radio programme with the correct preposition. Then listen and check your answers.

1 I'm still looking _____ a permanent job.
2 We argue _____ the rules.
3 He can always rely _____ us.
4 I help _____ the housework.
5 I can talk _____ her.

Verb + preposition

Some verbs can be used with different prepositions to mean different things.

argue + about + something

• *We often argue **about** housework.*

argue + with + someone

• *I often argue **with** my parents.*

It is possible to join the sentences together:

• *I often argue **with** my parents **about** housework.*

B Complete the email to Stella with the prepositions from Exercise A.

Re: Help?!
Sent: Friday 10th November, 2017, 2.19 pm
To: stella_28@logbox.com
From: d.smith@screen.nett

Hi Stella,

Thanks for phoning this morning. Sorry to hear you're having money problems, but we're happy you decided to talk ¹___*to*___ us about it. You can always rely ²_____ us. I know you don't like borrowing money, but we'd like to help ³_____ your rent this month. Let's not argue ⁴_____ it this time. You can pay us back when you have a bit more money.

You said you'd like to look ⁵_____ somewhere cheaper to live. How about coming back to live ⁶_____ us for a while? It would only be a temporary solution, but we'd like you to think ⁷_____ it. Give us a call and let's talk ⁸_____ it.

Lots of love,

Mum and Dad

C SPEAK Work in pairs. What should Stella do? Move home or find somewhere else to live?

A: I think she should definitely …
B: I'm not sure she should …

GRAMMAR
Present simple and present continuous

A WORK IT OUT Read the sentences from *The boomerang generation*. Are they present simple (PS) or present continuous (PC)?

1 I love my parents. _____

2 I'm sleeping in my old room. _____

3 Mum cooks and does all my washing. _____

4 More and more of my friends are moving back home. _____

B Complete the rules with *simple* or *continuous*.

Present simple and present continuous
1 We use the present _____ to talk about routines (events that happen every day) and things which are always or generally true.
2 We use the present _____ to describe what is happening now and to talk about trends.
3 We do not usually use the present _____ with state verbs like *be, like, want, understand, believe, know, mean, need, cost.*
4 We often use the present _____ with time expressions like *at the moment, now, today, this year.*

C Go to the **Grammar Hub** on **page 124.**

D SPEAK Work in pairs. Complete the sentences with information about your country and discuss with your partner.

1 Recently, more people are living ___*in apartments in the big cities*___ .

2 People love _____, but they don't like _____.

3 Everyone's talking about _____ at the moment.

4 Many young people are studying _____ at the moment.

5 Some people are happy because _____ _____.

PRONUNCIATION
Consonant pairs at the beginning of words

A Listen to the words and add them to the correct consonant group.

2.5

sl	sm	sn	sp	st	sw
sleep					

B SPEAK Work in pairs. Practise saying these words. Can you add one more example to each group?

SPEAKING

A You are going to ask your partner about his/her life and routine. Use the prompts to make present simple or present continuous questions.

1 think about / moving back home again?
   Are you thinking about moving back home again?

2 save money / for anything this year?
   _____

3 like / cooking for yourself?
   _____

4 know / your neighbours?
   _____

5 your own question
   _____

B Work in pairs. Take turns to ask and answer your questions.

A: *Are you thinking of moving back home?*
B: *I'm not sure. I need to save some money, so maybe!*

○─ **Talk about your life and routine**

G— past simple – regular and irregular verbs   P— Past simple irregular verbs /ɔː/, /e/ and /eɪ/
V— life events   S— skimming for key words

READING

A Work in pairs. Read the sentence from the article and discuss the questions.

When I was young, … a year was such a long time. Now I'm an adult, time passes so quickly.

1 Do you agree with this sentence? Why/Why not?

2 Can you think of an example when time passed quickly or slowly for you?

B READ FOR MAIN IDEA Read *When did the years get shorter?* quickly and match the headings (a–e) with each theory in the text (1–4). There is one heading you do not need. Use the information in the box to help you.

Skimming for key words

When you read an article for the first time, look for clues to help you understand the main idea of each paragraph.

- Look for key words. These could be numbers or the same words repeated.
- Look for words connected to the main topic.
- Look at the first sentence of each paragraph to help you understand the topic.

a The race against time

b From spring to winter

c New experiences slow down time

d It's all about the numbers

e Counting the days

C READ FOR DETAIL Read again. Are the sentences true (T) or false (F)? Correct the false sentences.

1 Time moved more quickly when the writer was a child.   *T / F*

2 As we grow old, every year becomes a smaller percentage of our life.   *T / F*

3 Many adults feel they have too much free time.   *T / F*

4 Time slows down if we are looking forward to an event.   *T / F*

5 New experiences can help to slow down time.   *T / F*

6 All the theories agree that adults and children experience time differently.   *T / F*

D SPEAK Work in pairs. Which theories in the article best explain why time seems to fly as we get older? Why? Give examples from your own life.

A: I like the one about …
B: I think Theory 3 is best because …

When did the years get shorter?

By Stefan Nyberg   10th January 2019

Glossary

routine (n) your usual way of doing things
stressful (adj) involving or causing a lot of pressure or worry
theory (n) an idea that explains how or why something happens

When I was young, the school summer holidays were six weeks long – it felt like forever. A year was such a long time! Now I'm an adult, time passes so quickly. Why does time seem to fly as we get older? Psychologists have several theories about this. Here are the most popular ones:

Theory 1: ___
The first theory is mathematical. When you were 5 years old, a year was 20 per cent of your life, so it seemed like a long time. When you are 50 years old, a year is only 2 per cent of your life, so it seems much shorter. Time can feel very different if you are a child or an adult.

Theory 2: ___
As children, we didn't have as much to worry about – we went to school and studied, then we came home and played with our friends. Adult life is fast, busy and stressful – it's difficult to do everything we want to do. Days can be tiring. Many of us feel that there isn't enough time in the day. Time seems to pass very quickly because as adults we tend to rush to do something and then move on to the next job with no time to stop and think.

Theory 3: ___
As children we knew exactly how many days it was until our next birthday or holiday. All that counting and waiting made the days seem to pass much more slowly. Some psychologists suggest adults don't notice time passing because they are focused on 'boring adult stuff', like shopping or housework. The days, weeks and months pass quickly. Suddenly, another year is over and a new one is beginning.

Theory 4: ___
The routines of work and family life mean that, for many adults, the days all feel the same. This is different from our early lives, which were full of exciting first-time experiences. Back then, we started school and studied new things. Then we took exams, went on our first dates and learnt to drive. When we look back on all these first-time experiences, we feel that the years were much longer because so many new things happened.

All these theories have something in common: there is a clear difference between the way adults and children experience time. Perhaps we need to learn from children and slow down a bit more. Stop, look around, notice the blossom on the trees in spring and the leaves changing colour in autumn. The earth will keep spinning, but we are only here for a short time. Let's enjoy it!

GRAMMAR
Past simple – regular and irregular verbs

A WORK IT OUT Complete the sentences (1–4) from *When did the years get shorter?* Then match them with the correct past simple forms in the box below.

1 As children we _____ school and studied.

2 We _____ exactly how many days it was until our next birthday or holiday.

3 As children, we _____ have as much to worry about.

4 When _____ the years get shorter?

negative	regular	question	irregular

B Choose the correct options to complete the rules.

Past simple regular and irregular verbs

Past simple positive

1 To talk about *finished / unfinished* actions in the past.

2 For most regular past simple verbs, we add *-ed / -ing*.

Past simple negative

3 We make the past simple *negative / positive* with subject + *didn't* + infinitive without *to*.

Past simple questions

4 We *make / don't make* questions with *Did* + subject + infinitive without *to* + ?

5 Question words (*What, Where, When, Why* and *How*) come *before / after did*.

6 After *yes/no* questions, we use *did/didn't* in *short / long* answers.

C Go to the **Grammar Hub** on **page 124**.

PRONUNCIATION
Past simple irregular verbs /ɔː/, /e/ and /eɪ/

A Complete the table with the words in the box. Listen and check.

2.6

~~ate~~	~~bought~~	fought	made
paid	~~said~~	sent	taught

/ɔː/	bought
/e/	said
/eɪ/	ate

B SPEAK Make questions about your childhood using the prompts. Ask and answer them with a partner.

1 Where / meet / your best friend?

2 What / your parents / teach you?

3 You / a happy teenager?

4 Your idea.

VOCABULARY
Life events

A Look at *When did the years get shorter?* again. Find four important life events and match them with the pictures (a–d). How old were you when you did these things?

B Go to **the Vocabulary Hub** on **page 146**.

C SPEAK Work in pairs. At what age do people generally do these things in your country? At what age did your grandparents' generation do these things? Tell your partner.

- learn to swim
- get married
- have a baby
- retire

⬤ SPEAKING HUB

A Work in groups. You are going to tell your group about three first-time experiences. Two should be true and one should be false. Use the ideas in the box or your own ideas.

first holiday without your parents
first child   first important exams   first job
first romantic relationship   getting your own place
learning to ride a bike or drive   leaving home
starting school, university or college

B ORGANISE Answer the questions. Make notes.

- Where and when did you have this first-time experience?
- Who else was part of the experience?
- What happened? What went well? Were there any problems?
- How did you feel? Did you learn anything from the experience?

C DISCUSS Tell the group about your first-time experiences. Take turns. Can you guess which experiences are true and which are false?

◯– **Talk about life events**

Café Hub

COMPREHENSION

A SPEAK Work in pairs. Describe your neighbours to your partner. What are they like? Use words in the box to help you or your own ideas.

> friendly   noisy   old   quiet   unfriendly   young

B Look at the picture. Why do you think Neena, Gaby and Zac are going to see their neighbour like this? Make notes.

Neena's problem	The advice	The decision

C ▶ 00:00–03:40 Watch the first part of the video and check your ideas in Exercise B. What do you think the neighbour is like?

D ▶ 03:40–04:04 Watch the second part of the video. Why does everybody laugh?

FUNCTIONAL LANGUAGE
Ask for and give advice

A Complete the sentences with the correct verb forms. Then decide who said each sentence, Gaby (G), Neena (N) or Zac (Z).

1 What do you think I should *do / to do*? ___
2 You could *ask / to ask* them to turn the volume down. ___
3 How about *to use / using* some earplugs? ___
4 Let me *help / to help* you out here. Earplugs. ___
5 What *do / are* you suggest? ___
6 Why don't you *go / to go* upstairs and talk to them? ___
7 I think you should *go / to go* and talk to them. ___
8 And why don't we *come / coming* with you? ___

B ▶ Watch the video again and check your answers to Exercise A. Write the sentences in the correct place.

Ask for advice
What should I do?

1 _____
2 _____

Give advice
You should/shouldn't …

3 _____
4 _____
5 _____
6 _____
7 _____
8 _____

Reply
That's a good idea.
Thanks, I'll try them.
I'm not sure it's a good idea.

MILLY　　**SAM**　　**NEENA**　　**ZAC**　　**GABY**

C Complete the job interview advice for Neena with one word in each gap. Which do you think is the best piece of advice?

1 You _____ leave plenty of time to get there.
2 I _____ you should read about the company before the interview.
3 Here's one idea: you _____ practise a few typical interview questions with a friend.
4 Nervous? _____ don't you do some breathing exercises to relax?
5 I think you _____ dress for success.
6 You _____ have your phone on during the interview.
7 I _____ think you should ask about salary first.

USEFUL PHRASES

A Match the useful phrases (1–6) with the phrases that come after them in the video (a–f). Then watch the video again and check your answers.

1 Seriously?!
2 What's wrong?
3 Cool!
4 Here you go.
5 What's the problem?
6 You can rely on us.

a No, it's not cool.
b All of us.
c Cool, thanks, Gaby.
d Someone's playing dance music in the flat above my bedroom.
e (very loud dance music playing)
f Oh Zac, the people upstairs are playing loud music.

B How do you say these useful phrases in your language?

PRONUNCIATION
Disagreeing

A 00:38–00:49 Watch the scene where Neena disagrees with Gaby again. Read out the conversation at the same time as Gaby and Neena. Copy the word stress and intonation.

Gaby: Really? Cool!
Neena: No, It's not cool. I need to get to sleep.

B SPEAK Work in pairs. Make similar conversations. Take it in turns to comment, disagree and say why. Use the comments in the box or your own ideas.

That's cheap/expensive! That's fair/unfair!
That's funny/serious! That's good/bad!
That's lucky/unlucky!

A: That's cheap!
B: No, it's not cheap. It's really expensive.

SPEAKING

A Work in pairs. Choose one of the problems and write a conversation with one friend giving advice to another one.

1 I often forget my door keys.
2 My neighbour's dog barks all day.
3 The children in the apartment upstairs are very noisy.
4 My flatmate spends too much time in the bathroom.
5 I'm the only person who does the washing up.
6 My flatmate's always hot and I'm always cold.

B Practise your conversation. Take turns to give advice. Then perform it for the rest of the class.

A: I often forget my door keys.
B: Why don't you leave a key with your neighbour?
A: That's a good idea.

○– **Ask for and give advice**

➤ Turn to **page 159** to learn how to write an email of complaint.

VOCABULARY

A Complete the advert with the correct prepositions.

Samaritans is a UK charity that helps
[1] _____with_____ personal problems.
Every six seconds, someone calls looking
[2] _____ support. Callers can talk
[3] _____ volunteers 24 hours a day
and can rely [4] _____ them to listen
and help. Many callers don't want to talk
[5] _____ their problems with people
they know well or live [6] _____.
Samaritans volunteers keep all conversations
private and are always there to help.

www.samaritans.org

B Complete the profile with the past simple forms of the verbs in the box.

change   fall   get   go to   have   ~~leave~~

David
Attenborough

1926 – born in London

1945 – [1] _____left_____ school and
[2] _____ Cambridge University

1946 – met and [3] _____ in love with Jane
Ebsworth Oriel

1950 – [4] _____ married to Jane; the
couple later [5] _____ two children, Robert
and Susan

1952 – joined the BBC

1965 – became the head of television channel
BBC Two

1973 – [6] _____ jobs and became the
writer and presenter we know and love today

GRAMMAR

A Choose the best adverb of degree to complete the sentences. Use the information in brackets to help you.

1 The idea of a vertical forest building sounds *quite / really* interesting. (*STRONG*)

2 It's *almost / totally* impossible to add trees to every high-rise building. (*WEAK*)

3 The builders worked *extremely / a bit* quickly. (*STRONG*)

4 The problem with buildings like this is they can be *very / quite* expensive. (*WEAK*)

5 The trees are *almost / so* healthy because of rainwater. (*STRONG*)

B Complete the paragraph with the present simple or present continuous form of the verbs in brackets.

Dreaming of Tokyo

Friends Tatsuo and Daisuki shared a small flat in Tokyo for three years. Tatsuo [1] _____speaks_____ (*speak*) French and recently left for a temporary job in Paris. He [2] _____ (*work*) there as a tour guide for the summer.
Apartments [3] _____ (*cost*) a lot in Tokyo and Daisuki can't afford to stay. At the moment, he [4] _____ (*live*) with his parents outside the city. They get on well, but Daisuki [5] _____ (*not like*) the two-hour daily train journey into Tokyo.
He is not the only one in this situation. More of his friends [6] _____ (*leave*) the city these days because it's so expensive. Every morning, the train Daisuki [7] _____ (*catch*) is full of young people, making the long journey to work and dreaming of their own place in the city.

C There is one mistake with the past simple in each sentence. Correct the mistake.

1 I ~~falled~~ *fell* in love when I was 18.

2 I weren't good at sports when I was a teenager.

3 I didn't thought money was important when I was a child.

4 When I was young, my parents always knowed when I wasn't telling the truth.

5 I leaved home when I was 19.

6 My father teached me how to drive.

7 I wasn't meet my partner at work.

FUNCTIONAL LANGUAGE

A Complete the missing words in the conversation.

Sophie: Peter, I can't stand the course I'm studying at university. [1]W _h_ _a_ _t_ d__ you t__ __ __ __ I s__ __ __ __ __ do?

Peter: [2]M__ __ __ __ you s__ __ __ __ __ wait and see if things improve.

Sophie: [3]I s__ __ __ __ __ __ s__, but I'm pretty sure the course is not for me.

Peter: [4]W__ __ d__ __'__ y__ __ talk to your tutor about it?

Sophie: [5]T__ __ __ __'__ a good i__ __ __ __.

Peter: [6]D__ you w__ __ __ m__ t__ go with you?

Sophie: No, that's OK, but thanks.

3 TRAVEL

To travel is to live.
Hans Christian Andersen

Canoeing through the early morning mist near Port Angeles, Washington, USA.

OBJECTIVES

- talk about journeys and transport
- tell a story about a journey
- talk about the kind of holidays you like
- ask for travel information and check understanding
- write an email about a travel experience

Work with a partner. Discuss the questions.

1 What can people learn from travelling?
2 Look at the picture. Do you enjoy doing outdoor activities?
3 Where is the last place you travelled to?

British man Graham Hughes is the first person to visit all of the countries in the world without flying.

Hughes travelled by sea and over land to complete his record-breaking journey. He travelled on a budget of only US $150 a week and paid for everything himself. Thirty-three-year-old Hughes set off on New Year's Day 2009. His first stop was Argentina, and 1,492 days later, he arrived at his final destination, South Sudan. Hughes crossed the borders of all of the 193 United Nations countries. He travelled long distances by boat, and for shorter journeys went by train, got a bus or occasionally took a taxi. None of his journeys were by plane. Lots of people helped him on his journey. Some of them gave him directions and food or let him sleep on their sofa for free, and others gave him lifts.

Of course, not all his experiences were good. He also had some problems. He crossed the Sahara Desert, but had to go back 2,000 miles because he didn't have the correct visa. The most difficult place to get to was the Seychelles. Graham tried three times from three different countries before he finally made it to the islands.

Glossary

budget (n) the amount of money a person has to spend on something
visa (n) an official document that allows you to enter or leave a country for a specific time period

READING

A Work in groups. Think of a country beginning with each letter of the alphabet. You have two minutes.

B SCAN Work in pairs. Read the first line of the article about Graham Hughes. What might the information in the box refer to? Read the article and check your answers.

| 150 US dollars | 193 countries | 1,426 days | 2,000 miles |

C SPEAK Work in pairs. Would you like to do a similar journey to Graham? Why/Why not?

D READ FOR DETAIL Read again. Are the sentences true (T) or false (F)? Correct the false sentences.

1 The United Nations helped Graham pay for his journey. *T / F*
2 His journey finished in Argentina. *T / F*
3 People were kind to Graham during his journey. *T / F*
4 He didn't always pay for accommodation. *T / F*
5 He visited the Seychelles three times. *T / F*
6 He went on his journey because he wanted to help people from all over the world. *T / F*

E SPEAK Work in pairs. Discuss the questions.

1 Would you let a stranger sleep on your sofa? Why/Why not?
2 Graham says the world is full of people who want to help each other. Do you agree? Explain your answer.

GRAMMAR

all / some / most / no / none

A WORK IT OUT Look at these sentences from the article about Graham Hughes. Then choose the correct words to complete the rules.

Hughes crossed the borders of **all of** the 193 United Nations countries.

None of his journeys were by plane.

Some of them gave him directions and food …

Of course, not **all** his experiences were good.

He also had **some** problems.

all / some / most / no / none

1 We use *all, some, most, no* **before / after** nouns.
2 We **can / can't** use *all, some, most, none* with *of* + pronoun.
3 We **can / can't** use *all, some, most, none* with *of* + *the / this / that / these / those.*
4 We **can / can't** use *no* with *of* + pronoun or *the / this / that / these / those.*
5 With *all* we **have to / don't have to** use *of* before a pronoun or *the / this / that / these / those.*

B Go to the **Grammar Hub** on **page 126.**

C SPEAK Work in pairs. Make sentences of your own with *all / some / most / no / none.* Talk about:

- my friends
- my travel experiences
- types of transport
- Graham Hughes or people like him

VOCABULARY
Types of transport

A Find five types of transport in the article about Graham Hughes. Write them in the correct place. Then add the words in the box.

coach	ferry	helicopter	minibus	tram

Travel by air	Travel over land	Travel by sea
plane		

Transport collocations

With all the transport nouns in Exercise A, we can use the verbs *go* or *travel + by*. We don't use *a / an* before the noun. We can also use *take* or *get + a / an*.

- *He travelled long distances by boat, and for shorter journeys went by train, got a bus or occasionally took a taxi.*

When we talk about plane travel, we usually use the verb *fly*.

- *We flew to Portugal last summer.*

B Add (+) or remove (–) one word to make each sentence correct. Use the Transport collocations box in Exercise A to help you.

1 I go to work by a bus everyday. (–)

2 My brother occasionally gives a lift on the back of his motorbike. (+)

3 I took taxi home last Saturday night. (+)

4 I usually get by a tram to my English lessons. (–)

PRONUNCIATION
/p/, /b/, /v/

 A Listen and repeat.
3.1

1 /p/ plane   2 /b/ boat   3 /v/ visa

B Listen and write the words in the correct place.
3.2

/p/	/b/	/v/
	bus	

C Listen, check and repeat the words.
3.2

SPEAKING

A Interview your classmates about their travel habits. Find out about:

- daily travel to and from university or work
- journeys they often make at the weekend
- transport they use to go on holiday

B Work in pairs. Write questions to find out about:

- the different types of transport people use in each type of travel in Exercise A
- what they like and dislike about each type of transport they use
- how much they spend on transport in a normal week

C Interview another student and make a note of their answers to your questions.

D Work with your original partner again and compare the travel and transport habits of the people you interviewed.

1 Who uses more types of transport?

2 Who feels most positive about the transport they use?

3 Who spends the most on transport in a normal week?

○ **Talk about journeys and transport**

LISTENING

A What famous stories or films do you know that involve seas, oceans and islands? What happens?

B **PREDICT** Work in pairs. You are going to listen to a podcast about the Robertson family. Look at the pictures (1–4). What do you think happened?

 C Listen and check your answers to Exercise B.
3.4

Glossary

brave (adj) a brave decision, action or choice is one that you make even though it involves risk and may cause problems for you

life raft (n) a small rubber boat used for saving people whose boat is sinking

survival expert (n) a person who knows how to stay alive in emergencies if you are far away from help

survive (v) to stay alive, especially in a difficult or dangerous situation, for example injury, illness, war

D **LISTEN FOR DETAIL** Listen again and put the information in the order that you hear it (1–6).
3.4

___ The Robertsons got help.

_1_ One of the Robertsons' children asked an unusual question.

___ The Robertsons had no more food.

___ The Robertsons left their old life behind.

___ There was a serious accident.

___ The Robertsons made it back to land.

E **SPEAK** Work in pairs. Discuss the questions.

1 Do you think the Robertsons' decision to sail around the world was a good one? Why/Why not?

2 Why do you think some people do dangerous things?

3 Do you ever do dangerous things, or do you prefer to avoid danger? Give examples.

GRAMMAR
Past continuous and past simple

A **WORK IT OUT** Read the rules and complete the examples with the words in the box.

> bought   noticed   sold   started
> was passing   were living

Past continuous and past simple

We use the past continuous (*was / were* + verb + *-ing*) for actions or situations that were in progress.

- *In 1970, Dougal and Lyn Robertson and their four children* ¹_____ *on a farm, in northern England.*

We use the past simple for finished actions or situations, and things that happened one after another.

- *They* ²_____ *their business,* ³_____ *a boat and on 27ᵗʰ January 1971,* ⁴_____ *their journey across the Atlantic.*

When used together in the same sentence, the past continuous describes a long action and the past simple describes a shorter action.

- *Their boat* ⁵_____ *the Galapagos Islands when they* ⁶_____ *something large in the water behind them.*

when and *while*

We use *when* or *while* to link past continuous and past simple verbs.

We can use *when* or *while* before the past continuous.

- *When/While they were sailing out into the Pacific Ocean, things started to go very wrong.*

We always use *when* before the past simple.

- *They were sailing out into the Pacific Ocean when things started to go wrong.*

AMAZING — ADVENTURES

B Go to the **Grammar Hub** on **page 126**.

C **SPEAK** Think of an interesting or unusual thing that happened to you on a journey or holiday. Make notes using the questions below. Then work in groups and tell your story.

1 Where and when was the holiday?

2 Who did you go with?

3 What happened that was interesting or unusual?

4 What were you doing when this thing happened?

When I was a teenager, I went camping with my family in Spain. One morning, we were walking to the beach when I found a wallet full of money on the path …

PRONUNCIATION
was and *were* with past continuous

A Listen and repeat the sentences. What do you notice about *was* and *were*?

3.5

1 We were cycling to the beach when I fell off my bike.

2 I was swimming in the sea when I lost my car keys.

B **WORK IT OUT** Choose the correct words to complete the rules.

1 We usually use **weak** / **strong** pronunciation of *was* and *were* in positive sentences.

2 We do this because we **stress** / **don't stress** the main verb.

C **SPEAK** Work in pairs. Find out what your partner was doing at these times.

1 7 am this morning

2 last New Year's Eve at midnight

3 10 pm last night

VOCABULARY
Prefixes

A Look at the sentences from *Amazing Adventures*. Choose the correct words to complete the rules.

*I mean, they were very **un**lucky, weren't they, Luis?*

*It sounds like an **im**possible situation.*

1 We use prefixes before **adjectives** / **pronouns** to change their meanings.

2 Prefixes like *un-*, *im-*, *dis-* and *in-* give the original word a(n) **opposite** / **stronger** meaning.

B Complete the words with the correct prefix, *un-*, *im-*, *dis-* or *in-*.

1 I don't believe anything he says. I think he's ____honest.

2 Living on rainwater and turtles sounds very ____healthy to me.

3 I failed the test; a lot of my answers were ____correct.

4 Not many people go to the Galapagos Islands. It's a/an ____usual holiday destination.

5 He doesn't like waiting – he's very ____patient.

C **SPEAK** Work in pairs. Think of other examples of things or people that you can describe with the adjectives with prefixes in Exercises A and B.

SPEAKING

A Work in groups and describe a journey. Students A and B – go to the **Communication Hub** on **page 157**. Students C and D – go to the **Communication Hub** on **page 152**.

B Work in pairs. Take turns telling your story to your group.

C Work in groups. Look at all eight pictures as a group and think of a new story that uses them all. Then tell your story to another group.

3

4

◯– **Tell a story about a journey**

G— verb + -ing and to + infinitive   **V**— accommodation and facilities   **P**— /ʃ/, /tʃ/ and /dʒ/   **S**— identifying tone

READING

A Work in pairs. Discuss the questions.

1 When you are planning a holiday, how do you choose where to stay?

2 Do you find online reviews helpful or not? Why?

B Read two online reviews for a hotel. Which sounds real and which does not? Why?

★★★★☆

a I love to travel, but I can't afford to stay in five-star hotels or expensive apartments all the time. If you are on a budget like me, the three-star Hotel Jasmine is an excellent choice. The service is very good and the rooms are small but clean. The location is a little noisy but central. I hope to return to Hotel Jasmine soon.

★★★★★

b This hotel is FANTASTIC!!! The rooms are BEAUTIFUL and the staff are very kind and WONDERFUL!!! I love shopping and the hotel is in the city centre!!! I will definitely go on using this hotel – in fact, I refuse to stay anywhere else!!!!!

C **SCAN** Read *Tips for a happy holiday* quickly. Underline any of the ideas you discussed in Exercise B.

D Choose two words which describe the author's tone. Use the information in the box to help you.

1 serious   3 formal

2 informal   4 funny

Identifying tone

The tone of a text can help you understand the author's opinion on the topic. Notice words and phrases the author uses to communicate this.

• Look at the author's choice of adjectives and adverbs.

• Does the punctuation give you any clues? For example, 'inverted commas', exclamation marks, brackets or capital letters.

• Is the language formal or informal?

TIPS FOR A **HAPPY HOLIDAY**

You're **planning** to go on holiday and you've **decided** to try somewhere new. You could **consider** using a travel agent, but it's easy to organise your own holiday online these days. All you **need** to do is visit a travel review site, **spend time** reading travellers' comments and then choose the accommodation with the best reviews. Simple!

Or is it? How do you know that what you are reading is genuine? Research shows that some hotels and restaurants pay people to write fake reviews. Of course, the websites **manage** to find and delete some of these fake reviews, but they aren't always successful. So, before you **choose** to spend your holiday budget on that 'amazing beach resort' or cruise ship that scored ten out of ten, read our tips and learn how to spot a fake review.

TIP ONE: What you see is not always what you get. If the pictures of the apartment, guest house or campsite **seem** to be too good to be true, they probably are. For example, when you see the photo below, you **expect** to find a lovely quiet beach, but in fact, the beach and all the hotels are right next to a building site!

TIP TWO: Nowhere is perfect – fact! Most genuine reviewers **like** to include a mix of positive and negative comments, so a review that's 100 per cent positive or negative is more likely to be fake. If you **want** to know what a hostel or chalet is really like, don't read the very best and very worst reviews. Look at the ones in the middle.

TIP THREE: FANTASTIC!!!!!!!! Fake reviewers **like** using capital letters, exclamation marks (!) and lots of extreme adjectives like 'wonderful', 'amazing' and 'fantastic'. It can feel like you are being SHOUTED AT! Genuine reviewers usually **avoid** using so much extreme language. Instead, they often include helpful details like room size or prices.

Glossary

fake (adj) made to look like something real in order to trick people

genuine (adj) real, rather than pretended or false

E READ FOR DETAIL Read again and answer the questions.

1 Why isn't organising your own holiday online as simple as it seems?

2 Why might someone want to write a fake review?

3 What does the article aim to teach its readers?

4 What are the characteristics of a genuine review?

5 What are the characteristics of a fake review?

F SPEAK Work in groups. Discuss the questions.

1 What other kinds of online reviews do you read or write, for example, films, books, games, etc.?

2 Do people rely too much on online reviews? Explain.

GRAMMAR
verb + -ing and to + infinitive

A WORK IT OUT Look at the underlined verb patterns from the online reviews. Then complete the rules with the words in the box.

> either   to + infinitive   verb + -ing

1 I love to travel, but I can't afford to stay in five-star hotels or expensive apartments all the time.

2 I hope to return to Hotel Jasmine soon.

3 I love shopping and the hotel is in the city centre!!!

4 I will definitely go on using this hotel – in fact, I refuse to stay anywhere else!!!!!

verb + -ing and to + infinitive
1 We use _____ after these verbs: *agree, can't afford, hope, learn, refuse, would like, would prefer,* _____, _____, _____, _____, _____, _____, _____, _____.
2 We use _____ after these verbs: *(don't) mind, enjoy,* _____, _____.
3 We can use _____ after these verbs (there is little change in meaning): *hate, love, prefer, (can't) stand,* _____.

B Look at *Tips for a happy holiday* again. Write the verbs in **bold** in the correct place in Exercise A.

C Go to the **Grammar Hub** on **page 126**.

D SPEAK Work in pairs. Think about the best place you have stayed on holiday. Write a short review. Then swap with a partner and ask questions about your partner's review.

VOCABULARY
Accommodation and facilities

A Look at the words in the box. Which types of accommodation are included in *Tips for a happy holiday*?

> apartment   beach resort   campsite   chalet
> cruise ship   guest house   hostel   hotel

B Go to the **Vocabulary Hub** on **page 147**.

C SPEAK Work in groups. Take turns describing or drawing items from the **Vocabulary Hub**. The first person in the group to guess each item gets one point.

A: This keeps your room cool when the weather is hot.
B: Air con!

PRONUNCIATION
/ʃ/, /tʃ/ and /dʒ/

A Listen to the sounds. Are they the same or different? Then listen and repeat.
3.6

1 /ʃ/ chalet   2 /tʃ/ choose   3 /dʒ/ budget

B Complete the table with the words in the box. Listen, check and repeat.
3.7

> adjective   beach   genuine   language
> manage   picture   ship   shout   show

/ʃ/	/tʃ/	/dʒ/
ship	beach	adjective

C SPEAK Work in pairs. Practise saying the words. Listen and check your partner's pronunciation.

◯ SPEAKING HUB

A Work in groups. You are going on holiday together to Barcelona for two nights. Together, you have a budget of 600 euros for accommodation and spending money. Answer the questions:

1 What kind of accommodation would you like to stay in?

2 Which facilities are most important to your group?

B Read about holiday accommodation in Barcelona. Student A – go to the **Communication Hub** on **page 155** and read about Hotel Rambla Park. Student B – go to the **Communication Hub** on **page 156** and read about Gaudí House Hostel. Student C – go to the **Communication Hub** on **page 157** and read about Olympic Apartments.

C PRESENT Describe the accommodation you read about to your group. Decide where you will stay. How much spending money will you have left?

◯ **Talk about the kind of holidays you like**

3.4 Overslept

F – ask for travel information and check understanding
P – word stress and intonation

COMPREHENSION

A SPEAK Work in pairs. Are you usually early or late for things? Give examples.

B SPEAK Work in pairs. Number the pictures in order (1–6) to describe a morning when Gaby overslept. What do you think happened?

a

b

c

d

e

f

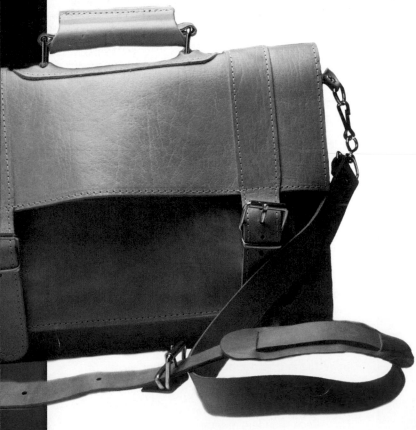

C ▶ Watch the video and compare it with your ideas in Exercise B. What does the ticket officer find? What do you think will happen next?

FUNCTIONAL LANGUAGE

Ask for travel information and check understanding

A Test your memory! Look at the conversation between a customer and a ticket officer. <u>Underline</u> five responses that are different from the video. Try to remember the correct information.

Ask for travel information – trains

Customer:	[1]Could I have a ticket to St Albans?
Ticket officer:	[2]Of course. Would you like a single or a return?
Customer:	[3]A single, please.
Ticket officer:	[4]No problem.
Customer:	[5]Do I have to change trains?
Ticket officer:	[6]Yes, you need to change at Watford.
Customer:	[7]What time's the next train?
Ticket officer:	[8]The next train's in about ten minutes. [9]The next train leaves from platform 4B.
Customer:	[10]What time does the train arrive in St Albans?
Ticket officer:	[11]At 9.13.

B ▶ Watch the video again and check your answers to Exercise A. Write the correct information.

MILLY

SAM

NEENA

ZAC

GABY

USEFUL PHRASES

A ▶ Watch the video without sound. Shout *Stop!* when you think the ticket officer is about to use one of the useful phrases. Then listen and check.

1 Here, let me help you.

2 Don't worry.

3 Follow me.

4 Don't forget this.

5 You don't want to miss your train.

6 Have a good trip.

B How do you say these useful phrases in your language?

PRONUNCIATION
Word stress and intonation

3.8

A Listen and repeat the conversation. Copy the word stress and intonation.

Ticket officer:	The <u>next</u> train's in about three <u>min</u>utes from platform <u>two</u>.
Anna:	I'm <u>sor</u>ry. Did you say <u>three</u> minutes?
Ticket officer:	Yes, <u>three</u> minutes!
Anna:	OK, thanks. Oh, and where's platform <u>two</u>?
Ticket officer:	Go past the <u>cof</u>fee shop, then turn <u>right</u>.
Anna:	OK. So I need to go past the <u>cof</u>fee shop and then ... turn <u>left</u>? Is <u>that</u> right?
Ticket officer:	No, you need to turn <u>right</u> after the coffee shop.

B SPEAK Work in pairs. Make a similar conversation.

SPEAKING

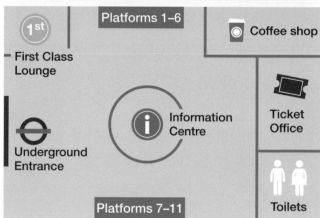

A Work in pairs. Student A is the customer. Student B is the ticket officer. Write a conversation. Use these ideas to help you.

Student A: Ask for information about trains to a place on the departure board.

Student B: Answer Student A's questions.

Student A: Check understanding and then ask for directions to the correct platform.

Student B: Look at the train station plan and give directions.

Student A: Check understanding.

B Practise your conversation. Take turns to be the customer and the ticket officer. Then perform it for the rest of the class.

○− **Ask for travel information and check understanding**

➤ Turn to **page 160** to learn how to write an email about a travel experience.

VOCABULARY

A Label the pictures with the correct forms of transport.

> coach   ferry   helicopter   minibus   plane   tram

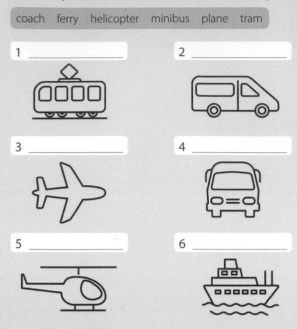

1 _____

2 _____

3 _____

4 _____

5 _____

6 _____

B Write the words in the box in the correct place. Some words can go in more than one place.

> accurate   happy   kind   likely   organised   polite

un-	im-	dis-	in-

C Complete the definitions with the words in the box.

> apartment   beach resort   campsite   chalet   cruise ship

1 A _____ is a place where people on holiday can stay in tents.

2 A _____ is a large, comfortable boat that has similar facilities to a hotel.

3 A _____ is a place that many people go to for a holiday by the sea.

4 A _____ is a wooden house built in a mountain area where people on holiday can stay.

5 An _____ is a set of rooms, usually on one floor of a large building, where people on holiday can stay and cook their own meals.

GRAMMAR

A Choose the correct words to complete the sentences.

1 *Most / Most of* the people I know want to visit other countries.

2 *Some / Some of* countries are difficult to get into.

3 *No / None* type of transport is completely safe.

4 *All the / All* my money was in my jacket.

B Complete the article with the past continuous or past simple forms of the verbs in brackets.

Lucky to be alive!

Today, we bring you the story of surfer Mick Fanning.

World champion surfer Mick Fanning is lucky to be alive. In 2015, he [1]_____ (surf) in a competition in South Africa when a shark [2]_____ (attack) him. Thousands of people [3]_____ (watch) on live television when the attack [4]_____ (happen). Mick [5]_____ (sit) on his surf board when he [6]_____ (notice) the shark next to him. The giant fish tried to pull him under the water, but Mick [7]_____ (hit) it on the back, and it [8]_____ (swim) away. A rescue boat [9]_____ (wait) and it brought Mick and another surfer safely back to land.

C Choose the correct form of the verbs to complete the questions. Both forms may be possible.

1 Do you ever refuse *to leave / leaving* a tip in a restaurant? Why?

2 Do you prefer *to go / going* on holiday in the summer or winter? Why?

3 What do you hope *to learn / learning* when you visit a new country?

4 Would you enjoy *to visit / visiting* a country where no one speaks your language? Why/Why not?

5 Do you like *to try / trying* new foods when you travel? Give an example.

FUNCTIONAL LANGUAGE

A Write the words in the correct order to make questions.

1 have / a / could / I / ticket / to / Central Station / ?

_____

2 a / single / you / like / would / a / return / or / ?

_____

3 does / train / what / the / arrive / in / time / Amsterdam / ?

_____

4 next / the / time's / train / what / ?

_____

5 do / trains / have / I / to / change / ?

_____

6 did / say / platform / sorry, / I'm / 30 / you / ?

_____

7 is that right / at the top of the stairs, / so it's left / ?

_____

8 do / get / you / to / platform / 9 / how / excuse me, / ?

_____

B Work in pairs. Think of different ways to answer the questions in Exercise A.

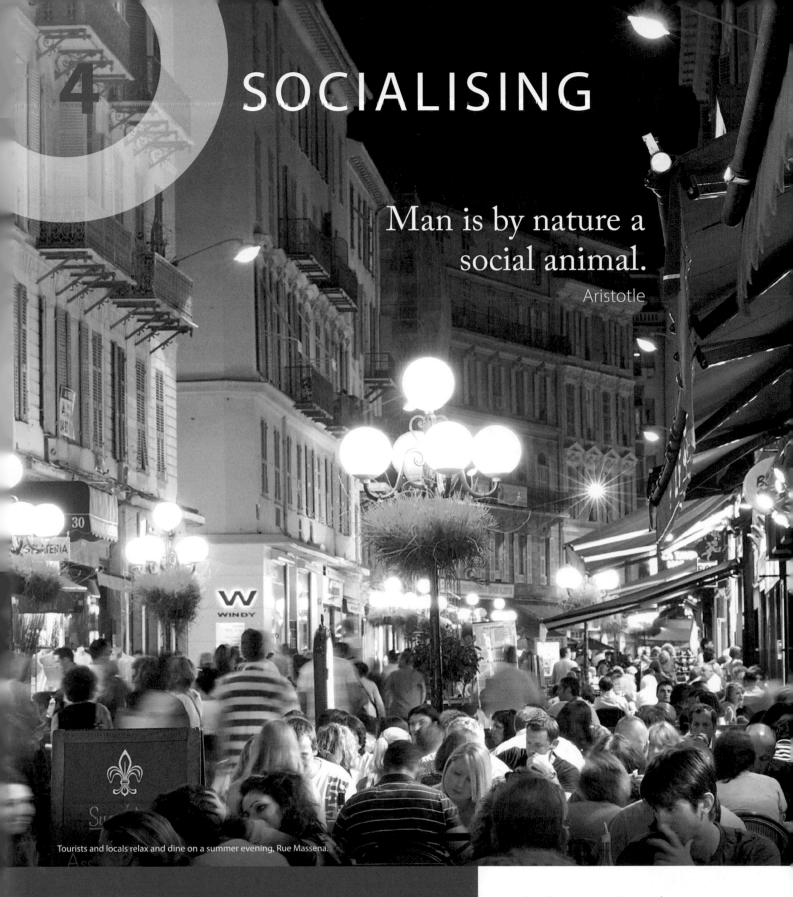

4 SOCIALISING

Man is by nature a social animal.

Aristotle

Tourists and locals relax and dine on a summer evening, Rue Massena.

OBJECTIVES

- talk about plans you have made for a weekend with visitors
- present reasons to support or argue against predictions
- ask and answer questions about how you like to spend your free time
- make arrangements to meet up with somebody
- write an invitation and reply

Work with a partner. Discuss the questions.

1 Where do people go out in your country?
2 Look at the picture. Which city do you think it is? Why?
3 What do you enjoy doing with your friends?

●—Talk about plans you have made for a weekend with visitors

V—free time   **G**—*be going to* + infinitive and present continuous for the future   **P**—*going to*

VOCABULARY
Free time

A SPEAK Work in pairs. Write down as many free time activities as you can in English. You have two minutes. Then compare your list with another pair.

B Complete the diagrams with the verbs in the box.

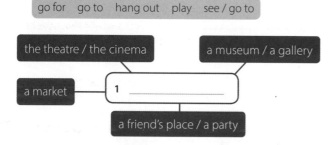

| go for   go to   hang out   play   see / go to |

the theatre / the cinema   a museum / a gallery

a market   1 _____

a friend's place / a party

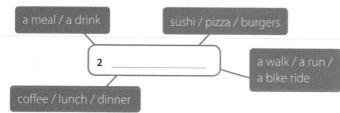

a meal / a drink   sushi / pizza / burgers

2 _____   a walk / a run / a bike ride

coffee / lunch / dinner

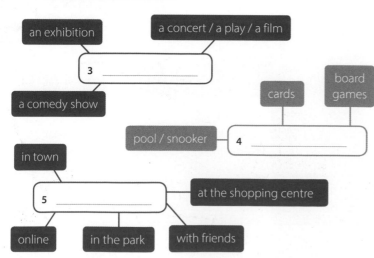

an exhibition   a concert / a play / a film

3 _____

a comedy show   cards   board games

pool / snooker   4 _____

in town

5 _____   at the shopping centre

online   in the park   with friends

C SPEAK Work in pairs. Which of the free time activities in Exercise B are your favourites, and why?

LISTENING

A Work in pairs. What kind of things do you like to do when you visit a city for the first time?

B LISTEN FOR GIST Listen to a conversation between Sylvia and Greg and circle seven free-time activities in Vocabulary Exercise B that they talk about.

4.1

> ### Glossary
> **arrange (v)** to make plans for something to happen, for example by agreeing a time and place
> **intelligent (adj)** good at understanding difficult ideas and subjects

C LISTEN FOR DETAIL Listen again and choose the correct answer a or b.
4.1

1 What is the relationship between Sylvia and Greg?
   a brother and sister
   b boyfriend and girlfriend

2 Who is Claire?
   a Greg's friend
   b Greg's girlfriend

3 Sylvia thinks that Greg will like her friend Duncan because they …
   a are both good cooks.
   b both enjoy eating.

4 After dinner, Sylvia and Greg are going to see …
   a a funny show.
   b a play by Shakespeare.

5 Greg stops Sylvia explaining the plan for the next day because he …
   a doesn't feel very well.
   b wants to order some food.

D SPEAK Work in pairs. When was the last time you visited friends or family for the weekend? Tell your partner.

GRAMMAR

be going to + infinitive and present continuous for the future

A **WORK IT OUT** Read the definitions. Then look at the sentences and decide if they are arrangements (A) or intentions (I).

Arrangements – you have probably booked a ticket or agreed a time with other people. You usually mention a time, date or place.

Intentions – you have already decided to do something and want to tell someone about it. You don't need to mention a time, date or place.

1 I'm going to introduce you to all my new friends as 'Greggy'. ____

2 Tomorrow evening, she's having dinner with some old friends. ____

3 I think I'm going to bring Mum and Dad here, too. ____

4 We're meeting Duncan and Alicia at three o'clock. ____

5 Alicia says she and Duncan are going to open a restaurant one day. ____

B Choose the correct words to complete the rules. Use Exercise A to help you.

> **be going to + infinitive and present continuous for the future**
>
> 1 We use *be going to* + infinitive to talk about *arrangements / intentions*.
> 2 We use the present continuous (*be* + verb + *-ing*) to talk about *arrangements / intentions*.

C Go to the **Grammar Hub** on **page 128**.

PRONUNCIATION

going to

A Listen and repeat the pronunciation of *going to* /ˈɡʌnə/ in informal speech.
4.2

1 She's going to call later.

2 I'm going to text Angie and Mark.

B **SPEAK** Work in pairs. Look at the sentences that you marked as intentions (I) in Grammar Exercise A. Practise saying the sentences in an informal way. Pronounce *going to* as /ˈɡʌnə/.

C **SPEAK** Ask questions about your partner's plans. Talk about your arrangements and intentions.

A: Are you going to have a party in the next few weeks?

B: Yes, I am! It's my birthday next weekend and I'm having a party.

SPEAKING

A Work in groups. Plan a weekend. Choose a group of visitors:

- older family members, for example, an aunt and uncle or grandparents
- younger family members, for example, a brother or sister with their partner and children
- a group of four friends from school or university

B Make plans for next weekend for you and your visitors in and around a city you know well. Make notes on:

- meeting
- sightseeing
- entertainment
- food and drink
- evening activities

C Explain your plan to students from other groups. Which weekend sounds like the most fun?

My old school friends are coming to visit next weekend. I'm meeting them at the train station. Then we're going to have breakfast in town, probably at Vincent Café. The food there is lovely and it isn't expensive.

○─ **Talk about plans you have made for a weekend with visitors**

READING

A Work in pairs. Do you agree with the following sentences? Why/Why not?

In the next ten years …

we will do less work and spend more time socialising.

we will do a lot of our socialising in virtual worlds.

we will socialise with artificial intelligence.

B **READ FOR MAIN IDEA** Work in groups. Student A go to **page 156**, Student B go to **page 153** and Student C go to **page 152**. Read your article and discuss the questions below.

1 What does the article say about our social lives?

2 What role will technology play?

3 Which expert or business leader is mentioned, and why?

4 What possible benefits of the development does the article mention?

C **SPEAK** Work in groups. Discuss your article and the following questions.

1 Which predictions do you think will happen?

2 Do you think these will be positive or negative developments for our social lives? Why?

GRAMMAR
Making predictions

A **WORK IT OUT** Look at the sentences from the articles about the future of our social lives. Underline the modal verbs used to make predictions.

1 The good news is some people think it might not be long until every weekend is a long weekend.

2 However, experts agree that the way we use social media will change in the future.

3 Some experts even believe that one day it may be possible for robots to feel love.

B Find and underline four more examples of modal verbs in one of the articles you read in Reading Exercise B. Then work in pairs and compare your answers.

C Complete the rules with *will* or *might/may*.

> **Making predictions**
>
> 1 We use _____ (*not*) + infinitive without *to* when we are certain about our prediction.
>
> 2 We use _____ (*not*) + infinitive without *to* when we are less certain about our prediction.

D Look at the sentences from *Robot relationships*. Then choose the correct words to complete the rules.

… humans will probably develop close relationships with robots.

… it definitely won't be long until robots look, sound and move like humans.

1 We use *probably* to make predictions with *will* and *won't* **less** / **more** certain.

2 We use *definitely* to make predictions with *will* and *won't* **less** / **more** certain.

3 We use *probably* and *definitely* **before** / **after** *will*.

4 We use *probably* and *definitely* **before** / **after** *won't*.

E Go to the **Grammar Hub** on **page 128**.

F Complete the predictions about artificial intelligence with the words in brackets.

          might not

1 Some people ₄want three-day weekends every week. (*might not*)

2 It _____ probably be harder to find a job in the future because of technology. (*will*)

3 I don't think we _____ have robot friends in my lifetime. ('*ll*)

4 We _____ control computers with our minds in the future. (*might*)

5 VR headsets _____ definitely get much cheaper in the next few years. (*will*)

6 Humans won't _____ fall in love with robots in the future. (*probably*)

7 I'm sure we all _____ have robots in our homes 20 years from now. ('*ll*)

8 We _____ stop working completely one day because of technology. (*may*)

G **SPEAK** Work in pairs. Are there any predictions in Exercise F that you do not agree with?

I think most people will want three-day weekends every week.

PRONUNCIATION
will and *won't*

A Stressed words are the ones that carry the information. Listen and <u>underline</u> the stressed words.
4.3

1 There will be fewer car journeys to work in the future.

2 Technology will do more of the work for us.

3 People won't be paid for working fewer days per week.

4 Do you think people will be happier in the future?

5 No, they won't.

6 Yes, they will. They won't have to work so hard.

B Listen again and repeat the sentences. Copy the stress.
4.3

VOCABULARY
Suffixes

A Go to the **Vocabulary Hub** on **page 147**.

B Add one of the suffixes in the box to the words in brackets to make nouns. You may need to change the spelling of some of the words. You will need to use some of the suffixes more than once.

> -ion   -ity   -ment   -ness

1 I think there is a _____ (*possible*) that robots will feel love in the future.

2 I agree with the _____ (*predict*) that virtual reality will be an important part of social media.

3 There is an _____ (*agree*) between many experts that technology will help our work–life balance.

4 An important _____ (*develop*) is that robots are now beginning to understand our feelings.

5 I don't believe that robots will be able to experience real _____ (*happy*) or _____ (*sad*).

C **SPEAK** Work in pairs. Look at sentences 1, 2 and 5 in Exercise B. Do you agree with these opinions? Why/Why not?

SPEAKING

A Discuss some predictions about the future. Read three predictions for the future and present reasons to support and argue against each.

Fifty years from now …

1 cash in the form of notes and coins will completely disappear.

2 all cars will be self-driving and there will be very few road accidents.

3 all European children will learn Mandarin at school.

B Work in groups. Discuss the predictions and note down reasons to support and argue against each prediction.

C Work in new groups. Take turns to speak for one to two minutes about one of the predictions.

◯ **Present reasons to support or argue against predictions**

G – subject and object questions　**V** – relaxing　**P** – linking a consonant to a vowel　**S** – summarising

READING

A Work in pairs. Which of these things have you done recently? What exactly did you do? Tell your partner.

1 spend the evening at a friend's home
2 relax at home on your own
3 invite people over to your home for the evening
4 get together with your extended family
5 have a night out with friends

B SPEAK Look at the pictures. What are the people doing? How do you think they feel? Use the words in the box to help you.

> a family gathering　a fire　a hot bath　a sleeping pet
> a cosy blanket　candles　warm socks　wool jumpers

C READ FOR MAIN IDEA The pictures all show the Danish idea of *hygge*. What do you think *hygge* means? Read the first paragraph of *Make yourself at home* to check your answer.

Make *yourself* at home

What is *hygge*?

Winters in Denmark are long, dark and cold, but according to the 2016 UN World Happiness Report, Danish people are amongst the happiest in the world. One reason might be *hygge*, the Danish attitude that focuses on enjoying the simple things in life, such as enjoying a coffee in a relaxed atmosphere with easy-going friends or family.

How do you pronounce *hygge*?

Hygge is easy enough to pronounce – 'hue-gah' – but much more difficult to translate. No single English word describes the idea completely, but being cosy is a big part of it. There may be a connection between the word *hygge* and the English word *hug*, and in Danish *hygge* can be an adjective, verb or noun.

How do I know if it's *hygge*?

Your friends come over on a cold winter evening to sit by the fire, eat homemade food and play board games. That's definitely *hygge*. You have a quiet night in, have a bath, light some candles, then sit down with a good book and a cosy blanket. That's *hygge*, too. You argue about politics, check your phone, play video games and listen to thumping techno music. That's definitely not *hygge*! So how do you know if it's *hygge*? Think warm socks, wool jumpers, sleeping pets and happy family gatherings. Got it now?

Why *hygge*?

Research shows that people who are kind to themselves and take some time out to relax have better mental health and feel happier. *Hygge* encourages us to do this and also to get together with friends and family. Happy groups of people make more caring communities and a happier society. It's no surprise that the Danes are always smiling!

> **Glossary**
>
> **cosy (adj)** warm and comfortable, and making you feel relaxed
> **family gathering (phrase)** when a family meet and spend time together
> **translate (v)** to change spoken or written words into another language

D READ FOR DETAIL Read the whole article. Then complete the summary with the words in the box. Use the information in the box to help you.

Summarising

A summary gives the most important points of a text.

Highlight or underline key points and take notes as you read the text. Try to use your own words rather than copy the writer's.

comfortable   explain   health   important   technology

Hygge is a Danish custom for people who want to relax and feel ¹_____. It is usually at home and no ²_____ is involved! *Hygge* can be with other people or by yourself – the ³_____ thing is to feel happy and cosy. Feeling this way is good for your mental ⁴_____. This might ⁵_____ why Danish people were described as some of the happiest people in the world by the 2016 UN World Happiness Report.

E SPEAK Work in pairs. Discuss the questions.

1 When did you last do something '*hygge*'? What was it and who were you with?

2 Is there a word in your language that means *hygge* or something similar?

GRAMMAR
Subject and object questions

A WORK IT OUT Read the rules and look at the questions from *Make yourself at home*. Then look at the examples and answer the questions (1–3).

Subject and object questions

We ask subject questions when we don't know *what/who/which/whose* something or someone is.

We ask object questions when we want to know more information about something or someone.

What is hygge?

How do you pronounce 'hygge'?

1 Which is the subject question?

2 Which is the object question?

3 Which question includes an auxiliary verb?

B Look at the questions and possible answers. Then choose the correct words to complete the rules.

What is hygge? It is an attitude that focuses on enjoying the simple things in life.

How do you pronounce 'hygge'? You pronounce it 'hue-gah'.

1 With subject questions, we **change** / **don't change** the word order in the answer.

2 In **subject** / **object** questions, the question word is the object of the sentence.

C Go to the **Grammar Hub** on page 128.

D Choose the best question word and decide if an auxiliary verb is needed to complete the questions. Then choose the correct question type: subject (S) or object (O).

1 *Who* / *Why* is *do* / – your best friend? **S / O**

2 *When* / *What do* / – you do with your best friend? **S / O**

3 *What* / *Who does smile* / *smiles* more, you or your best friend? **S / O**

4 *What* / *Which do* / – you do to relax? **S / O**

E SPEAK Work in pairs. Ask and answer the questions in Exercise D.

VOCABULARY
Relaxing

A Work in pairs. Make a list of different ways of relaxing. You have one minute.

B Go to the **Vocabulary Hub** on page 148.

PRONUNCIATION
Linking a consonant to a vowel

A SPEAK Work in pairs. Which letters of the alphabet are vowels and which are consonants?

B Listen and repeat the phrases. Which words link together? (4.4)

1 light a candle

2 have a bath

C Say the phrases and draw an arrow where a consonant sound links to a vowel sound. Then listen and check your answers. (4.5)

1 have some friends over   3 the simple things in life

2 a relaxed atmosphere   4 friends and family

⭘ SPEAKING HUB

A Work in pairs. You are going to write a quiz with the title *Are you a home bird or a party animal?*

B PLAN Ask five questions and give two or three possible answers for each. Use the topics below:

- a favourite way of celebrating
- a typical Saturday night
- your ideal holiday
- going to or having parties
- eating out or cooking at home

C Swap quizzes with another pair and answer their questions. Do you agree with the results?

◯– **Ask and answer questions about how you like to spend your free time**

Café Hub

4.4 Would you?
- **F** make arrangements to meet up with somebody
- **P** saying *yes* or *no*

COMPREHENSION

A SPEAK Work in pairs. Look at the pictures and discuss where the characters are and what you think happens. Then choose the correct words to complete the sentences.

1 Zac and Milly *have / haven't* met before.

2 Zac *knows / doesn't know* what to say to Milly.

3 Zac *wants / doesn't want* to buy a T-shirt.

4 Milly *likes / doesn't like* Zac.

5 Zac *likes / doesn't like* Milly.

6 Zac and Milly *arrange / don't arrange* to go out together.

B ▶ Watch the video and check your answers to Exercise A.

C ▶ 02:58–04:19 Watch part of the video again. When are Milly and Zac free to meet? Put a tick (✓) or a cross (✗) in the correct place.

	Milly	Zac
1 tonight		
2 on Saturday after 1.30		
3 on Sunday at midday		

D SPEAK Work in pairs. Why are they not able to meet tonight or on Saturday?

FUNCTIONAL LANGUAGE
Make arrangements to meet up with somebody

A Complete the questions with the words in the box. There are three words you do not need.

> are   can   could   do   how   maybe
> what   will   ~~would~~   would

Make arrangements (invitations)
1 *Would* you like to hang out tonight?
2 _____ you like to do something, then?
3 We _____ go for a coffee, or eat something?
4 _____ you free on Saturday?
5 _____ about Sunday instead?
6 _____ time?
7 _____ you want to meet at the park?

Say *yes*
Yeah! Sure. / Sounds great. / Awesome!
I'd love to!
Great. Twelve o'clock it is!

Say *no*
I'm so sorry, I can't.
Oh! Wait a minute. I just remembered …

B ▶ Watch the video again and check your answers to Exercise A.

MILLY

SAM

NEENA

ZAC

GABY

USEFUL PHRASES

A Match the useful phrases (1–6) with the phrases which show the correct meaning (a–f).

1 Are you looking for anything in particular?

2 I'm sorry, I need to get that.

3 So, you were saying.

4 Well, it was nice to see you again.

5 Wait, hold on!

6 Sounds great!

a I'm leaving.

b That's a good idea.

c Stay here!

d Do you want to buy something?

e Please continue.

f The phone is ringing.

B How do you say these useful phrases in your language?

PRONUNCIATION

Saying *yes* or *no*

A Listen and write the replies in the correct place.
4.6

Saying *yes*	Saying *no*

B Listen and repeat. Can you hear the difference in intonation between saying *yes* and saying *no*? Copy the word stress and intonation.
4.6

C **SPEAK** Work in pairs. Practise saying the replies. Listen and check your partner's pronunciation.

SPEAKING

A Work in pairs. Look at some things you could arrange to do. One item in each word set is not correct. Cross it out and replace it with your own idea.

1 go for … a drink / a meal / a walk / a drive / a shop

2 go to … the cinema / swim / a gig / the beach

3 go … shopping / eating / swimming / dancing / cycling

B Work in pairs. Practise making arrangements using the ideas in Exercise A. Take turns to invite each other.

Student A: Invite B to do something.

Student B: Say *no*.

Student A: Suggest another time.

Student B: Say *no*.

Student A: Suggest *another* time.

Student B: Say *yes*.

○─ Make arrangements to meet up with somebody

➤ Turn to **page 161** to learn how to write an invitation and reply.

VOCABULARY

A Write the missing words to complete Olivia's email.

To: Natalie

Subject: This weekend

Hi Natalie,

I've got a great weekend planned for us. On Friday, I'll meet you at the station – then let's ¹_____ for sushi and go ²_____ a drink in town.

On Saturday, we can go for a bike ³_____. I've got two bikes, so let's take them and go ⁴_____ the market.

After we can hang ⁵_____ in the park and chat or ⁶_____ cards.

On Saturday evening, we're going ⁷_____ my friend Alex's place. Then on Sunday, maybe we can ⁸_____ a film before you go.

Can't wait!

Olivia xxx

B Choose the correct words to complete the sentences.

1 This robot can do a lot of different *active / activities*.

2 I think we should have a *discussion / discuss* about what will happen in the future.

3 What kind of *abilities / able* do you think machines will have in 50 years?

4 In my opinion, *happiness / happy* is one of the most important things in life.

5 There is the *possible / possibility* that people will stop using social media.

GRAMMAR

A Complete the sentences with *be going to* + infinitive or the present continuous form of the verbs in brackets. Use contractions.

1 I _____ (*not forget*) my friend's birthday again this year.

2 We _____ (*meet*) the others tonight on the corner by the coffee shop.

3 Mia _____ (*take*) her friend out for dinner tomorrow.

4 I think I _____ (*lie down*) for a while before we go out.

5 Go to bed early because we _____ (*get up*) at 6 am to drive to the airport.

B Find and correct the mistake in each sentence.

1 It will be easier to meet people in the future probably because of technology.

_____

2 People might going on virtual dates online in the future.

_____

3 A virtual date probably won't very romantic.

_____

4 We might to use technology to help us choose the perfect partner.

_____

5 The way people meet and fall in love not may change very much.

_____

C Complete the questions and answers with the words in the box. You need to use some of the words more than once.

did   do   don't   it's   make
spend   went   what   which

1 '_Which_ country is *hygge* from, Denmark or Sweden?'
   '_____ from Denmark.'

2 'Who _____ you spend time with?' 'I _____ a lot of time with my best friend.'

3 '_____ is your favourite book?' '_____ *The Lord of the Rings*.'

4 'Which board games _____ you play?' 'I _____ play board games.'

5 'How _____ you celebrate your last birthday?'
   'I _____ out for dinner.'

FUNCTIONAL LANGUAGE

Look at the beginning and end of the telephone conversation. Put the rest of the conversation in the correct order.

John: Dean, it's your brother. You OK?

Dean: Yep, fine thanks, and you?

___ **John:** That's great. There's just one thing … Jenny and I are going out.

___ **Dean:** Not really. No plans. Why?

___ **John:** Well, yes.

___ **John:** Well, we got an invitation to a new restaurant and …

___ **Dean:** And, you need a babysitter!

_1_ **John:** I'm great, thanks. Listen, are you doing anything this evening?

___ **John:** Do you fancy coming over? Jenny has made a curry and little Sam says he misses his Uncle Dean.

___ **Dean:** Curry and my favourite nephew? I'd love to!

___ **Dean:** What?

___ **Dean:** Fine, fine. What time?

John: You are the best. How about seven o'clock?

5 WORK

> There is no substitute for hard work.
>
> — Thomas Edison

Electrical lineman Chen Qi cleans snow from a high-voltage transmission tower, Baima Mountain, Wulong County, China.

OBJECTIVES

- talk about the pros and cons of different jobs and say how they help society
- decide on the rules for a workplace or classroom
- answer questions on topics in which you are an expert
- give information about your work experience in a job interview
- write a covering email

Work with a partner. Discuss the questions.

1 What do you like about your job or the subjects you study?

2 Read the quote. What do you think Edison meant? Do you agree with him?

3 Look at the picture. Would you like to have this man's job? Why/Why not?

READING

A Match the definitions (1–4) with the words in the box.

> pay rise   salary   self-employed   well-paid

1 working for yourself _____
2 a fixed amount of money that you earn each month or year from your job _____
3 paid a lot of money _____
4 an increase in the amount of money you are paid to do your job _____

B SPEAK Work in pairs. What are four things, apart from money, that can make people happy at work?

C SCAN Read *What really makes us happy in our jobs?* quickly. Which of your ideas from Exercise B can you find?

D READ FOR DETAIL Read again. Who says these things make them happy in their job, Helen (H), Lena (L), Bret (B) or Ken (K)?

1 they have flexible holidays and working hours ____
2 they learn and use special skills ____
3 their employer gives them clear aims ____
4 they are independent ____
5 they have a relaxed manager ____
6 they have time for the family ____

E SPEAK Work in pairs. Which of the four jobs in the article would you rather have? Why?

What really makes us *happy in our jobs?*

In a recent survey about jobs and work, 75 per cent of children under ten said 'yes' to the question 'Can money buy happiness?' But is being **well-paid** really so important? Can you still be happy at work if you earn a **low hourly wage**? We asked four working adults what, apart from money, they like about their jobs.

Helen Police Officer

I don't work regular office hours – I do shifts. This means I often work in the evenings and sometimes do the night shift. In my last job I could choose when I wanted to work and I found that I liked working in the evenings. I also like that I am able to use all the different skills I learnt when I was training to be a police officer.

Bret Waiter

My job is badly paid, but I only work weekends, so I can study during the week. I work in a big restaurant. When there are no problems, the boss is usually very easygoing.

Lena Sales Manager

I earn an average salary. However, if I make a lot of sales, I get a bonus and I find that motivating. I also enjoy having clear goals, even when I have to work long hours to achieve them. I recently got a promotion which meant a lot of extra work, but I don't mind. I got a small pay rise and as a manager I was able to take an extra afternoon off each week to spend with my kids.

Ken Architect

The best part of my job is being my own boss. Because I'm self-employed, I can choose when I work and can take long holidays when I want to. The only bad part is I don't get a company car!

> **Glossary**
>
> **bonus (n)** extra money you are paid in addition to your usual salary, often because you have done well, for example, *a New Year bonus*
> **promotion (n)** a move to a higher level in your job, often because you have done well

GRAMMAR
can, could, be able to

A **WORK IT OUT** Look at the sentences from *What really makes us happy in our jobs?* Then complete the rules with *can*, *could* or *be able to*.

I only work weekends, so I can study during the week.

I am able to use all the different skills I learnt when I was training.

In my last job I could choose when I wanted to work.

I was able to take an extra afternoon off each week.

can, could and be able to
1 We use *can* and _____ to talk about possibility and ability in the present.
2 We use _____ and *was / were able to* to talk about possibility and ability in the past.
3 We often use _____ or *was / were able to* for possibilities and abilities at a particular time or for a particular reason.
4 We use _____ immediately before the main verb because *can* has no *-ing* form or *to* + infinitive form.

B Go to the **Grammar Hub** on **page 130**.

C **SPEAK** Work in pairs. Discuss the questions.

1 What are some of your abilities?

2 What were some of your abilities as a child?

VOCABULARY
Work collocations

A Complete the questions with the correct form of the verbs in the box. Sometimes more than one answer is possible. You need to use some verbs more than once.

be   earn   get   take   work

1 Do you or anyone you know _____ shifts? How often do they do a night shift?

2 Do you know anyone who _____ a very high salary? What do they do?

3 Do you think people should _____ an automatic pay rise every year they stay in the same job?

4 Who _____ the longest hours out of all the people you know? What do they do?

5 When was the last time you _____ a day off? What did you do?

6 Would you prefer to _____ a company car or more money?

7 Do people who _____ unemployed get money from the government in your country?

8 Would you be motivated by a job where you earn an average salary, but have the chance to _____ a bonus? Why/Why not?

B **SPEAK** Work in pairs. Would you like to be your own boss? Why/Why not? Tell your partner.

PRONUNCIATION
/w/ and /v/

 A Listen to the sounds. Are they the same or different? Listen and repeat.
5.1

1 /w/ work   2 /v/ very

 B Listen and write the words in the correct place.
5.2

/w/	/v/
wage	involve

C Listen and check your answers. Then listen and repeat.
5.2

D **SPEAK** Work in pairs. Can you think of more words with the sounds /w/ and /v/? Make a list.

SPEAKING

A Work in groups. Go to the **Communication Hub** on **page 157** and look at your group's list of jobs. Discuss the questions for each job.

1 Who do you know that does these jobs? How do they feel about them?

   My brother is a social worker. He works with people that have serious problems, but he still enjoys it.

2 Is each job paid a high, medium or low wage or salary?

3 What are the best and worst parts of each job?

4 Give each job a category which describes how it helps society, for example, *important for entertainment, health, education.*

B Work in new groups. Tell the group about the jobs you discussed and the categories you chose in Exercise A. Discuss which categories of jobs are most valuable to society and why.

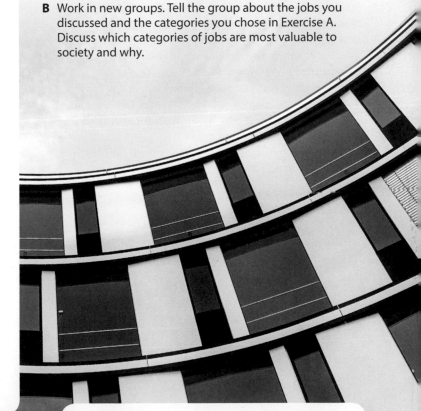

○– **Talk about the pros and cons of different jobs and say how they help society**

5.2 Flip-flopentrepreneurs

●— Decide on the rules for a workplace or classroom

G— obligation, necessity and permission: *must, have to* and *can*   **P**— *can / can't* and *must / mustn't*   **V**— adjectives for appearance

READING

A SPEAK Work in pairs. How important to you are the things on the list when you are buying new clothes? Decide whether they are very important (1), quite important (2) or less important (3). Compare your ideas.

The product …

a   is available in different colours and designs.   ____

b   is fashionable.   ____

c   is popular with celebrities.   ____

The company …

a   pays its staff fair wages.   ____

b   gives money to charity.   ____

c   does charity work.   ____

B SCAN Read *How do you build a children's home out of flip-flops?* Which things in Exercise A are mentioned?

C READ FOR DETAIL Read again and answer the questions.

1   What was unusual about Rob and Paul's education?

2   How did the brothers become orphans?

3   Why did the brothers start Gandys?

4   Which six adjectives are used to describe the company's flip-flops?

5   What was unusual about the brothers' visit to Buckingham Palace?

D SPEAK Work in groups. Discuss the questions.

1   Who do the biggest charities in your country help? What do they do to help?

2   Do you give money to charity? Why/Why not?

How do you build a children's home out of flip-flops?

British brothers Rob and Paul Forkan have experienced tragedy and success in their short and unusual lives. When they were still children, their parents took them out of school in the UK and moved the family to India to travel and do charity work. The experience taught them about life in other places and made them confident and independent.

Tragedy struck in 2004 when the Asian tsunami hit the coast of Sri Lanka, where the Forkans were staying. The giant wave killed their parents, but Rob (17), Paul (15) and their younger brother and sister survived. The children, now orphans, managed to hitchhike across Sri Lanka to the airport. From there, they flew back to Britain, where friends and family were waiting.

Six years later and now adults, the brothers decided to do something in memory of their parents. Their idea was simple. Make and sell attractive casual footwear and use the profits to help other orphans. Their company *Gandys* and their charity *Orphans for Orphans* were born.

After a lot of hard work and with the support of celebrity customers such as Richard Branson and Jamie Oliver, the comfortable rubber flip-flops became a hit. Customers love *Gandys'* stylish and fashionable designs and that the brothers give ten per cent of the profits to their charity. In 2014, three years after *Gandys* began, *Orphans for Orphans* opened its first children's home in Sri Lanka.

Gandys' head office now employs a large team and is possibly the only office in London where you can wear flip-flops to work! Rob and Paul's charity work even got them an invitation to meet British princes William and Harry. Normally of course, you must wear smart clothes at Buckingham Palace, but the brothers ignored the dress code and looked cool in their colourful flip-flops!

Rob and Paul's story shows that positive can follow negative and that you don't have to wear a smart suit to be successful in business!

Glossary

hitchhike (v) to have people give you a ride in their car, usually by standing at the side of the road and holding out your thumb or a sign

in memory of someone (phrase) in honour of someone who has died, so that people will remember them

tragedy (n) a very sad event that causes people to suffer or die

GRAMMAR
Obligation, necessity and permission:
must, have to and can

A WORK IT OUT Look at the last two paragraphs of *How do you build a children's home out of flip-flops?* and complete the sentences.

1 You _____ wear flip-flops to work.

2 You _____ wear a smart suit to be successful in business.

3 You _____ wear smart clothes at Buckingham Palace.

B Match the modal verbs (1–4) with the meanings (a–d).

Obligation, necessity and permission: *must, have to and can*	
1 *don't have to*	a This is necessary or is a rule.
2 *must / have to*	b This is not necessary but allowed.
3 *can*	c This is allowed but not necessary.
4 *can't / mustn't*	d This is not allowed.

C Choose the correct word to complete the rule.

Obligation, necessity and permission: *must, have to and can*
Modal verbs, such as *have to*, *can* and *must* are followed by an infinitive **with** / **without** to.

D Go to the **Grammar Hub on page 130**.

PRONUNCIATION
can / can't and must / mustn't

5.4 A Listen to the pairs of sentences. Can you hear the differences?

1 a You can wear casual clothes.
  b You can't wear casual clothes.

2 a Staff mustn't wear sportswear.
  b Staff must wear sportswear.

5.5 B Listen and tick (✓) the sentence you hear.

1 a You must wear large earrings. ☐
  b You mustn't wear large earrings. ☐

2 a You can wear a baseball cap. ☐
  b You can't wear a baseball cap. ☐

3 a You must leave your coat downstairs. ☐
  b You mustn't leave your coat downstairs. ☐

4 a You can hang your coat on your chair. ☐
  b You can't hang your coat on your chair. ☐

VOCABULARY
Adjectives for appearance

A SPEAK Work in pairs. Make a list of adjectives to describe appearance. You have one minute.

cool, casual …

B Match the adjectives (1–7) with the definitions (a–g).

1 attractive — a show good judgement about how to dress well
2 casual — b relaxed and comfortable
3 colourful — c pleasant to look at
4 cool — d impressive and modern
5 fashionable — e clean and neat
6 smart — f popular at a particular time
7 stylish — g has bright or many different colours

C Choose the words that you agree with most. Then work in pairs and explain why.

1 I *do / don't* think it's important to wear smart clothes to work.

2 I think that flip-flops are **too casual / perfect** for wearing around town.

3 I prefer clothes with **colourful / cool and simple** designs.

4 I think it *is / isn't* important to wear fashionable clothes.

5 You *can / can't* be stylish without wearing expensive clothes.

6 People *spend too much / don't spend enough* time and money trying to look attractive.

SPEAKING

A Work in groups. Think about the place where you work or study. Answer the questions.

1 What are the most important rules?
2 What annoying or unnecessary rules are there?
3 What rules would you add to make it a better place to work or study?

B Work in groups. Write ten rules for the perfect workplace or classroom. Think about what is/isn't allowed and what is/isn't necessary. Use these ideas:

Workplace: rules for workers, managers and directors; working hours; pay; dress code, etc.

Classroom: rules for students and teachers; during lessons; homework; tests and exams, etc.

C Look at the rules written by other groups. Which are the most useful? Why? Are there any you do not agree with? Why?

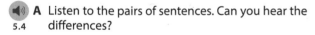

○─ Decide on the rules for a workplace or classroom

G— present perfect with *for* and *since*   **P**— *has, have, for, since*   **V**— *work* + preposition   **S**— listening for inference

LISTENING

A Work in groups. Complete the tips for job interviews with *do* or *don't*.

1 _____ eat smelly food or smoke before the interview.

2 _____ arrive ten minutes before your appointment.

3 _____ listen carefully to introductions and try to remember names.

4 _____ answer your telephone or check messages during the interview.

5 _____ be negative about yourself or your last job.

6 _____ ask one or two questions at the end.

B **LISTEN FOR GIST** Barry has a job interview with Gemma. Listen and choose the summary (1–3) that best describes the interview.

5.6

1 The interview goes well. Gemma and Barry have a good conversation. Barry will probably get the job.

2 The interview goes quite well. Barry has lots of experience working in a team. Barry might get the job.

3 The interview does not go well. Barry lies. Gemma is annoyed. Barry will definitely not get the job.

Glossary

call centre (n) a place where a large number of people are employed to deal with customers by telephone, either in order to sell something or to answer questions

CV (curriculum vitae) (n) a document giving details of your qualifications and the jobs you have had in the past that you send to someone when you are applying for a job

teamwork (n) work that you do together with other people

telemarketing (n) the activity or job of using the telephone to sell goods or services

C Test your memory! Tick (✓) the things Barry has done and cross (✗) the things he has not. Listen and check.

5.6

1 worked in a call centre ☐

2 worked in a team ☐

3 worked for a telemarketing company ☐

4 been skydiving ☐

5 read French poetry ☐

D Listen to three extracts from the interview. Then answer the questions about each extract. Use the information in the box to help you.

5.7

Listening for inference

When you listen to a foreign language, use vocabulary and context clues and your wider knowledge to work out the meaning of what you hear.

Think about the speaker's tone and attitude, as well as what they don't say.

Extract one

1 Does Barry check whether he needs to tell the truth?   *yes / no*

2 Does he give a real example?   *yes / no*

3 Do you think he has ever worked as part of a team?   *yes / no*

Extract two

4 Is Barry interested in skydiving?   *yes / no*

5 Does he think it's exciting?   *yes / no*

6 Do you think he has ever actually done it?   *yes / no*

Extract three

7 Does Barry remember what he wrote on his CV?   *yes / no*

8 Does he tell the truth about what he wrote on his CV?   *yes / no*

9 Do you think he enjoys French poetry?   *yes / no*

E **SPEAK** Work in groups. Have you ever had an interview for a job, course or scholarship? Tell your group about it.

GRAMMAR
Present perfect with *for* and *since*

A **WORK IT OUT** Look at the sentences from Barry's interview and answer the questions.

I left my old job in June.

1 Does Barry still do his old job?
2 Is the action *leave* finished or unfinished?
3 What tense is the verb *leave* in?

I've worked at the call centre for six weeks.

4 Does Barry still work at the call centre?
5 Is the action *work* finished or unfinished?
6 What tense is the verb *work* in?

B Choose the correct words to complete the rules.

Present perfect and past simple
1 We use the *present perfect / past simple* to talk about actions or situations that started and finished in the past.
2 We use the *present perfect / past simple* to talk about actions or situations that started in the past, but are unfinished and so continue until the present.

C Look at the words in **bold** in the sentences from Barry's interview. Complete the rules with *how long*, *for* or *since*.

How long have you worked there?

Actually, I've been here since 9 am.

You've been here for three hours?

Present perfect with *how long*, *for* and *since*
1 We use _____ + present perfect to ask about the duration of an action.
2 We use _____ to talk about the point in time when something started, e.g. *yesterday, I was young.*
3 We use _____ + present perfect to talk about a length of time until the present time, e.g. *three hours, two weeks.*

D Look at the sentence from Barry's interview and choose the correct words to complete the rule.

I've liked skydiving since I was a teenager.

since
After *since* we often use a verb in *present perfect / past simple*.

E Go to the **Grammar Hub** on **page 130**.

PRONUNCIATION
has, have, for, since

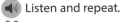 Listen and repeat.

5.8
1 How long has he lived there?
2 How long have you worked there?
3 He's lived there for three years.
4 I've worked there since last summer.

VOCABULARY
work + preposition

A Go to the **Vocabulary Hub** on **page 148**.

B **SPEAK** Work as a class. Talk to as many different people as possible in five minutes about their job or the job of someone they know. Make notes for each person you talk to.

Cassie: She works in IT for a software company. She's a computer programmer. She works in their city centre office.

C **SPEAK** Work in pairs. Compare your notes. Which jobs were the most unusual or interesting?

⬤ SPEAKING HUB

A You are going to talk about a topic in which you are an expert. Consider the following areas:

• your profession and/or studies
• a skill you've learnt, e.g. cooking, skiing, car mechanics, piano

B **PLAN** Think of some questions you could ask your classmates about their topics.

How long ...?
What can/can't you do?

C **DISCUSS** Work in a group. Interview each student in your group about their expertise. What were the most interesting things you learnt about your classmates?

◯– **Answer questions on topics in which you are an expert**

5.4 The cat

F – give information about your work experience in a job interview
P – singular and plural forms

C ▶ 00:27–03:06 Complete the job interview form for Neena. Then watch part of the video again and check your answers.

JOBS, JOBS, JOBS AND JOBS

Job interview

Name: ___Neena Patel___

Current job: Working for a ¹_____ firm.

Responsible for international ²_____ .

Time in current job: ³_____ years.

Reasons for changing job: Is looking for a
⁴_____ challenge.

Strengths: Is good at working ⁵_____ pressure. Can ⁶_____ her time.

Is very organised. Is good at ⁷_____ management. Works well in a ⁸_____ .

Weaknesses: Is a perfectionist – enjoys getting everything ⁹_____ .

A good candidate for the job: ¹⁰ Yes / No

COMPREHENSION

A ▶ **SPEAK** Work in pairs. Look at the pictures above from Neena's job interview. What do you think goes wrong in the interview? Watch the video and check.

B ▶ 03:09–05:00 Watch the last part of the interview again. Answer the questions.

1 Whose cat was it?

2 What was the cat's name?

3 What is Neena doing on Monday?

MILLY

SAM

NEENA

ZAC

GABY

FUNCTIONAL LANGUAGE
Give information about your work experience in a job interview

A Cross out the word that is NOT possible to complete the sentences.

1 Currently, I'm working for *a law firm* / *Citibank* / *architect*.

2 I have to manage *a team* / *five sales representatives* / *a company car*.

3 I've worked there for *last year* / *a long time* / *four years*.

4 People say I'm good at *working under pressure* / *manage my time* / *my job*.

5 I've learnt how to *manage my time* / *working in a team* / *deal with clients*.

6 I work well *in a team* / *under pressure* / *my job*.

B Look at Exercise A. Think of another word for each sentence to replace the one you crossed out.

USEFUL PHRASES

A ▶ Complete the conversations with the useful phrases in the box. Then watch the video again and check your answers.

> Go on.   How did it go?   It was going so well …
> Just go!   Let me think.   Please take a seat.
> Tell me about yourself.   That's a good question.

Gaby:	1 _____
Neena:	Oh, Gaby, it was awful.
Gaby:	What happened?
Neena:	2 _____
Interviewer:	Good afternoon, Neena. 3 _____
	So Neena, 4 _____
	What have you learnt from your current job?
Neena:	5 _____
Interviewer:	And any weak points?
Neena:	6 _____
	Well, I have one question.
Interviewer:	7 _____
Neena:	So, will you call me?
Interviewer:	8 _____

B How do you say these useful phrases in your language?

PRONUNCIATION
Singular and plural forms

🔊 5.9 **A** Listen and repeat the singular and plural forms of the nouns in the box. Which noun has an extra syllable in the plural form?

> account(s)   challenge(s)   job(s)   perfectionist(s)
> pressure(s)   project(s)   question(s)   strength(s)

B **SPEAK** Work in pairs. Practise saying the words in Exercise A. Listen and check your partner's pronunciation.

SPEAKING

A Think about the things you are good at. Write down three strengths and one weakness. Then work in pairs and compare your ideas.

B Work in pairs. Write down three important skills for each of the jobs in the box.

> accountant   football team manager
> teacher   website manager

C Roleplay a job interview. Use the job interview form in Comprehension Exercise C to help you. Include at least two useful phrases. Take turns.

Student A: Choose a job from Exercise B and interview Student B for the job.

Student B: Answer Student A's questions.

Student A: Decide if Student B is suitable for the job.

⭕ **Give information about your work experience in a job interview**

➤ Turn to **page 162** to learn how to write a covering email.

VOCABULARY

A Match beginnings of the sentences (1–5) with the ends of the sentences (a–e).

1 What advantages are there to a job where you work
2 How important do you think it is to earn
3 What are the disadvantages of being
4 When did you last take
5 Do you think people should get

a a day off work or study and what did you do?
b shifts, so sometimes you start at night or early in the morning?
c a pay rise every year or only when they have done well at work?
d your own boss?
e a high salary in your job?

B Write the missing words to complete the sentences.

1 My brother is very c___ ___ ___; he always looks good.
2 She's not allowed to wear c___ ___ ___ ___ ___ clothes to work.
3 I love those high-heeled shoes – they have a very s___ ___ ___ ___ ___ ___ design.
4 I don't like that T-shirt. I don't think those colours look a___ ___ ___ ___ ___ ___ ___ ___ ___ .
5 In our country, you must wear s___ ___ ___ ___ clothes to a wedding.

C Choose the correct prepositions. In three examples, both are possible.

1 They work *at / for* the IT department.
2 He works *in / at* marketing.
3 She works *at / for* Bluemoon Software Services.
4 She works *at / for* an advertising firm.
5 I work *at / in* a library.
6 We work *in / for* a telemarketing company.

GRAMMAR

A Choose the best words to complete the sentences.

1 When I was young, I *can / could* stay up late, but these days I get tired early.
2 I really enjoy *being able to / can* work for myself.
3 Johann *able to / can* speak four languages.
4 I *was able to / could* speak to my boss last Friday about getting a pay rise.
5 I'd like *can / to be able to* speak perfect English one day.

B Match the rules (1–8) with the meanings (a–d).

Memo: Information for palace staff

1 ___ You can park your car in the staff car park.
2 ___ You mustn't bring your own mobile phone inside the palace.
3 ___ You can't take any pictures while at work.
4 ___ You have to be smartly dressed at all times.*
5 ___ You must call the Queen 'Your Majesty'.
6 ___ You mustn't mention anything you see or hear at work to anyone.
7 ___ You can smoke in the staff smoking area.
8 ___ *If the Royal family are away, you don't have to wear the full uniform.

a This is necessary or is a rule.
b This is not necessary but allowed.
c This is allowed but not necessary.
d This is not allowed.

C Complete the conversations with the past simple or present perfect form of the verbs in brackets.

Erin: How long ¹_____ (*you / work*) here?
Paulie: Oh, not long. ²_____ (*I / start*) work last December. But, you see that lady there? Well, ³_____ (*she / be*) here for 20 years. ⁴_____ (*she / become*) a cook when she was only 17.

Karl: I thought you worked for a newspaper? When ⁵_____ (*you / change*) jobs?
Crystal: Years ago! ⁶_____ (*I / not work*) in journalism since about 2004.

Pippa: ⁷_____ (*I / want*) to be a doctor when I was a child, but now I'm a vet.
Gianni: A vet? That's so cool. ⁸_____ (*I / love*) animals since I was little.

FUNCTIONAL LANGUAGE

A Complete the phrases to use in job interviews with the words in the box.

enjoy   learnt   problem   question   responsible   team

1 I've _____ how to motivate other people.
2 Well, I have one _____ I'd like to ask.
3 I'm _____ for customer service.
4 I _____ working in a busy office.
5 I work well in a _____ .
6 Well, I have a _____ with the weekend hours.

HEALTH

Health is not
valued until
sickness comes.

Thomas Fuller

Yoga enthusiasts take part in the annual Times Square event celebrating
the Summer Solstice, the longest day of the year, New York.

OBJECTIVES

○ give a presentation on health dos and don'ts

○ plan an exercise event for your local community

○ encourage people to make a lifestyle change

○ talk about your symptoms at a pharmacy

○ write a product review

Work with a partner. Discuss the questions.

1 What do you do to stay healthy?

2 Read the quote. Do you agree with it?

3 Would you like to take part in an event like
the one in the picture? Why/Why not?

G— quantifiers *too* and *enough* **V**— minor illnesses **P**— /ʌ/, /ɔː/, /uː/, /eɪ/ and /ɜː/

LISTENING

A Match the definitions (1–7) with the words in the box.

> a balanced diet antibiotics confused
> expert liquid myth reality

1 something that people wrongly believe to be true
2 someone who has a particular skill or who knows a lot about a particular subject
3 a fact, event or situation as it really exists
4 a range of food that a person eats to provide all the good things their body needs
5 drugs that cure illnesses and infections caused by bacteria
6 unable to understand something or think clearly about it
7 a substance (such as water) that can flow, has no fixed shape and is not a solid or a gas

B SPEAK Work in pairs. Tick (✓) the sentences about health you have heard before. Which ones do you think are true and which ones are myths? Give reasons.

1 Everyone should drink eight glasses of water per day. ☐
2 Eating fatty food makes you fat. ☐
3 Eggs are bad for your heart. ☐
4 Cold weather causes colds. ☐
5 Take antibiotics when you have a cold. ☐

C LISTEN FOR GIST Look at the glossary. Then listen to the introduction of *Live with Pippa* and answer the questions.
6.1

Glossary

calorie (n) unit for measuring how much energy you get from food
carbohydrate (n) a substance found in foods such as sugar, bread and potatoes. Carbohydrates supply your body with heat and energy.
fatty (adj) containing a lot of fat
virus (n) a thing that can enter your body and make you ill

1 How many experts does Pippa speak to?
2 Choose the best summary of Pippa's message in the introduction to the show.
   a It is better to ask a medical professional than look online for information about health.
   b It is difficult to know which online information about health is true.
   c Bad online advice about health is making healthy people ill.

D LISTEN FOR DETAIL Listen again and choose a, b or c.
6.1

1 Doctor Singh says that …
   a most headaches are due to a lack of water.
   b we get some of the water we need from our food.
   c more than eight glasses of water per day is dangerous.

2 Michael says that …
   a everyone needs some fat in their diets.
   b most people get fat because they eat too much sugar.
   c we shouldn't eat fatty food.

3 Dr Tremblay says you are more likely to catch a cold or flu …
   a if you spend time outside in cold weather.
   b if you don't get enough vitamins in your diet.
   c if you spend time indoors with a lot of people.

4 Lia says that …
   a advice on eating eggs changes regularly.
   b advice on eating eggs is not the same as it was in the past.
   c advice on eating eggs is the same as it has always been.

GRAMMAR
Quantifiers *too* and *enough*

A WORK IT OUT Complete the sentences from the radio show (1–5) using the audioscript on **page 173**. Then match the sentences with the rules (a–c).

1 You drink too _____ coffee. rule ___
2 You don't sleep _____. rule ___
3 It's because you go to bed _____ early. rule ___
4 Make sure you are getting _____ vitamins. rule ___
5 Too _____ eggs are bad for your heart. rule ___

Quantifiers *too* and *enough*

a We use *too* + adjective or adverb, *too much* and *too many* to mean more than the right amount.
b We use *enough* to mean the right amount.
c We use *not enough* to mean less than the right amount.

B Look at the sentences from the radio show in Exercise A and complete the rules.

> **too much and too many**
>
> 1 We use **too much** / **too many** with countable nouns.
>
> 2 We use **too much** / **too many** with uncountable nouns.

C Go to the **Grammar Hub** on **page 132.**

D **PRACTISE** Complete the sentences so they are true for you.

1 I spend too much time _____ and not enough time _____.

2 I eat too much/many _____ and not enough _____.

3 I don't _____ enough and I _____ too much/often.

4 I find _____ too difficult.

5 I have enough _____, but not enough _____.

E **SPEAK** Work in pairs. Discuss your answers to Exercise D.

VOCABULARY
Minor illnesses

A Read Dr Tremblay's audioscript on **page 173** and <u>underline</u> six health problems he talks about.

B Label the pictures (1–10) with the health problems in the box.

> a broken bone   a-cold   a cough
> a headache   a temperature   a sore throat
> flu   stomach ache   sunburn   toothache

PRONUNCIATION
/ʌ/, /ɔɪ/, /uɪ/, /eɪ/ and /ɔɪ/

6.2
A Listen and repeat.

1 /ʌ/ but	4 /eɪ/ pay
2 /ɔː/ caught	5 /ɜː/ fur
3 /uː/ do	

6.3
B Each word contains one of the sounds in Exercise A. Listen and match the words with the sounds. Then <u>underline</u> the letter(s) that make the sounds.

1	burn	a	/ʌ/
2	ache	b	/ɔː/
3	stomach	c	/uː/
4	flu	d	/eɪ/
5	sore	e	/ɜː/

C **SPEAK** Work in pairs. What do people usually do for each of the problems in Vocabulary Exercise B? Use ideas below to help you and your own ideas.

- go to bed
- take medicine
- go to the doctor's
- take painkillers
- put on cream
- stay off work

SPEAKING

A Work in pairs. Plan and give a short presentation called *The dos and don'ts of staying fit and healthy.*

B Write a list of dos and don'ts for each of the topics:

- food and drink
- sleep
- exercise
- stress
- avoiding and recovering from illness

C Present your advice to the class. Ask them to guess which piece of advice is a myth or bad advice.

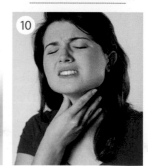

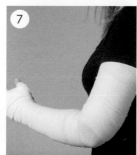

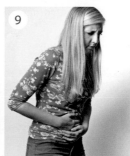

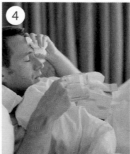

1 _____ a cold _____

2 _____

3 _____

4 _____

5 _____

6 _____

7 _____

8 _____

9 _____

10 _____

○– **Give a presentation on health dos and don'ts**

V — exercise   **P** — /ŋ /, /n/ and /m/   **G** — -ing forms

VOCABULARY
Exercise

A Work in pairs. Make a list of different ways of exercising. You have one minute.

Walking, swimming …

B Go to the **Vocabulary Hub** on **page 148**.

C **SPEAK** Look at the **Vocabulary Hub** Exercise B on **page 149**. Go around the class and ask the questions. If someone answers *yes*, write their name and ask a follow-up question.

A: Do you hate working out at the gym?
B: Yes, I do.
A: Why?
B: I like to exercise outdoors and I don't like to exercise with so many other people watching me. I find most gyms too busy.

PRONUNCIATION
/ŋ/, /n/ and /m/

A Listen to these sounds. Do they sound the same or different?

6.4

   1 /ŋ/ cycling   **2** /n/ run   **3** /m/ team

B Listen again and repeat the sounds.

6.4

C Listen and complete the table with the words you hear. Do the words have an /ŋ/, /n/ or /m/ sound? Some words have more than one of the sounds.

6.5

/ŋ/	/n/	/m/

READING

A Tick (✓) the sentences you agree with. Then work in pairs and explain your choices.

Running is great exercise and great fun. ☐

I'd like to run a marathon one day. ☐

I prefer team sports, like squash or hockey. ☐

Jogging is exercise, not fun. ☐

Running is boring. ☐

The only time I run is to catch the bus. ☐

B **SCAN** Read texts 1–3. What is the purpose of each?

Text ___: to inform   Text ___: to persuade

Text ___: to entertain

1 Funny fitness

Did you know that laughing for 15 minutes can burn up to 40 calories? We hope these jokes and quotes will keep you smiling as you walk to the shop, jog round the park or run your next marathon.

Q What is a runner's favourite school subject?
A Jog-raphy

'If you are in a bad mood, go for a walk. If you are still in a bad mood, go for another walk.'
Hippocrates

Patient: Doctor, can you give me something to stop sleepwalking?
Doctor: I'm afraid I can't, sir. You need the exercise!

Parkrun

Are you looking for an easy way to keep fit and lose weight? Would you like to run 5 km in a family-friendly atmosphere? Would you like to compare your results with other runners from all over the world? If so, then check out *Parkrun*.

Parkrun organises free weekly timed runs in parks all over the world. The 5 km runs take place on weekend mornings and are open to everyone. After each race, runners receive detailed results via email.

Parkrun is an international community of over one million runners in 17 countries and there is always space for more! So come and join the *Parkrun* family and get fit for free!

Glossary
atmosphere (n) the mood or feeling in a place

MARATHON MAN

What do you think it takes to become a running master? Fauja Singh, from east London, finished a 10 km race in Hong Kong in one hour 32 minutes – and he did it at the age of 101.

In 2011, Singh became the oldest person to run a marathon. At 100 years of age, he completed the Toronto Marathon in just over eight hours.

As a young man, Mr Singh was a farmer in Punjab, India. Then in the 1960s, he went to live in Britain and only began running when he was 89 years old.

Mr Singh plans to run again for charity, but the Hong Kong 10 km was his final competitive race. 'I will remember this day. I will miss it,' Mr Singh said after the event.

C READ FOR DETAIL Read again and answer the questions. Write *Funny fitness* (FF), *Parkrun* (PR), *Marathon man* (MM) or none of the texts (N).

Which text …

1 tells the story of an individual? _____
2 offers readers the chance to read more online? _____
3 tries to sell readers something? _____
4 reports the results of a research project? _____
5 tries to make readers laugh? _____
6 describes the purpose of a particular organisation? _____

D SPEAK Work in pairs. Discuss the questions.

1 Why is running such a popular form of exercise?
2 Would you like to do a parkrun? Why/Why not?

GRAMMAR
-ing forms

A Look at the examples of different -*ing* forms used in the texts. Then complete the rules with the words in the box.

1 Did you know that **laughing** for 15 minutes can burn up to 40 calories? (gerund)
2 Are you **looking** for an easy way to keep fit and lose weight? (present participle)
3 What do you think it takes to become a **running** master? (adjective)

> adjectives   gerunds   present participle

-ing forms

1 We use the _____ -*ing* form with the verb *to be* to talk about things that are happening now or around now, and are not finished.
2 We use -*ing* form as _____ to describe nouns.
3 We use -*ing* form as _____ to make nouns.

B Go to the **Grammar Hub** on **page 132**.

C SPEAK Work in pairs. Discuss the questions.

1 What is your favourite form of exercise?
2 Do you like working out? Why/Why not?

SPEAKING

A Work in groups. Plan an event to encourage local people to start doing more exercise. Think about:

- who your event is for
- how it will help people get fit or start exercising
- what people need to bring to the event
- how you will promote the event

B Describe your event to the rest of the class. Which event is the most popular. Why?

◯– Plan an exercise event for your local community

● Encourage people to make a lifestyle change

G present perfect with *just, already* and *yet*   **V** food groups   **P** /s/ and /ʃ/   **S** scanning for key words

READING

A Match the words in the box to pictures (1–6).

avocado   broccoli   fur   grain   kale   wheat

B **READ FOR GIST** Read *A fresh start*. Which three reasons for going vegetarian or vegan are given in the article?

A fresh start 🕴

Large numbers of people are saying 'never again!' to meat and becoming vegetarian or vegan. For some it's about health, for others it's about concern for the environment. Whatever the reason, many people are changing the way they eat forever.

Research by the Vegan Society states that in 2016 there were around 542,000 vegans in the UK alone. Veganism is also on the rise thanks to celebrity supporters including Ellie Goulding, Liam Hemsworth and Venus and Serena Williams.

There are various reasons why people decide to go vegetarian or vegan. Some do it for their health. Vegans get all the vitamins, minerals and other things they need for a balanced diet from grains, fruit, seeds, nuts and vegetables such as kale, broccoli, beans and avocados. A vegetarian diet can help people lose weight because it is low in fat. High-fat diets are linked to serious health problems including diabetes, heart disease and cancer.

Some people give up meat because they are worried about the environment. A 2006 FAO (The Food and Agriculture Organization of the United Nations) study reported that 18 per cent of greenhouse gases come from farm animals such as cows, sheep and chickens. That's more than all of the world's cars, trains and planes put together. We use over 36 per cent of the world's grain to feed farm animals, yet a quarter of the people in the world do not have enough food. If we made food for people from the grain instead, there would be enough for everyone.

Other people go meat-free because they feel it is wrong to kill animals. Animals feel pain and fear. Many farmed animals are kept in poor conditions with little space and no time outdoors. In the UK, around 990 million farmed animals are killed for food each year.

With so many supermarkets and restaurants now offering vegetarian and vegan goods, it's easier than ever to give up or reduce the amount of meat we eat. Why not try a few meat-free days a week – you could help reduce world hunger and even help with climate change!

Are you vegan or vegetarian?

We want your comments!

Nora_27
 I've just changed to a vegetarian diet after years of eating meat. It's only been a week, but I feel much healthier and I highly recommend it!

M-M-Maxine
I feel bad about killing animals, but I really enjoy meat. **I've already eaten two sausages and a chicken sandwich today, and it's only lunchtime!** I don't think I'd last very long without meat.

Cool_keith2
I've been vegetarian for a while, but I haven't managed to go vegan yet. It seems like a lot of work to plan and prepare the food. Any advice?

Kellykale
Great article. Vegan food is great! **Have you tried kale chips yet?** They are really tasty and great as a healthy snack.

Glossary

billion (number) the number 1,000,000,000

greenhouse gas (n) a gas that stops heat from escaping the atmosphere and causes the greenhouse effect, the gas that makes global warming worse

mineral (n) a natural substance in some foods that you need for good health, for example, iron and calcium

vitamin (n) natural substances found in food that are necessary to keep your body healthy

C SCAN Read again. Are the sentences true (T) or false (F)? Use the information in the box to help you.

Scanning for key words

When you are reading to find specific information, such as names, dates and statistics, move your eyes quickly over the text and look for titles, numbers, symbols and names. Read around these items to find the information you are looking for. This is called scanning.

Scanning helps save time in exams and is useful for previewing texts to decide whether to read them in more detail.

1 There are about half a million vegetarians in the UK. **T / F**

2 Quite a few famous people are vegans. **T / F**

3 Vegans need to take extra vitamins to stay healthy. **T / F**

4 Transport vehicles produce less air pollution than farming animals for meat. **T / F**

5 If we produced less meat, there would be more food for those people who do not have enough. **T / F**

6 It is difficult to buy vegan products. **T / F**

D SPEAK Work in pairs. What are the arguments for and against farming and killing animals for food?

GRAMMAR
Present perfect with *just*, *already* and *yet*

A WORK IT OUT Look at the sentences in **bold** in the comments section of *A fresh start*. Then complete the rules with *just*, *already* or *yet*.

Present perfect with *just*, *already* and *yet*

1 We use the present perfect with _____ in positive statements to say something happened very recently.

2 We use the present perfect with _____ in positive statements to say that something happened before now or earlier than expected.

3 We use the present perfect with _____ :
   • in negative statements to say that something hasn't happened, but it still might.
   • in questions to ask if something has happened.

B Look again and choose the correct words to complete the rules.

1 *Just* comes **before / after** the past participle in a sentence.

2 *Already* usually comes **before / after** the past participle in a sentence.

3 *Yet* comes at the **beginning / end** of a sentence or question.

C Go to the **Grammar Hub** on page 132.

D SPEAK. Work in pairs. Have you done any exercise today? Make true sentences with present perfect and *just*, *already* or *yet*.

VOCABULARY
Food groups

A Work in pairs. Make a list of different food items. You have one minute.

B Go to the **Vocabulary Hub** on page 149.

C SPEAK Work in pairs. Have you eaten any healthy food today? Who has been kinder to their body?

I had two oranges with my breakfast, and I've just eaten an apple and two kiwis, so I've already had five pieces of fruit today.

PRONUNCIATION
/s/ and /ʃ/

A SPEAK Work in pairs. Write the words in the box in the correct place. Use the examples to help you.

chefs   fish   fresh   lettuce   ~~lobster~~   rice
sandwich   sauce   spinach   sushi   ~~sugar~~

/s/	/ʃ/	/s/ and /ʃ/
lobster	*sugar*	

B Listen and check. Then listen again and repeat the words.

6.6

C SPEAK Work in pairs. Student A – point to a word in Exercise B. Student B – say the word. Take turns.

⃝ SPEAKING HUB

A Work in groups. You are going to design a leaflet to help other students make a lifestyle change. Choose one of the following:

• eat less meat
• stop drinking bottled water
• use more fresh ingredients when cooking
• eat less sugar

B PLAN What information will you include on the leaflet? Think about the areas below and then design your leaflet.

• health benefits
• environmental benefits
• how your school or university will help
• how you or someone you know changed their lifestyle in this way and how they benefitted

C REFLECT Read the other groups' leaflets. Which do you think would be most successful and why?

⃝ **Encourage people to make a lifestyle change**

Café Hub

6.4 Painful experience
- F — **talk about your symptoms at a pharmacy**
- P — **vowel sounds**

COMPREHENSION

A ▶ 00:00–02:13 Watch the first part of the video without sound and answer the questions.

1 How does the pharmacist feel?

2 How does Gaby feel?

3 Tick (✔) the parts of their bodies that hurt.

arm ☐   back ☐   ears ☐   eyes ☐   foot ☐
hand ☐   head ☐   leg ☐   nose ☐   throat ☐

B ▶ 00:00–02:13 Watch the first part of the video again with sound and check your answers to Exercise A.

C **SPEAK** Work in pairs. What advice would you give Gaby? What advice would you give the pharmacist?

D ▶ 02:26–04:54 Watch the second part of the video and check your answers to Exercise C.

FUNCTIONAL LANGUAGE
Talk about your symptoms at a pharmacy

A Write the headings in the box in the correct place (a–c).

> Explain symptoms   Ask about health   Give advice

Useful language

a _____

Are you OK?

Are you ¹_____?

What's painful?

What are your symptoms?

Do you have anything for a sore throat / a ²_____?

Do you have sore eyes / ³_____?

Are you allergic to anything?

b _____

It's very painful.

My nose / ⁴_____ hurts.

I'm not feeling very well.

I have a terrible cold.

You don't have a cold, you have hay fever / ⁵_____.

c _____

I suggest these tablets / ⁶_____.

Take one every eight hours.

You could try drinking a hot lemon and honey.

I think you should rest / ⁷_____.

MILLY **SAM** **NEENA** **ZAC** **GABY**

B Write the words and phrases in the box in the correct place in Exercise A.

> back   flu   a temperature   headache   relax
> sure you're OK   this medicine

USEFUL PHRASES

A Match the useful phrases (1–6) with similar phrases which show the meaning (a–f).

1 I know how you feel.
2 We are both not very well today.
3 It's common at this time of year.
4 I'll be fine.
5 Is one enough?
6 That usually makes me feel better.

a A lot of people get this in summer.
b Don't I need more?
c I have the same symptoms as you.
d It's my favourite cure.
e You and I are ill today.
f Don't worry about me.

B How do you say these useful phrases in your language?

PRONUNCIATION
Vowel sounds

A Match the words which have the same vowel sound.

1 cough
2 hurt
3 pain
4 sore
5 throat

a allergic
b jaw
c nose
d same
e wrong

🔊 **B** Listen and check. Then listen again and repeat the words.
6.7

C **SPEAK** Work in pairs. Practise saying the words. Listen and check your partner's pronunciation.

SPEAKING

Work in pairs. Roleplay a conversation about health. Take turns to be Student A and Student B.

Student A: Choose an ailment from the pictures and explain the symptoms.

You must use the following words: *feeling, have, hurt(s), painful.*

Student B: Ask questions and give advice.

You must use the following words: *allergic, take, temperature, try.*

○─ **Talk about your symptoms at a pharmacy**

➤ Turn to page 163 to learn how to write a product review.

VOCABULARY

A Complete the crossword.

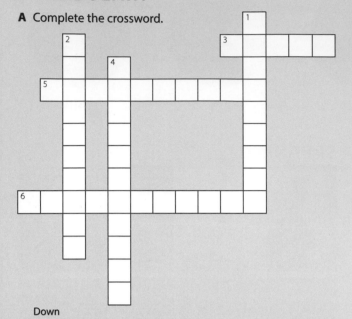

Down

1 See the dentist with this problem.

2 Leg, arm, finger? Go to the hospital. (two words)

4 You are warmer than you should be.

Across

3 Cover your mouth with your hand when you do this.

5 Try not to talk. Drink hot drinks. Suck a sweet. (two words)

6 Did you eat too much? (two words)

B What are the missing words? Choose a, b or c to complete the survey.

WELCOME TO *SUNNY'S GYM*

Tick (✓) your fitness goals.

1 ___ weight ☐

2 get or ___ fit ☐

Do you …

3 ___ at a gym? ☐

4 ___ jogging? ☐

5 ___ a team sport? ☐

6 ___ yoga? ☐

1 a get	b put	c lose
2 a keep	b work	c go
3 a work it	b work out	c work on
4 a run	b do	c go
5 a go	b play	c join
6 a play	b go	c do

C Choose the correct words to complete the sentences.

1 Pasta is made from *nuts / wheat*.

2 You can eat the shell of *shrimp / lobster*, but a lot of people choose not to.

3 Pizza is made with bread, cheese and *avocado / tomato* sauce.

4 British-style fish and chips usually includes *tuna / cod*.

5 One of the main salad ingredients is *rice / lettuce*.

GRAMMAR

A Complete the sentences with *too many*, *too much* and *not enough*.

1 We can't make a cake today. There are _____ eggs in the fridge.

2 There are _____ flavours of ice cream – I can't decide!

3 There are _____ chairs here. I'll get two more from the kitchen.

4 We shouldn't eat _____ sugar in our diets. It's unhealthy.

5 I've eaten _____ pies. I don't feel well.

B Write the word in brackets in the correct place. Then circle the correct *-ing* form. Choose gerund (G), adjective (A) or present participle (PP).

1 She left the gym because of the ˄*rising* prices. (rising)   **G / Ⓐ / PP**

2 Lucien is very fit these days. (becoming)   **G / A / PP**

3 He isn't any exercise at the moment. (doing)   **G / A / PP**

4 My brother loves marathons. (running)   **G / A / PP**

5 I want to try yoga by myself. (practising)   **G / A / PP**

C Complete the comments from a health website with *just*, *already* or *yet*.

HART_27: I became vegetarian about two weeks ago. I feel lighter and I've [1]_____ got clearer skin. I've [2]_____ weighed myself but I haven't lost any weight [3]_____.

KENNYKEN: This morning, I finally decided to go vegan. I've [4]_____ come back from the shops with vegan ingredients and a cookbook. Actually, I've [5]_____ got one vegan cookbook, but I haven't made anything from it [6]_____.

FUNCTIONAL LANGUAGE

A Complete the words in the conversation at a pharmacy.

Pharmacist: Good morning. [1]H__ __ can I h__ __ __ __ ?

Customer: Oh, good morning. [2]I f__ __ __ __ terr__ __ __ __ __ .

Pharmacist: [3]Wh__ __ are your sym__ __ __ __ __ __ ?

Customer: [4]I've g__ __ __ a s__ __ __ __ thr__ __ __ __ and a cou__ __ __ . [5]It really hu__ __ __ __ .

Pharmacist: Oh, dear. Anything else?

Customer: Well, I think [6]I've g__ __ __ a tem__ __ __ __ __ __ __ __ __ , too, because I feel hot all the time.

7 MIND

The greatest thing in life is
to keep your mind young.

Henry Ford

A little boy tries to solve the Sunday crossword puzzle, Lancashire, United Kingdom.

OBJECTIVES

- discuss what makes you happy
- write an online comment about the effects of the internet
- talk about intelligence and achievements
- describe an object and say what you use it for
- write a survey report

Work with a partner. Discuss the questions.

1 How can people 'stay young'?
2 Look at the picture. Who is helping whom?
3 What do you do to keep your mind healthy?

G— articles   **P**— /ə/ (schwa) in *a* / *an*   **V**— feelings

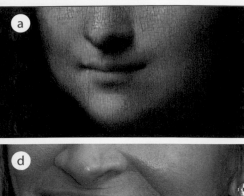

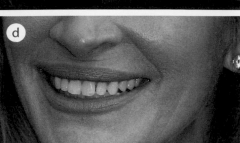

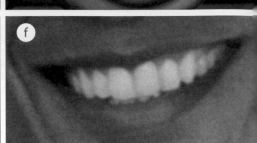

READING

A Work in groups. Discuss the questions.

1 Do you recognise these famous smiles? What do you know about them?

2 'Laugh and the world laughs with you.' What does this saying mean? Do you agree with its message? Do you have a similar saying in your language?

3 How many times a day do you think a person laughs on average?

4 How is laughing good for our health?

5 How do smiling and laughing help social relationships?

B **READ FOR GIST** Read *A smile a day …* quickly and check your answers to questions 3, 4 and 5.

C **READ FOR DETAIL** Are the following statements true (T) or false (F)? Correct the false sentences.

1 Happy people are likely to live to an older age.   *T / F*

2 Laughing can have a similar effect to working out in the gym. *T / F*

3 Laughing slows our heartbeat and blood flow.   *T / F*

4 Laughing can prevent small health problems.   *T / F*

5 The production of chemicals in our brain causes laughter.   *T / F*

6 Smiling and laughter began in humans to show there was danger.   *T / F*

D **SPEAK** Work in pairs. Discuss the questions.

1 How many times do you think you laugh each day? When did you last laugh? What did you laugh at?

2 What everyday things make you feel good and put you in a positive mood? (For example, good food, music, new clothes)

A *smile* a day …

We all know that a cheerful state of mind makes us happy but it could also help us to live longer.

Laughing out loud, something we do on average 17 times a day, is particularly good for you. Laughter is a short sound which is repeated, on average, five times a second. It is widely believed that laughing 100 times is equal to ten minutes' light exercise in the gym. In addition, a 2005 study by the University of Maryland School of Medicine showed that laughter lowers blood pressure and there is a healthy increase in heart rate and blood flow. This can lead to a healthier heart and also make you less likely to catch colds and other minor illnesses. The research also suggests that people who are happy are likely to live longer. Laughing also produces chemicals in the brain that make us feel pleased and puts us in a positive mood. Smiling and laughing are also important for social relationships. Experts believe that smiling and laughing in humans began as a way to show relief when danger had passed. It helped the mind and body to feel relaxed and therefore showed trust between people. This stopped people from feeling scared of each other and helped people to connect. So the next time you want to connect with someone, why not start with a smile? It will help them to feel at ease and you might even make a new friend!

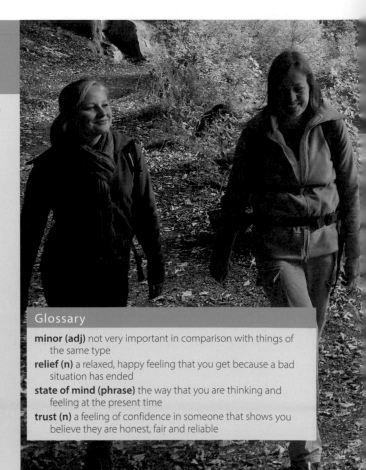

Glossary

minor (adj) not very important in comparison with things of the same type

relief (n) a relaxed, happy feeling that you get because a bad situation has ended

state of mind (phrase) the way that you are thinking and feeling at the present time

trust (n) a feeling of confidence in someone that shows you believe they are honest, fair and reliable

GRAMMAR
Articles

A WORK IT OUT Look at the sentences from *A smile a day …* Then complete the rules with *a/an*, *the* or – (no article).

The research also suggests that people who are happy are likely to live longer.

*Laughter is **a short sound*** which is repeated, on average, five times a second.

*Smiling and laughing are also important for **social relationships.***

Articles
1 We use _____ to refer to something indefinite when it is one of many. We often use it when we refer to something for the first time.
2 We use _____ to refer to something definite and which we know. This is often because it has already been mentioned.
3 We use _____ to refer to a plural or uncountable noun or something in a general sense.

B Go to the **Grammar Hub** on **page 134**.

C PRACTISE There are two mistakes in each question. Correct the mistakes.

1 The smiley is a famous image all over world. Why do you think an image is so successful and popular?

2 Do you own or have you ever owned anything with smiley on it, such as the T-shirt? Where else do we see it?

3 Do you use an emojis or icons in your online messaging? Do you have a favourite emoji? Are there the emojis for your country or culture?

D SPEAK Work in pairs. Ask and answer the questions in Exercise C.

PRONUNCIATION
/ə/ (schwa) in *a* / *an*

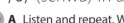

A Listen and repeat. What do you notice about the pronunciation of *a* and *an*?

1 Have **a** nice day.
2 We had **a** great time.
3 She's **an** old friend.
4 **A** smile **a** day keeps the doctor away.

B SPEAK Work in pairs. Student A – go to the **Communication Hub** on **page 156**. Student B – go to the **Communication Hub** on **page 153**.

VOCABULARY
Feelings

A WORK IT OUT Look at the sentences from *A smile a day …* Then choose the correct words to complete the sentences (1–3).

*We all know that a **cheerful** state of mind makes us happy …*

*It helped the mind and body to feel **relaxed** and therefore showed trust between people.*

*This stopped people from feeling **scared** of each other and helped people to connect.*

1 The words in bold are *adjectives* / *nouns*.
2 They describe *opinions* / *feelings and states of mind*.
3 Words like these *are always positive* / *are always negative* / *can be positive or negative*.

B Go to the **Vocabulary Hub** on **page 149**.

C SPEAK Work in pairs. When was the last time you felt anxious, confused, pleased, relaxed? Tell your partner.

SPEAKING

A Work in pairs. Do a class survey about what everyday things make people happy. Think of three everyday things that make you happy. Write them down and tell your partner about them.

A: *I feel happy when I have a cup of tea in the morning. How about you?*
B: *Me, too, but I prefer a coffee. And going for a walk on a sunny day with a clear blue sky makes me feel good.*
A: *I agree. A nice day makes everyone feel good!*

B Go around the class and ask your classmates what three everyday things make them happy. Write down their answers.

A: *Getting into bed after a long day.*
B: *When I find a bargain in the shops.*
C: *Relaxing with a good book.*

C Work in pairs. Compare your findings. What were the most common answers? What were the most interesting or unusual answers? Work with other pairs and share your answers.

◯— **Discuss what makes you happy**

READING

A Work in pairs. Discuss the questions.

1 Look at the picture on the opposite page. What are the people doing?

2 How much time do you spend online? Which devices do you use?

3 What do you like or dislike about the internet?

B Match definitions (1–4) with the words in the box.

> addicted   attention span   distracted   memory

1 the length of time that you can pay attention to one thing without becoming bored or thinking about something else _____

2 the ability to remember things _____

3 not able to concentrate on something _____

4 enjoying a particular activity very much and spending as much time as you can doing it _____

C READ FOR MAIN IDEA Work in pairs. Look at the title of the programme and think of three ways the internet could be killing or damaging our brains. Then read the blog and check your answers.

D READ FOR DETAIL Read the comments. Match the comments with the person.

Who …

1 doesn't think the internet is a negative thing?
Tom6 / JennyH / Sue123

2 is losing the ability to concentrate on something for long periods?
Tom6 / JennyH / Sue123

3 thinks the internet has many negative effects on people?
Tom6 / JennyH / Sue123

4 can't remember some things as well as in the past?
Tom6 / JennyH / Sue123

5 thinks it's normal to change the way we use our memory?
Tom6 / JennyH / Sue123

E SPEAK Work in pairs. What does 'use it or lose it' mean? What other skills could 'use it or lose it' apply to?

Glossary

adapt (v) to change your ideas or behaviour so that you can deal with a new situation

approval (n) a positive opinion feeling that you have towards someone or something that you think is good or suitable

impress (v) if someone or something impresses you, you admire them

Did you see ...?
The TV blog for the TV lover *by Anna Frese*

Programme: *Is the internet killing our brains?*

Did anyone see that TV programme last night, *Is the internet killing our brains?* It was really interesting! First, it looked at the human memory in the 21st century and at how the internet is destroying our memory. This is because today most information is instantly available online and we don't need to remember things. And it said that over time, this could have a negative effect on the brain's memory system – a case of use it or lose it. The programme then focused on how the human attention span is decreasing. It said that the brain is naturally easily distracted, and on the internet there is a lot of opportunity for this distraction. Evidence suggests that this is negatively affecting our attention spans and our ability to concentrate.

Finally, the programme examined how the 'likes' and other positive comments and approval we receive on social media can be addictive. As a result, people are constantly trying to impress, and social network addiction is becoming a serious issue.

What do you think? Add your comments below:

> **Tom6**   I don't agree with all the points. But, as soon as I start using the net, I find myself looking at site after site. It's quite addictive. I can spend hours online and I suddenly realise it's dark outside! I didn't use to be like that. I really do think my attention span is decreasing because of the net. However, they used to say the same thing about the radio and TV when they became popular.

> **JennyH**   The Greek philosopher Socrates said that writing would destroy memory because we would not have to remember things. However, Einstein believed that remembering facts was not a good use of our brains or our time. He said we had books to do that for us. What's different about the internet? Humans will adapt to it as they have in the past. I don't see a problem.

> **Sue123**   I disagree with JennyH. I read somewhere that more than 70 per cent of people don't know important phone numbers. I used to know all my friends' numbers. Now, I don't know any. We rely on our devices and the internet too much. So I do think it's killing our brains, and in a lot of ways, not just our memories.

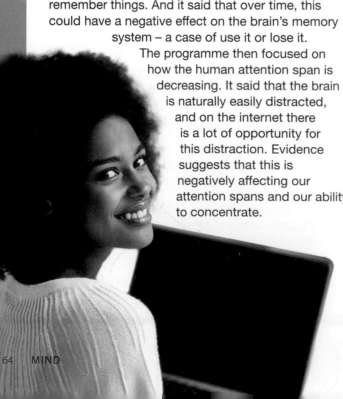

GRAMMAR
used to

A WORK IT OUT Look at the sentences from *Did you see …?* Find the missing words and complete the sentences. Then choose the correct words to complete the rule.

1 I can spend hours online, and I suddenly realise it's dark outside! I _____ be like that.

2 However, they _____ say the same thing about the radio and TV when they became popular.

3 I _____ know all my friends' numbers. Now, I don't know any.

---

used to

We use *used to* to talk about past situations that **do not exist now** / **continue now**. The negative form is *didn't use to*.

• I used to work in a phone shop.

• She used to have long hair.

• I didn't use to like chatting online.

B Go to the **Grammar Hub** on **page 134**.

C PRACTISE Write five sentences that are true for you with *used to* or *didn't use to*. Use the verbs in the box or your own ideas.

> be   be able to   buy   drive   eat   go   have
> like   listen to   live   play   read   smoke   watch

I used to read comics a lot when I was younger.
I didn't use to enjoy learning English.

D SPEAK Work in pairs. Discuss your answers to Exercise C.

PRONUNCIATION
used to

A Listen and repeat. What do you notice about the pronunciation of *used to*?
7.2

1 used to

2 I used to play video games.

3 Phones used to be much bigger.

B SPEAK Work in pairs. Practise saying the sentences. Then listen and check your pronunciation.
7.3

1 We used to speak on the phone a lot more.

2 Computers used to be much bigger.

3 I didn't use to go online much.

VOCABULARY
Shortened words

A Look at the words in **bold** in the sentence from *Did you see …?* They are shortened words. What are the words short for?

*But, as soon as I start using the **net**, I find myself looking at **site** after **site**.*

B Go to the **Vocabulary Hub** on pages **149** and **150**.

C SPEAK Work in pairs. Discuss the questions.

1 Why do you think we shorten some words?

2 Is it better to use shortened words in an informal or a formal situation?

3 Can you think of any other shortened words in English?

SPEAKING

A Read *Did you see …?* again. Comment on the blog or one of the comments.

B Make notes. Include at least one example of *used to* or *didn't use to*.

C Write about 50 words. Read your comment carefully and check for spelling and grammar.

D DISCUSS Work in pairs. Swap your comments and say whether you agree or disagree with your partner then add a further point.

E Display the comments for your classmates to read. Which ideas and opinions are the most common?

○– **Write an online comment about the effects of the internet**

V— phrasal verbs　　**G**— no article (*school, the school*)　　**P**— practising *the*: /ði:/ or /ðə/　　**S**— listening for the order of events

Wolfgang Amadeus Mozart

Pablo Picasso

Venus Williams

William James Sidis

Garry Kasparov

LISTENING

A SPEAK Work in pairs. Look at the pictures. What do you know about these people? What do they all have in common?

B Match the words (1–2) with the correct definitions (a–b).

1 intelligence
2 knowledge

a all the facts that someone knows about a particular subject
b the ability to understand and think about things

C LISTEN FOR KEY WORDS Listen to the podcast about William James Sidis. Tick (✓) what the presenter talks about.
🔊 7.4

1 Sidis's IQ ☐
2 where he was born ☐
3 his grandparents ☐
4 his language skills ☐
5 his university studies ☐
6 his jobs ☐
7 his friends ☐
8 how he died ☐

Glossary

child prodigy (n) a child who is extremely skilful at something that usually only adults can do
in/out of the public eye (phrase) well known or not well known to people in general
IQ = intelligence quotient (n) a number that represents a person's intelligence, based on the results of a particular type of test
turning point (n) a time when an important change takes place in a situation

D Number the events (a–h) in William James Sidis's life in the order they happened (1–8). Use the information in the box to help you. Then listen again and check.
🔊 7.4

Listening for the order of events

Listen for words and phrases to help you follow the order of events in a story.

• Words and phrases that tell us when something happened:

when he was nine　by four years old　at 11 at age 16　in 1898

• Words and phrases that tell us that something happened before, at the same time or after something else:

before　before that　earlier　previously

while　during　at the same time

after　after this　soon after　then　next

• Words and phrases that tell us that one thing was a consequence of another:

as a result　therefore

a He received a prison sentence. ___
b He became interested in politics. ___
c He taught maths at Rice University. ___
d He studied maths at Harvard University. ___
e He went to Harvard University to study law. ___
f He gave a lecture in maths at Harvard University. ___
g He travelled around the USA doing different jobs. ___
h He learnt seven languages and also invented one. ___

E SPEAK Work in pairs. Discuss the questions.

1 What were the key events and turning points in William James Sidis's life?

2 Sidis didn't go to school, his mother taught him at home. What are the advantages and disadvantages of this?

VOCABULARY
Phrasal verbs

A Look at the phrasal verbs in **bold** from the podcast about William James Sidis. Match the phrasal verbs (1–6) with the correct meanings (a–f).

1 He was born in 1898 and **grew up** in New York.
2 They **brought** him **up** to have 'a love of knowledge'.
3 His mother **gave up** her job and taught him at home.
4 He also **made up** his own language.
5 He **dropped out** of university before he finished his degree.
6 He **fell out** with his parents and lost contact with them.

a invented
b spent his childhood
c stopped doing something
d left something before finishing it
e stopped being friendly because he had had a disagreement with them
f looked after him until he became an adult

B **PRACTISE** Complete the sentences with the correct form of a phrasal verb from Exercise A. Use each phrasal verb once.

1 Where did you _____? What is the neighbourhood like? Do you still live there?
2 Who _____ you _____? Do you have a big family or a small family?
3 Name something you have _____. When and why did you stop doing it?
4 When you were a child, did you play traditional games or did you _____ your own games?
5 Do you know anyone who _____ of school or university? Why didn't they finish?
6 Have you ever _____ with someone? Did you become friends again?

C **SPEAK** Work in pairs. Ask and answer the questions in Exercise B.

GRAMMAR
No article (*school, the school*)

A **WORK IT OUT** Look at the sentences from the podcast. Then choose the correct words to complete the rules.

No article (*school, the school*)

Sometimes we use an article (*a, the*) with the words *school, university, hospital* and *prison*. But sometimes we use no article.

- *He didn't go to school.*
- *News reporters followed him everywhere at the university.*
- *At 11, he went to university to study maths.*
- *It was actually the hospital where his parents worked.*
- *He didn't go to prison and instead he spent a year in hospital.*

1 When we are referring to the *activity* associated with the place (studying / being a student, being a prisoner, being a patient) we use *an article / no article*.
2 When we are referring to the *physical* place, we use *an article / no article*.

B Go to the **Grammar Hub** on **page 134**.

C **PRACTISE** Choose the correct words to complete the texts.

Most people go to ¹*the university / university* aged 18 or 19. However, in 1981, at the age of just 12, Ruth Lawrence became the University of Oxford's youngest ever student. She didn't go to ²*the school / school* and her father gave up his job to teach her at home. He also accompanied her everywhere at ³*the university / a university*.

Artist Vincent van Gogh spent several weeks in ⁴*a hospital / hospital* after he cut off part of his ear. While he was there, he produced several paintings of ⁵*the hospital / hospital* and some of the people who worked there.

Nelson Mandela was president of South Africa from 1994 to 1999. Before that, he spent 27 years in ⁶*the prison / prison* for crimes against the government. Eighteen years of this was in ⁷*the prison / prison* on Robben Island, which is seven kilometres out to sea from Cape Town.

D **SPEAK** Work in pairs. Close your books. Tell your partner a story from Exercise C.

PRONUNCIATION
Practising *the*: /ðiː/ or /ðə/

A **SPEAK** Work in pairs. Practise saying the sentences.

1 Have you ever been to the East coast of America?
2 No, but I've been to the West coast.

B 7.5 Listen and compare your pronunciation. What do you notice about the pronunciation of *the* in each sentence? Why is there a difference?

⭕ SPEAKING HUB

A You are going to give a short presentation about a child prodigy. Student A – go to the **Communication Hub** on **page 152**. Student B – go to the **Communication Hub** on **page 157**.

B **PLAN** Read the biography and makes notes about:
- the person's early life and education
- his/her talents and abilities
- any key moments or turning points in his/her life
- achievements he/she is famous for
- what he/she did later in life

C **ORGANISE** Work in groups. Decide who is going to present which topics and practise your presentation. Use words and phrases from the Listening box to help you.

D **PRESENT** Give your presentation to your classmates.

◯ **Talk about intelligence and achievements**

Café Hub

7.4 Neena's dinner

F— describe an object and say what you use it for   **P**— objects

COMPREHENSION

A SPEAK Work in pairs. Look at the picture. Who do you think says the following, Zac (Z), Gaby (G) or Neena (N)? What do you think happens and who cooks Neena's dinner?

1 Gaby, what's wrong?   ____

2 And we promised to cook dinner for her tonight.   ____

3 And it's 6.30!   ____

4 Who's going to cook?   ____

5 I can make pizza!   ____

6 I can't think of the word in English.   ____

7 A knife?   ____

8 You used to work at Pizza Roma?   ____

9 Yeah, but I ate too much pizza.   ____

10 It looks like Pizza Roma!   ____

B ▶ Watch the video and check your answers to Exercise A. What is *rallador* in English?

FUNCTIONAL LANGUAGE
Describe an object and say what you use it for

A Complete the phrases with the verbs in the box. You need to use one verb twice.

> called   forgotten   know   made   think   use

Find out the English word for something
Problem
I've ¹ _____ the name of it.
I can't ² _____ of the word in English.
It's *rallador* in Spanish.
Oh, what's it ³ _____ of?
Description
You ⁴ _____ it to …
It's a thing you ⁵ _____ to …
It's ⁶ _____ of metal.
Check understanding
Do you ⁷ _____ what I mean?

B ▶ 01:09–02:43 Watch part of the video again and check your answers to Exercise A.

USEFUL PHRASES

A ▶ Match the useful phrases (1–5) with the phrase that comes before or after it (a–e). Then watch the video again and check your answers.

1 Let me think …

2 Who's going to cook?

3 You can be my assistant chef.

4 You know! 'Un rallador'.

5 Neena says she'll be home soon.

a I'm sorry, I don't understand Spanish.

b Oh, no! We have no time!

c Who's going to cook?

d Cool, good plan.

e Me, for sure.

B How do you say these useful phrases in your language?

MILLY   **SAM**   **NEENA**   **ZAC**   **GABY**

SPEAKING

1   2   3
4   5
6   7   8

PRONUNCIATION
Objects

A Match the pictures (a–c) with the conversations (1–3). Then listen and repeat the conversations.
7.6

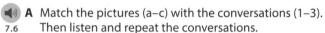

a   b   c

1 **A:** What's it made of?
  B: It's made of metal. You use it to beat eggs.
2 **A:** What's it made of?
  B: It's made of wood. You use it to roll pastry.
3 **A:** What's it made of?
  B: It's made of plastic. You use it to wash the dirty dishes.

B SPEAK Work in pairs. Choose another object and write a conversation. Practise saying your conversation.

Work in pairs. Take turns to be Student A and B.

Student A: Look at the pictures and choose an object. Tell your partner:
  • the word in your language
  • what it's made of
  • what you use it for

Student B: Listen and guess the object you partner describes. Tell him/her the number of the object and the name in English.

○─ **Describe an object and say what you use it for**

➤ Turn to **page 164** to learn how to write a survey report.

VOCABULARY

A Choose the best adjective to complete the sentences. Use the information in brackets to help you.

1 I feel really *anxious / cheerful* now the holidays have started. (*positive*)

2 Lola is a little *nervous / glad* about the interview tomorrow. (*negative*)

3 I always feel *scared / pleased* when I get a lot of 'likes' for my posts on Twitter. (*positive*)

4 I'm really *nervous / glad* that you liked the cake I made. (*positive*)

5 Casper didn't go to the top of the building because he was too *relaxed / scared*. (*negative*)

B Look at the shortened words. Write the missing letters to complete the full words.

1 mobile *p h o n e*

2 info___ ___ ___ ___ ___ ___ ___

3 uni___ ___ ___ ___ ___ ___ ___

4 ___ ___ ___ plane

5 ___ ___ ___ ___ ___ net

6 mic___ ___ ___ ___ ___ ___ ___

7 ___ ___ ___ case

8 ___ ___ ___ site

C The phrasal verbs are in the wrong places in the texts. Write them in the correct place. Change the tense if necessary.

I [1]**brought up** in Sheffield. It was just me and my mum, so she [2]**made** me **up** on her own. We had a good relationship, although we argued sometimes and [3]**gave up** from time to time. Because I was an only child, I played on my own a lot of the time. This was OK because I had a good imagination and I used to [4]**grew up** my own games. To be honest, I had a really good childhood.

I didn't enjoy university. I found it really difficult. Studying took up all of my time and I had to [5]**drop out** a lot of my hobbies and other activities. I just went to lectures in the day and then studied all evening. So, I decided to [6]**fall out** and get a job instead. It was the best decision I ever made.

GRAMMAR

A Choose the correct article or no article to complete the text.

Humans are not [1]*the / –* only animals that laugh. Other animals such as [2]*the / –* gorillas, chimpanzees and orang-utans also laugh. [3]*A / The* main reason for laughter in [4]*the / –* animals is when they are playing. [5]*A / The* laughter indicates that it is [6]*a / the* game and that no one is going to get hurt. [7]*A / –* Laughter has also been observed in [8]*the / –* rats.

B Think about everyday life forty years ago. For each pair of words of phrases, write what we *used to* and *didn't use to* do. Use the verbs in the box.

chat ~~use~~ use watch write and send

1 online maps and satnavs / paper maps

We didn't use to use online maps and satnavs. We used to use paper maps.

2 on social media / on the phone

3 videos / films online

4 emails / letters

C Complete the questions about school and university with *a/an*, *the* or *–* (no article).

SCHOOL AND UNIVERSITY QUESTIONNAIRE

1 Where did you go to ____ school as a child? Was ____ school near to where you lived?

2 Did you enjoy ____ school? What were your favourite subjects at ____ school?

3 Did you, do you or will you go to ____ university? If so, is ____ university well known for anything?

4 Is there ____ university in the town or city where you grew up? Do most cities in your country have ____ university?

FUNCTIONAL LANGUAGE

Write the missing letters to complete the words. Then match the conversations (1–3) with the pictures (a–c).

a   b   c

1 **A:** What's a protractor?

B: It's a thing you u___ ___ to measure and draw angles. It's shaped like half a circle and usually m___ ___ ___ of plastic.

2 **A:** I can't t___ ___ ___ ___ of the English word for *agrafeuse*. Do you know?

B: Yes, it's stapler, I think.

3 **A:** What's this for?

B: You u___ ___ it to draw circles. It's c___ ___ ___ ___ ___ a compass.

8 ART

Art is not what you
see, but what you
make others see.

Edgar Degas

School children play at *The Tinnies* – a public art sculpture
on the outskirts of Strabane, Northern Ireland.

OBJECTIVES

○ **talk about taste in music and your favourite songs**

○ **talk about art and artists**

○ **describe films and books**

○ **show interest in a topic**

○ **write a review**

Work with a partner. Discuss the questions.

1 What different types of art can you name?

2 Look at the picture. Would you like to visit
this place?

3 Do you think museums and art galleries
should be free? Why/Why not?

G— reflexive pronouns   **V**— music   **P**— consonant clusters in words

LISTENING

🔊 **A** Listen to the music extracts (1–7) and match them with the
8.1   different types of music (a–g).

a rap   ___   e blues   ___
b jazz   ___   f reggae   ___
c rock   ___   g classical ___
d disco   ___

B SPEAK Work in pairs. Discuss the questions.

1 Can you think of any other types of music?
2 What types of music do you like? What don't you like? Why?
3 Who are your favourite bands or musicians?
4 Why do we like certain types of music? Think of three reasons.

🔊 **C LISTEN FOR MAIN IDEA** Listen to the podcast *Music matters*
8.2   with Professor Suzy Harrison. What are the three things which
explain our taste in music?

Glossary

comforting (adj) making you feel less sad, worried or disappointed
energise (v) to make someone feel excited and enthusiastic
influence (v) to affect the way someone thinks or behaves, also *be influenced by*

🔊 **D LISTEN FOR DETAIL** Choose the correct answer a, b or c,
8.2   to complete the sentences. Then listen again and check
your answers.

1 When we are older, the music from our childhood makes
us feel …
  a old.
  b sad.
  c happy.

2 Our first big music influence is generally …
  a our younger brothers and sisters.
  b our older brothers and sisters.
  c our school friends.

3 Music brings people together because we can share …
  a music files and records.
  b our opinions of the music.
  c the mood it creates.

4 We sometimes choose a particular type of music …
  a to create the right conditions for an activity.
  b to give us a break from an activity.
  c to help us forget about an activity.

5 Compared with the past, people today generally like …
  a fewer kinds of music.
  b more kinds of music.
  c the same variety of music.

E SPEAK Work in groups. Discuss the questions.

1 Who has influenced your taste in music, your
parents, brothers and sisters, friends or someone or
something else?

2 Do you generally like the same kinds of music as
your friends? Do you think music is an important
part of your friendships?

3 Do you tend to play different kinds of music at
different times and when you are in different
moods? Give some examples.

GRAMMAR
Reflexive pronouns

🔊 **A** Complete the sentences from the podcast *Music*
8.3   *matters* with the pronouns in the box. You need
to use one of the pronouns more than once.
Then listen and check.

> ourselves (x2)   themselves   yourself

1 **We** don't choose this music _____,
of course.

2 So, when **we** start to discover music by
_____, it is influenced by what we
listened to when we were growing up.

3 In contrast, for **other people**, musical taste is a
way to make _____ different from
other people.

4 And when you're preparing for a night out, **you**
might want to energise _____ and
play something loud and full of energy.

B WORK IT OUT Match the sentences in Exercise A (1–4) with the rules (a–c).

> **Reflexive pronouns**
>
> There are several ways we can use reflexive pronouns. The most usual are:
>
> **a** We use a reflexive pronoun as the object of a verb. This is when the subject and the object are the same person or thing. ___ ___
>
> **b** We also use a reflexive pronoun after the object of a verb. This is to emphasise the person or thing that does the action. ___
>
> **c** We use *by* + reflexive pronoun to say we do something alone or with no help. ___

C Go to the **Grammar Hub** on page 136.

D SPEAK Work in pairs. Have you ever …

1 taught yourself to do something (for example, play a musical instrument, do a sport, learn a skill)?

2 designed and/or built something yourself?

3 bought yourself something special?

VOCABULARY
Music

A Go to the **Vocabulary Hub** on page 150.

B Replace the words in **bold** with words in the box with the same or similar meaning.

> album   band members   catchy   cover songs
> gig   live   lyrics   on tour

1 It's a great song. I love the **words**. _____

2 It's the best **concert** I've been to. _____

3 They play their own songs and **songs by other bands**. _____

4 This song is **very easy to remember**. _____

5 They are **doing a series of concerts** soon. _____

6 Their first **collection of songs** is their best. _____

7 I would love to see them **performing a concert**. _____

8 They have some great **people in the group**, who are excellent musicians. _____

C SPEAK Work in pairs. Replace the pronouns in Exercise B to make true sentences. Tell your partner.

PRONUNCIATION
Consonant clusters in words

 A <u>Under</u>line the consonant clusters in each word.
8.4 Then listen carefully. Are all the letters in the consonant clusters pronounced?

1	background	4	influenced
2	electric	5	keyboards
3	individual	6	ourselves

B Listen again and repeat the words.
8.4

SPEAKING

A Read the text about a radio programme. Do you have a similar programme in your country?

Desert Island Discs is a BBC Radio 4 programme in the UK. It was first broadcast in 1942 and since then 3000 episodes have been recorded. Each week, a guest is asked to choose eight songs or other pieces of music they would take if they had to go on a desert island. The guest explains the reasons for their choices.

B Choose three songs or pieces of music to take to a desert island. Which is your number one song?

C Think about how to describe the songs and what you like about them, for example, the lyrics. Make notes about:

- what type(s) of music the songs are
- where the singers or bands are from
- the instruments they play
- what other songs or music the singers or bands are famous for

D Work in pairs. Tell each other what songs you have chosen. Describe the songs and say what you like about them.

> ◯─ **Talk about taste in music and your favourite songs**

— types of art — /ɪ/ and /iː/ **G**— infinitive of purpose

VOCABULARY
Types of art

A SPEAK Work in pairs. How many artists can you name? What do you know about them or their paintings? Who are the most famous artists from your country?

B Go to the **Vocabulary Hub** on **page 150**.

PRONUNCIATION
/ɪ/ and /iː/

🔊 Listen to the sounds /ɪ/ and /iː/. Then listen and <u>underline</u>
8.5 the word you hear.

	/ɪ/	/iː/			/ɪ/	/iː/
1	slip	sleep		4	sit	seat
2	ship	sheep		5	pitch	peach
3	live	leave		6	bit	beat

READING

A Work in pairs. Look at the works of art (a–d). What material do you think the artist uses in each one? Tell your partner.

B SCAN Read *Unusual art* quickly and check your answers to Exercise A. Then match the works of art (a–d) with the correct paragraphs (2–5).

C READ FOR DETAIL Read again. Are the following sentences true (T) or false (F)?

1 Anastassia Elias cuts up toilet rolls to produce her works of art. *T / F*

2 Max Zorn uses different coloured tape to produce light and dark. *T / F*

3 Stanislav Aristov uses more than one picture to create his art. *T / F*

4 Scott Wade mostly creates images of cars and things connected with motoring. *T / F*

D SPEAK Work in pairs. Which of the works of art do you like best? Why?

UNUSUAL ART

1 Art and artists come in many forms. In this post, we look at four artists who use unusual materials to produce their art.

2 French artist Anastassia Elias uses toilet rolls and paper to create everyday scenes of life. She cuts out the image from paper and places it inside the roll. She then illuminates the images from the back, which creates a silhouette.

3 Max Zorn uses brown packing tape to create his works of art. He sticks the tape on glass sheets and illuminates them from the back. He creates dark and light by using thick or thin layers of tape. Originally, he used street lights in Amsterdam in the Netherlands, which is where he is from.

4 Russian artist Stanislav Aristov uses burnt matchsticks to create his art. First, he photographs a match after it has finished burning. He then photographs a separate burning flame. Aristov then combines these two images to produce the final picture using picture software. He produces images from nature, such as flowers and animals, as well as everyday objects.

5 Scott Wade creates works of art on the dirty windows of cars. He often uses artificial dirt to make the car dirty. Wade creates his own images and also recreates famous paintings, such as landscapes and still life. He also produces portraits of famous people. Wade has displayed his work at car shows and other motoring events around the world. He believes that 'dirt is beautiful'.

Glossary

artificial (adj) made by people and used instead of something natural
illuminate (v) to shine a light on something
layer (n) an amount or sheet of a substance that covers a surface
silhouette (n) the dark shape of something

Little Dancer by Edgar Degas

The Scream by Edvard Munch

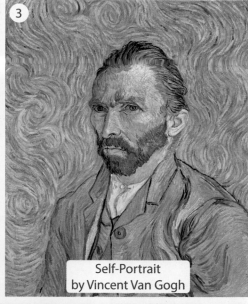

Self-Portrait by Vincent Van Gogh

THERE IS ALWAYS HOPE

Girl with Balloon by Banksy

GRAMMAR
Infinitive of purpose

A Complete the sentences from *Unusual art*. Write two words in each gap.

1 Max Zorn uses brown packing tape _____ his works of art.

2 Aristov then combines these two images _____ the final picture.

3 He often uses artificial dirt _____ the car dirty.

B **WORK IT OUT** Look at the sentences in Exercise A and complete the rule. Then find and <u>underline</u> three more examples in the article.

Infinitive of purpose
We use _____ + _____ to express the purpose or reason for doing something.

C Go to the **Grammar Hub** on **page 136**.

D **SPEAK** Complete the sentences with your own ideas to express purpose or reason. Then work in pairs and compare your ideas.

1 I go to museums and galleries …

2 We take pictures …

3 People go on holiday …

SPEAKING

A Look at the pictures above. What do you know about the works of art and the artists (1–4)? Which do you like the best? Why? What other famous works of art do you know?

B Choose one of the works of art or the artist who produced it (1–4) or use your own ideas. Make notes about:

Work of art

- What is the title?
- Who painted or made it? When?
- Is it in a museum or gallery? Where?
- What does it show?

- What materials are used?
- How does it make you feel?
- Have you seen the original?
- Any other information?

Artist

- What is his name?
- Where is he from?
- When was he alive?
- What is his style?
- What are his famous works of art?

- Do you have a favourite picture by him?
- Do you like this artist? Why/Why not?
- Any other information?

C Work in groups. Give your presentation to the group.

〇 **Talk about art and artists**

V — film and book genres; adjectives for describing films and books   P — word stress in longer words
G — first conditional   S — identifying contrasts

VOCABULARY
Film and book genres

A Match the pictures (1–6) with the genres in the box. Then work in pairs to think of films and books which match the other genres in the box.

> action adventure animated
> autobiography biography biopic comedy
> costume drama fairy tale fantasy historical
> horror musical romantic comedy (rom-com)
> science fiction (sci-fi) thriller western

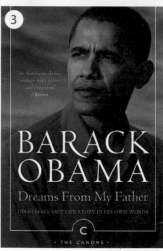

PRONUNCIATION
Word stress in longer words

A Write the film and book genres in the box in the correct place.

> adventure animated biography comedy fantasy
> historical musical romantic comedy science fiction

1 ○●○	2 ●●○○	3 ○●○○
adventure		

4 ●○○	5 ○●○●○	6 ●○●○

B Work in pairs. Compare your answers. Then listen and check.
8.6

C SPEAK Work in pairs. What genres of films and books do you enjoy?

LISTENING

A Match the definitions (1–5) with the words in the box.

> engaging gripping memorable sense visualise

1 easy to remember because of being special in some way
   _____

2 attracting and keeping someone's attention
   _____

3 to form a picture of something in your mind
   _____

4 one of the natural abilities most people have to see, hear, smell, taste and feel things _____

5 very exciting and interesting _____

B PREDICT Do you think the following statements refer to films (F) or books (B)?

1 They allow us to imagine and see things in our own way. ___

2 We get to know the characters more. ___

3 They connect with our different senses at the same time. ___

4 It is an experience we often share with friends. ___

C LISTEN FOR GIST Listen to a podcast comparing films and books and check your answers to Exercise B.
8.7

> **Glossary**
>
> **book club (n)** a group of people who meet regularly to discuss books
> **chapter (n)** one of the sections into which a book is divided; a chapter usually has a number or a title
> **character (n)** a person in a book or film
> **dialogue (n)** the words that characters speak in a book or film

D Match the sentences (1–5) with their contrasting ideas
(a–e). Then listen again and check your answers. Use the
information in the box to help you.

8.7

Identifying contrasts

Listen for linking words and phrases that express a contrast
between two ideas:

but, though, however, although	*(but) at the same time*
on the other hand	*compared to*

Listen for phrases that introduce a further contrast:

another (important) difference is	*and one more thing*

---

1 Books allow the reader
to use their imagination.

2 With books, the story
generally moves more
slowly.

3 We generally watch a
film with other people.

4 Reading is a less
sociable activity.

5 People often say they
are disappointed by
the film.

a Book clubs are very
popular these days.

b In many cases people
actually prefer the film.

c Reading a book is more
individual and personal.

d With a film the whole
story needs to start and
finish in 90 minutes.

e With films we see what
the director and the
actors want us to see.

E LISTEN FOR KEY WORDS Listen to the extracts. Which
linking words or phrases express the contrasting ideas in
Exercise D? Make a list.

8.8

VOCABULARY
Adjectives for describing films and books

A Look at the sentences from the podcast. Complete the
adjectives with the missing vowels (*a, e, i, o, u*).

1 I think this makes the experience more personal and
_e_ng_a_g_i_ng.

2 A film can be much more ___xc___t___ng and
gr___pp___ng than a book.

3 Music can also make the film more
___nt___r___st___ng and m___m___r___bl___.

4 Compared to the book, people often say they are
d___s___pp___ ___nt___d by the film.

B Read the information in the box and choose the correct
option in the sentences below. Listen and check.

8.9

Adjectives for describing films and books

We use adjectives ending in *-ing* to talk about what caused
the feeling.

- *The film was disappointing.*

We use adjectives ending in *-ed* to talk about how we feel.

- *I was disappointed.*

---

1 It was totally *engaged / engaging* and the acting was
amazed / amazing.

2 I was, well, a bit *bored / boring* by the end. It isn't very
memorable I'm afraid.

3 You won't be *disappointed / disappointing*. The singing
was incredible.

4 It's really *gripped / gripping*. And it's quite *moved /
moving* and sad, too.

GRAMMAR
First conditional

A WORK IT OUT Look at the first conditional sentences
below. Then choose the correct words to complete
the rules.

*If you **want** a great night out, you **should see** this film.*

*If you **remind** me, I'll **lend** it to you.*

*If you **like** musicals, you'**ll love** it.*

First conditional

1 We use the first conditional to talk about *impossible /
possible* situations in the future.

2 Conditional sentences usually have two clauses: the
if-clause and the main clause. To make a first conditional
sentence, we use:

- If + *present tense / will* and *present tense / will* +
infinitive without *to*.

3 We *can / can't* use other modal verbs (for example, *can,
could, might, should*) instead of *will* in the main clause.

B Go to the **Grammar Hub** on page 136.

 SPEAKING HUB

A Listen to Salli recommending a film. What does she
talk about?

8.10

1 the film type or genre

2 the main story

3 the actors, the director, the writer

4 what she likes about it

5 how it made her feel

B PLAN You are going to recommend a film or book.
Decide which film or book you are going to talk
about and make notes about the topics in Exercise A.

C ORGANISE Use adjectives for describing films or
books and at least one first conditional sentence
(*If you like …, you'll love …*).

D DISCUSS Work in groups. Recommend the film or
book you chose to your group.

○– **Describe films and books**

COMPREHENSION

A ▶ **SPEAK** Work in pairs. Which topics do you think Milly and Zac will talk about on their first date? Then watch the video and check your answers.

> children   culture   family   food   home
> marriage   money   music   the weather   work

B ▶ Are the sentences true (T) or false (F)? Correct the false sentences. Then watch the video again and check your answers.

1	Zac arrives first at the park.	*T / F*
2	Milly knows the band Zac is listening to.	*T / F*
3	Zac and Milly have tickets to the same show.	*T / F*
4	It's Milly's birthday today.	*T / F*
5	Zac loves English food.	*T / F*
6	Milly likes English culture.	*T / F*
7	Zac thinks Milly is shy.	*T / F*
8	Milly wants to go home.	*T / F*

FUNCTIONAL LANGUAGE
Show interest in a topic

A Complete the replies (1–11) with the words in the box.

> are   believe   did   do   for   kidding
> neither   no   really   so   too

Comment	Reply
	Show surprise
[music playing]	1 _____ way! Is this Gold Sounds?
It's their new record.	2 _____ real?
I have tickets to their show.	You're 3 _____! I don't 4 _____ it!
I'm going with my sister.	5 _____ you?
She got the tickets for my birthday.	She 6 _____?
It's today.	7 _____? It's your birthday today?
I like that about you.	You 8 _____?
	Show you understand
I miss my family.	9 _____ do I.
I'm not crazy about English food.	10 _____ am I.
I feel like I can be myself here.	Me, 11 _____.

B ▶ Watch the video again and check your answers.

MILLY

SAM

NEENA

ZAC

GABY

Glossary

for real? (phrase) (American) really?
you're kidding! (phrase) (American) you're joking!

PRONUNCIATION
Intonation

 A Listen to the replies from Functional language Exercise A.
8.11 Write them in the correct place. Then listen again and check your answers.

Rising intonation	Falling intonation
	No way!

 B Listen again and repeat the replies. Copy the intonation.
8.11

SPEAKING

A Write a short sentence about the following topics:

1 something surprising
I've got tickets for Rihanna!

2 something shocking
_____

3 something that isn't true
_____

4 something about the past
_____

5 something about the future
_____

6 something you like
_____

7 something you don't like
_____

B Work in pairs. Take turns. Student A – read out your sentences. Student B – show interest and reply.

◯– **Show interest in a topic**

➤ Turn to **page 165** to learn how to write a review.

Unit 8 Review

VOCABULARY

A Rearrange the letters of the words in **bold**. The first and last letters are in the correct place.

1 Do you listen to whole **ablmus** or do you usually listen to individual songs?

2 Do you pay much attention to the **lriycs** of a song or do you mostly listen to the music?

3 Do you have a favourite **sigenr** or musician (**giuristat, dmruemr**)?

4 Do you go to many **ggis**? What was the last band you saw **lvie**? Was there a good **lhgit sohw**? Where were you in the **aduenice** – near to the **satge** or far away from it?

B Complete the quiz questions with the words in the box. There is one word you do not need. Then do the quiz.

> abstract exhibition gallery landscape
> portrait sculpture still life

ART QUIZ
How much do you know?

1 Which is the world's most visited art _____?
  a The British Museum, London
  b The Metropolitan Museum of Art, New York
  c The Louvre, Paris

2 It toured the world in the 1970s and is the most visited _____ of all time. What was it?
  a *The Treasures of Tutankhamun*
  b *The Art of the Aztecs*
  c *The Visions of Van Gogh*

3 *David* by Michelangelo is perhaps the most famous _____ in the world. How tall is it?
  a 5.17 metres
  b 7.15 metres
  c 1.75 metres

4 *Sunflowers* is one of the world's most famous collections of _____ paintings. Who painted them?
  a Leonardo da Vinci
  b Vincent van Gogh
  c Pablo Picasso

5 *Girl with a Pearl Earring* by Johannes Vermeer is a famous _____ painting. When did Vermeer paint it?
  a 1465
  b 1665
  c 1865

6 Pablo Picasso was most famous for his _____ art. Where was Picasso born?
  a France
  b Italy
  c Spain

C Match the film and book genres (1–5) with the descriptions (a–e). Then choose the correct adjectives. Which of the descriptions are positive (P) and which are negative (N)?

1 comedy
2 thriller
3 biography
4 fantasy
5 horror

a It isn't scary at all and I was pretty *bored / boring* for most of it.
b It's really funny. Go see it, you won't be *disappointed / disappointing*.
c It's got lots of strange creatures in it. The visuals are *amazed / amazing*.
d The story of his life was very *engaged / engaging* and quite *moved / moving*.
e It's very *excited / exciting* and *gripped / gripping*. I couldn't stop reading it.

GRAMMAR

A Complete the conversations with the correct reflexive pronouns.

1 A: Great gig! Who's the last song by?
  B: We wrote it _____.
2 A: I like Jenny's website. Who designed it for her?
  B: I think she designed it _____.
3 A: Did you have guitar lessons or teach _____?
  B: I taught _____.

B Complete the sentences with the best verb to express purpose. Use *to* + infinitive.

1 We're going to the museum _____ the Picasso exhibition.
2 I mostly use my laptop _____ films.
3 I took up a hobby _____ new people.
4 Can I use your phone _____ my friend?

C Complete 1–3 with the correct form of the verbs in brackets.

1 If you _____ (see) Janice this evening, _____ (you / say) hello from me?
2 A: If we _____ (miss) the bus, we _____ (get) a taxi.
  B: OK, or if it _____ (stop) raining, we _____ (walk). It isn't far to the cinema.
3 If you _____ (like) reggae, you _____ (love) this band. I _____ (get) you a ticket if you _____ (like).

FUNCTIONAL LANGUAGE

A Complete the conversations with the words in the box.

> believe did do real so too

1 A: Alice got a place on the art course.
  B: She _____? That's great news.
2 A: Jimmy's band have got a record contract.
  B: For _____?
3 A: Did you know that the film won three Oscars?
  B: Really? I don't _____ it! It was terrible.
4 A: I'm going see Jake's new band tonight.
  B: Yeah. Me, _____.
5 A: I want to go to the Damien Hirst exhibition.
  B: You _____? I didn't think you liked his stuff.
6 A: I love musicals.
  B: _____ do I!

9 MONEY

Money often costs too much.

Ralph Waldo Emerson

The money mounts up in a museum's voluntary donation box, Milan, Italy.

OBJECTIVES

- talk about attitudes to money and about spending money
- talk about philanthropy and charities
- discuss your skills and how they could help others
- go shopping for clothes and ask for a refund
- write a 'for sale' advert

Work with a partner. Discuss the questions.

1 Is money important?
2 Read the quote. What do you think Emerson meant? Do you agree?
3 Do you spend money every day? What do you buy?

READING

A Match the words (1–4) with the definitions (a–d).

1	obsessed	a	something that you own
2	gain	b	to get something
3	inspire	c	to give someone the enthusiasm to do something
4	possession	d	considering something so important that you are always thinking about it

B **READ FOR MAIN IDEA** Read *How to buy happiness*. Write the paragraph headings in the correct place. There is one heading you do not need.

a Try something new

b Discover yourself

c Take your time

d Open your mind

C **READ FOR DETAIL** Read again and answer the questions.

1 Which make us feel better for longer, possessions or experiences?

2 In what three ways does Julie benefit from travelling?

3 What does Carmen learn from meeting people?

4 According to Carmen, how can travelling improve our character?

5 What does Hugo think can make us lazy?

6 Why does Hugo think experiences inspire us to do more?

D **SPEAK** Work in pairs. Discuss the questions.

1 Do you agree with the article? Why/Why not?

2 Have you spent money on experiences such as travel? What did you do? Were the experiences positive or negative? Why?

HOW TO BUY HARAPPINESS

We live in a society that is obsessed with spending money – a society that is obsessed with materialism. When we buy things, it gives us happiness. But this feeling often lasts only for a short time. Experiences, on the other hand, stay with us for a long time after they have finished. Therefore, if we spent more of our money on experiences, we would gain something that can last a lifetime. Here are three more reasons we should spend more time and money on experiences and three people who agree with this advice.

1 _____

Julie from the UK believes travel is an important experience. She says, 'Travelling helps us to discover our interests. I'm always saving up so I can go away at least once or twice a year. It helps me to discover what I like and what I don't like. It helps me to understand who I am. I think we wouldn't find out these things if we didn't spend money on experiences.'

2 _____

Carmen from Italy also believes that travel is important. She says, 'I spend a lot of my money on travelling. It helps us to see different points of view. As you travel, you meet new people with different ideas and opinions to your own. This teaches us some important life lessons and helps us to understand the world.' Carmen also believes that travelling helps you to become more independent and more confident.

3 _____

According to Hugo from Brazil, our experiences can inspire us. He says, 'It's always good to do something that is new. If we didn't do anything different, we might become lazy. We don't have to climb Mount Everest, but we can do things like learn to play a musical instrument, start a new sport or simply do something new for the first time. This will make us feel good and give us a sense of achievement. This will then inspire us to try more things in life. So, my attitude to money is to spend it on experiences as much as possible!'

So, before you buy your next possession, ask yourself 'Is there an experience I can spend my money on instead?' This could be a night out with friends, a concert or a sports event, or maybe a weekend away or a holiday. Whatever we choose, it will make us rich with memories and life lessons.

Glossary

materialism (n) the belief that money and possessions are the most important aspects of human existence

PRONUNCIATION
/ɑː/, /ʌ/ and /æ/

A Look at the <u>underlined</u> letters in each word. What sound do they make? Write the words in the correct place.

after disc<u>o</u>ver happiness last
m<u>o</u>ney m<u>u</u>ch p<u>a</u>st tr<u>a</u>vel up

/ɑː/	/ʌ/	/æ/
past		

B Listen and check. Then listen again and repeat the words.

9.1

C **SPEAK** Work in pairs. Practise saying the sentences. Listen to your partner and check their pronunciation.

1 Happiness often lasts only for a short time.

2 Travelling helps us to discover our interests.

3 Is there an experience I can spend my money on instead?

GRAMMAR
Second conditional

A **WORK IT OUT** Look at the second conditional sentences from *How to buy happiness*. Write the missing words. Then choose the correct words to complete the rules.

1 If we _____ more of our money on experiences, we _____ something that can last a lifetime.

2 We _____ these things if we _____ money on experiences.

3 If we _____ anything different, we _____ lazy.

Second conditional

1 We use the second conditional to talk about *real / unreal or impossible* situations in the present or future.

2 Conditional sentences usually have two clauses: the *if-*clause and the main clause. To make a second conditional sentence, we use:

• *If + past simple / would* and *past simple / would + infinitive without to*.

3 We *can / can't* use other modal verbs (for example, *can, could, might, should*) instead of *would* in the main clause.

B Go to the **Grammar Hub** on page 138.

VOCABULARY
Prepositions in money phrases

A Complete the sentences with the correct prepositions. Then read *How to buy happiness* again and check your answers.

1 I'm always saving _____ so I can go away at least once or twice a year.

2 I spend a lot of my money _____ travelling.

3 My attitude _____ money is to spend it on experiences as much as possible.

B Complete the sentences with the prepositions in the box.

by   for   from   in   out   out of   to

1 I usually take money _____ the ATM once or twice a week. I take _____ 20 or 30 euros each time.

2 For things under, say, five euros, I generally pay _____ cash. I usually pay _____ things over five euros _____ card.

3 I occasionally borrow money _____ my friends and I also sometimes lend it _____ them. But it's never usually more than 10 or 20 euros.

C **SPEAK** Work in pairs. Change the sentences in Exercises A and B so they are true for you. Ask your partner questions to find out more information.

A: *I'm always saving up so I can go to concerts and music festivals.*

B: *My attitude to money is spend a little and save a little.*

SPEAKING

A Work in groups. Think about different situations and make choices. Group A – go to the **Communication Hub** on **page 157**. Group B – go to the **Communication Hub** on **page 153**.

B Work in pairs. Ask your partner your new questions and make a note of their answers.

C Work in groups. Compare your findings. How similar or different are they? What are the most common or unusual answers?

○— Talk about attitudes to money and about spending money

V— verbs connected with money **P**— /s/ and /z/ **G**— defining relative clauses

VOCABULARY
Verbs connected with money

A Complete the facts below with the correct form of the verbs in the box.

> donate   earn   give away   lose
> make   owe   raise   support

MONEY facts

1 In 1979, baseball player Nolan Ryan became the first professional sportsperson to _____earn_____ $1 million a year.

2 Microsoft's Bill Gates, businessman Warren Buffett and Facebook's Mark Zuckerberg have all said they will _____ 95 per cent of their money to charity. A number of other philanthropists have also made the same promise.

3 Spanish actress Penélope Cruz _____ many charities (organisations that give money and help to people who need it). In fact, she gave all of her salary from her first Hollywood film to charity.

4 On 16th September 1992, Hungarian-born businessman George Soros _____ $1 billion. This is the biggest single-day profit in history.

5 Eike Batista was once Brazil's richest person with $30 billion. However, unfortunately he _____ it all. In fact, in 2014, he _____ $30 billion to the banks.

6 The London Marathon _____ more money for charity than any other sports event. In 2016, this was almost £60 million.

7 Philanthropy is about giving money to people who need it. Philanthropists across the world _____ around $500 billion a year to charity and other organisations. The main givers include the United States, China, United Kingdom, Russia, Australia and Switzerland.

B Complete the questions with the correct verbs. Use the *Money facts* to help you.

1 Have you ever **d**_____ money to a charity? If so, what does the charity **r**_____ money for?

2 If you could give a lot of money to charity, which charities or organisations would you **s**_____? Why?

3 Do you agree that all people who **e**_____ a lot of money or who have **m**_____ a lot of money should **g**_____ some of it **a**_____ to charities? Why/Why not?

C SPEAK Ask and answer the questions in Exercise C.

PRONUNCIATION
/s/ and /z/

A SPEAK Work in pairs. Look at the words in the box. Do the letters in **bold** make a /s/ or a /z/ sound? Underline the /s/ sounds and circle the /z/ sounds.

> across   also   baseball   Facebook   givers   organisation
> promise   raises   salary   same   supports   Switzerland

B Listen and check. Then listen again and repeat the words.
9.2

LISTENING

A Work in pairs. Discuss the questions.

1 What you know about the people in the pictures? What do you think they have in common?

2 Which other philanthropists do you know?

Andrew Carnegie

John D Rockefeller

Bill Gates, Melinda Gates, Warren Buffett

Oprah Winfrey

B LISTEN FOR KEY WORDS Listen to Part 1 of a lecture about philanthropists. Complete the first column with the people in the pictures on page 84.

Names of philanthropists	Numbers	What the numbers mean
John D Rockefeller	$540m, 1937	John D Rockefeller gave away about $540 million. He died in 1937.
	$350m, 90 per cent	
	half a billion dollars	
	tens of billions of dollars, 2010	

C LISTEN FOR KEY INFORMATION Listen again. What do the numbers mean? Write your answers in the third column in Exercise B.

D LISTEN FOR GIST Listen to Part 2 of the lecture. Which is the best explanation of the Giving Pledge? Choose a, b or c.

The Giving Pledge asks people to give at least 50 per cent of their wealth to charity …

a when they die.

b before they die.

c in the next ten years.

E LISTEN FOR MAIN IDEA Listen again. Tick (✓) the names of the philanthropists who have joined the Giving Pledge. Cross (✗) the ones who have not.

1 Mark Zuckerberg ☐   5 Sara Blakely ☐
2 Richard Branson ☐   6 Li Ka-shing ☐
3 Ann Gloag ☐   7 Meg Whitman ☐
4 Carlos Slim ☐   8 Azim Premji ☐

F LISTEN FOR DETAIL Listen again. Write the names of the philanthropists.

1 _____Azim Premji_____ has started a university.

2 _____ has given away a quarter of his or her wealth.

3 _____ would refuse to join the Giving Pledge if he or she was invited.

4 _____ believes that there should be more women in powerful positions.

5 _____ believes the best way to end poverty is through education and jobs.

6 _____ is mostly concerned with education and health in his or her own country.

GRAMMAR
Defining relative clauses

A WORK IT OUT <u>Underline</u> the relative clauses in the sentences from the lecture. Then complete the rules with *who*, *which* or *that*.

1 And today, there are many celebrities <u>who have given money to charity</u>.

2 Let's now look at five modern-day philanthropists that you may or may not have heard of.

3 Instead she has her own charity that focuses on the environment and education.

4 He has also set up a university which promotes educational thinking.

Defining relative clauses

1 A defining relative clause gives information about and identifies a noun (a person or thing). It comes after the noun and starts with a relative pronoun.

We use ª _____ when the noun is a person.

We use ᵇ _____ when the noun is a thing.

We can use ᶜ _____ for a person or a thing.

2 We can miss out the relative pronoun when the word following the noun is a subject (*I, you, people, the charity*).

- *Let's now look at five modern-day philanthropists that you may or may not have heard of.*

B Go to the **Grammar Hub** on **page 138**.

C You are going to write some definitions. Student A – go to **page 152**. Student B – go to **page 154**.

D SPEAK Complete the sentences with the correct relative pronouns and your own ideas. Miss out the relative pronoun if possible. Then, work in groups and share your ideas.

1 A famous person _____ I admire is …

_____A famous person I admire is Michelle Obama._____

2 A charity _____ does a lot of good is …

3 Someone _____ has influenced me a lot is …

4 A global issue _____ I think is important is …

5 A person _____ has positively influenced society is …

SPEAKING

A Work in groups and discuss the questions.

1 Which charities do you know?

2 What do you know about them?

3 Why do people give to charity?

4 Do you think it is better to give time or money? Why?

○ **Talk about philanthropy and charities**

G— gerunds　　**V**— *make* and *do* expressions　　**P**— /ʒ/ and /dʒ/　　**S**— using context to guess unknown words

READING

A Did you exchange anything with other people when you were younger, for example, toys, books or football cards? What about later in life?

B PREDICT Look at the title of the article and at the glossary. What do you think the article is about?

C SCAN Read *Bartering is back* and complete the notes.

1　Kyle McDonald started a website, and after one year exchanged a _____ for a _____.

2　Websites such as Craigslist.org: People can exchange _____ with each other.

3　Antonio Puri exchanged a _____ for _____.

4　Time banks: For every _____ you work, you earn _____.

5　Basic rule: Ask a _____ for what you are offering. Need to agree what is _____.

BARTERING IS **BACK**

Back in 2005, Canadian Kyle MacDonald was making a living delivering pizzas, but he dreamt of owning his own house. So, one day he set up a website and offered a red paperclip in exchange for 'something bigger and better'. One year later, and after 14 exchanges, he had swapped the paperclip for a house! First, he swapped the paperclip for a pen. After that, the trades included a snowmobile, a van, an afternoon with rock star Alice Cooper and a role in a Hollywood film. Finally, he swapped the film role for a house.

But trading or bartering one item for another is nothing new. It was how people 'shopped' before the invention of money. And today, bartering is back. The number of people who use websites such as Craigslist.org, where you can exchange one item or service for another, is increasing. Some websites, such as babysitterexchange.com, provide just one service, while other sites cover a range of items and services. People have exchanged yoga lessons and language lessons for decorating, offered dog-walking and lifts to the airport in exchange for theatre and concert tickets, and some people will offer to do your shopping, cleaning or ironing in exchange for items they need. People also offer to trade professional services such as legal advice and accountancy. Antonio Puri, an artist based in Philadelphia in the USA, was in his dentist's chair when he noticed there were no paintings on the walls. He told his dentist 'You need art. How about doing a trade?' Puri made him an offer and swapped a $1200 painting for his dental treatment.

Glossary

barter (v) to exchange goods or services for other goods or services instead of using money

Time banks are another recent development. You register at your local *Time Bank*'s website and list the services you have to offer or like doing. For each hour of work you provide to another member, you earn a certain number of 'time credits'. You can then spend your 'time credits' on another service on the site that someone else enjoys doing.

Doing your research and suggesting realistic prices are the basic rules with both barter sites and time banks. It's important not to try to make a profit. At the same time, if someone does you a favour, don't give them something below its value. If you do this, the system will break down and stop working. If you are bartering, it is important to agree with the other person what is a fair exchange. So, for example, you might agree that a driving lesson is equal to two haircuts or that fixing someone's washing machine is equal to a half-hour guitar lesson.

So, next time you need something, don't reach for your wallet or bankcard. Who needs money when you can trade?

D Do you know the meaning of the words and phrases in the box? Find them in the text and use the information in the box to work out or check their meaning.

> break down   dental   favour   making a living
> set up   swapped   treatment

Using context to guess unknown words

If there is a word or phrase in a text that you don't know or understand, try to guess the meaning from context. Read the sentence before and the sentence after to help you.

Think about the wider context, for example, the topic and message of the paragraph.

Identify the word's grammatical form and function to help give it meaning.

If you can't work out the meaning, keep reading. You may read something later which helps you to understand the word.

E Guess the meaning of the words in **bold** (1–3). Then match them with their definitions (a–c).

> Bartering is about communities. It connects people. It ¹**fosters** human contact. For something ²**tangible**, like a sofa or a bike, it is easy to decide a price. But to work out a price for a service is more ³**tricky**.

a difficult to do

b helps something to develop over a period of time

c something that you can touch

F **SPEAK** Work in groups. Do you think bartering items and services is a good idea? What are the pros and the cons?

GRAMMAR
Gerunds

A Look at the gerunds in **bold** in the phrases from *Bartering is back*. Then choose the correct words to complete the rules.

> … but he dreamt of **owning** his own house.

> … that someone else enjoys **doing**.

> **Doing** your research and suggesting realistic prices are the basic rules …

> … the system will break down and stop **working**.

Gerunds

1 Gerunds are types of *nouns / verbs*.

2 We use gerunds *after / before* prepositions.

3 We can use gerunds directly after *some / all* verbs.

4 We can use gerunds as *subjects only / objects only / subjects or objects*.

B Go to the **Grammar Hub** on **page 138**.

C **SPEAK** Work in pairs. Discuss the questions.

- What are you looking forward to doing this weekend?
- What do you like/dislike spending your money on?
- Are you good at saving money? Why/Why not?

VOCABULARY
make and *do* expressions

A Complete the sentences from *Bartering is back* with the correct form of *make* or *do*. Then check your answers in the article.

1 Back in 2005, Canadian Kyle MacDonald was ____*making*____ a living delivering pizzas.

2 Some people will offer to _____ your **shopping, cleaning** or **ironing** in exchange for items they need.

3 Puri _____ him **an offer** and swapped a $1200 painting for his dental treatment.

4 _____ your **research** and suggesting realistic prices are the basic rules with both barter sites and time banks.

5 It's important not to try to _____ **a profit**. At the same time, if someone _____ you **a favour**, don't give them something below its value.

B Go to the **Vocabulary Hub** on **page 151**.

PRONUNCIATION
/ʒ/ and /dʒ/

A Listen to the sounds /ʒ/ and /dʒ/. They are very similar. Then listen and say whether you hear the sound /ʒ/ or /dʒ/ in each word.

9.5

1	exchange	3	decision	5	suggest
2	language	4	Asia		

B Listen, check and repeat the words.

9.6

⭕ SPEAKING HUB

A You are going to swap skills and services with your classmates. Follow the instructions.

- Think about two or three skills and services that you can offer (music, language or driving lessons; help with cleaning, gardening; accounting advice).

- Decide on the price of your service. For example, a one-hour driving lesson = $30, or an hour's ironing = $10.

B **SPEAK** Walk around the class and find out what skills and services your classmates are offering and how much they cost.

C **PLAN** When you have spoken to at least five people, decide which three skills and services you would like.

D **DISCUSS** Try to exchange skills or services with your classmates. For example, you could offer a one-hour driving lesson in exchange for three hours of ironing.

⭕– **Discuss your skills and how they could help others**

Café Hub

COMPREHENSION

A **SPEAK** Work in pairs. Think of a time when you bought something in a clothes shop (or any shop) and then returned it. Discuss the questions.

1 What was the item?

2 What was the problem?

3 What happened in the end?

B ▶ Watch the video and answer the questions in Exercise A.

C How would you describe Milly? How would you describe the customer? Choose adjectives from the box or use your own ideas.

> anxious   dishonest   friendly   kind   relaxed   scared   shy

FUNCTIONAL LANGUAGE
Go shopping for clothes and ask for a refund

A Work in pairs. Change the highlighted words for more polite words in the box.

> Can you enter   Here's your refund   I'd like a refund   I'd like to   I'll take it   I'm looking for   kind of thing   would you like

Shop assistant	Customer
Can I help you?	I want ¹_____ a gift for my nephew. He's 15.
What exactly ²_____ are you looking for?	A blue sweater.
	How much is this sweater?
£15	Great. I want it ³_____.
How do you want ⁴_____ to pay, cash or card?	Card, please.
Put in ⁵_____ your pin?	
Would you like me to gift wrap it for you?	Yes, please.
OK.	
Two weeks later	
	I want to ⁶_____ return this, please. It doesn't fit my nephew. It's the wrong size.
	I want my money back ⁷_____, please.
Have you got your receipt?	It's in here somewhere.
Don't worry about it. Take your money. ⁸_____	

B ▶ Watch the video again and check your answers to Exercise A.

MILLY   **SAM**   **NEENA**   **ZAC**   **GABY**

USEFUL PHRASES

A Complete the useful phrases. Who says them, Milly (M) or the customer (C)?

about   be   must   only   over   right

1	You're a yoga teacher, _____?	*M / C*
2	The sweaters are _____ there.	*M / C*
3	It says 'hand wash _____' on the label.	*M / C*
4	I have to _____ quick.	*M / C*
5	It _____ be here!	*M / C*
6	Don't worry _____ it.	*M / C*

B How do you say these useful phrases in your language?

PRONUNCIATION
Adding emphasis

A To emphasise a point, you can change the stressed word.
Listen and <u>underline</u> the stressed word in each sentence.
9.7

1 a He is so <u>spec</u>ial to me.
   b He is <u>so</u> special to me.

2 a My niece is really tall.
   b My niece is really tall.

3 a These shoes are very comfortable.
   b These shoes are very comfortable.

4 a You've been extremely helpful.
   b You've been extremely helpful.

B Listen again and repeat the sentences.
9.7

C **SPEAK** Work in pairs. Student A – say a sentence from Exercise A. Student B – point to the sentence. Take turns.

SPEAKING

A Work in pairs. Roleplay buying a gift for your mother, father or best friend. Take turns to be the customer and the shop assistant. Use the Functional language box to help you.

- Customer: Tell the shop assistant you want to buy a gift. Choose one of the items in the pictures. Ask for the price and for gift-wrapping.

- Shop assistant: Answer the customer's questions and sell the item.

B Roleplay returning the gift you bought in Exercise A.

Customer: Tell the shop assistant you want to return something. Choose one of the following problems:

- it is the wrong size
- it is damaged
- the person you bought it for doesn't like it

Shop assistant: Listen to the customer and give them a refund.

○– **Go shopping for clothes and ask for a refund**

➤ Turn to **page 166** to learn how to write a 'for sale' advert.

VOCABULARY

A Complete the questions with the prepositions in the box.

> by   for   from   in   ~~on~~   out of   to   up

1 What do you **spend** most money __on__ ?
2 Do you ever **lend** money _____ your friends? Or **borrow** it _____ them?
3 How often to you **take money** _____ the ATM?
4 Do you **pay** _____ things mostly _____ **card**, cash or do you use your phone?
5 What kind of things do you pay for _____ **cash**?
6 What kind of things do you **save** _____ for?

B Complete the sentences with the correct form of *make* or *do*. Then finish the sentences so they are true for you.

1 I need to ____*make*____ **a decision** about *what to do at the weekend.*
2 I often _____ **mistakes** when …
3 I _____ **a mess** when I was …
4 I usually _____ **my homework** …
5 I'd love to be able to _____ **a living** as a …
6 I _____ my friend **a favour** when …

GRAMMAR

A What would you do in these situations? Write sentences using the second conditional.

> ⊖ ⊡ ⊗

If I were you …

Get answers to your dilemmas.

1 The other day, I found a €100 note in the street. What would you do? Would you keep it or take it to the police?

> *If I found a €100 note in the street,*
> *I'd take it to the police.*

2 I bought a phone from an online company, but they sent me two by mistake. What would you do? Would you tell them or keep both phones?

3 I am the best at maths in my class. Some of my classmates want to give me money to copy my homework. What would you do? Would you accept the money or tell the teacher?

4 I saw someone who looked homeless steal some food from the local shop that I shop at regularly. Would you offer to pay for the food for them or tell the shopkeeper?

B Complete the news report with the relative clauses in the box.

> that Matt has hidden   which is useful
> who finds one   who has received a favour
> who needs food   you don't know   you spend it on

Man hiding tenners in Cardiff

A man from Cardiff in South Wales has hidden twenty £10 notes around the city. Anyone
[1] _____ has to use the £10 to do something good for someone else. And this has to be someone [2] _____.
The man behind the idea, Matt Callanan, says that you could give it to a person
[3] _____ or, if it's raining when you find the note, you could buy something
[4] _____, like an umbrella, and give it to someone! Callanan believes that a person [5] _____ will then do something good for someone else, and so on. So, if you find a tenner [6] _____, you could be helping more than just the person
[7] _____.

FUNCTIONAL LANGUAGE

Put the words in the correct order to complete the conversations.

Shop assistant: [1] I / help / you / can / ? ___*Can I help you?*___

Customer: [2] for / I'm looking / for / a gift / my mother
_____. It's her birthday.

Shop assistant: [3] thing / kind / what / of / are you looking for / ?
_____

Customer: Well, maybe a scarf or some gloves perhaps … I like these gloves. [4] much / they / are / how / ?
_____

Shop assistant: Let me see. They're £20.

Customer: Great. [5] them / I'll / take _____

Shop assistant: [6] for / would you like me to / gift-wrap / you / them / ? _____

Customer: Yes, please.

Shop assistant: [7] like / you / how / would / pay, / to / cash or card / ? _____

Customer: Card, please.

Shop assistant: Thanks a lot!

SCIENCE AND TECHNOLOGY

Be less curious about people
and more curious about ideas.

Marie Curie

Engineers of the future – two young Serbians work together to repair a robot.

OBJECTIVES

- describe and compare personal possessions
- describe types of technology
- discuss the requirements for a job
- make and receive formal and informal phone calls
- write a recommendation

Work with a partner. Discuss the questions.

1 Look at the picture. What were you curious about when you were a child?

2 What was your dream job when you were younger? Is it different now or the same?

3 What would you like to learn more about?

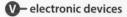 **V— electronic devices** 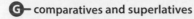 **G— comparatives and superlatives** **P— /ɪst/ and superlative adjectives**

VOCABULARY
Electronic devices

A SPEAK Work in pairs. Make a list of words to name or describe electronic devices. You have one minute.

A: Can you think of anything?
B: OK, a tablet and a mobile phone.

B Go to the **Vocabulary Hub** on **page 151**.

LISTENING

 A LISTEN FOR MAIN IDEA Listen to four people talking about devices. What question are they answering?
10.1

  a Which device do you use every day?

  b What is the most useful device you own?

  c What device do you most regret buying?

> **Glossary**
>
> **package (n)** an object or set of objects wrapped in a box or in paper and sent or given to someone
>
> **regret (v)** to feel sorry or sad about something that has happened or about something you have said or done
>
> **reliable (adj)** a reliable vehicle, piece of equipment or system always works well

B LISTEN FOR DETAIL Listen again and match the speakers (1–4) to the devices (a–h) they are describing. There are four devices you do not need.
10.1

a	drone	___	**e**	power bank	___
b	e-reader	___	**f**	tablet	___
c	fitness tracker	___	**g**	USB drive	___
d	GPS	___	**h**	laptop	___

C SPEAK Work in groups. Discuss the questions.

  1 Which of the devices in the list in Exercise B do you own or would you like to own?

  2 Which do you think is most useful and why?

GRAMMAR
Comparatives and superlatives

A <u>Underline</u> the comparative and superlative adjectives and adverbs in the sentences from the radio show.

  1 My bag is a lot lighter than it used to be.

  2 It's the best gadget I've ever bought.

  3 I got the cheapest one.

  4 You can check words so much more quickly than in a paper dictionary.

  5 This is definitely the most useful piece of technology I own.

  6 It was more expensive than an old-fashioned paper map.

  7 We spend a lot of time arguing about which turns the most quickly.

B WORK IT OUT Write the words you <u>underlined</u> in Exercise A in the correct place.

Comparatives and superlatives				
	Comparative	Example	Superlative	Example
one syllable adj	adjective + -er (+ than)	cheaper 1 _____	the + adjective + -est	the ⁴ _____ the lightest
adj with two + syllables	more + adjective (+ than)	more useful 2 _____	the most + adjective	the ⁵ _____ the most expensive
adj with two + syllables ending in -y	we cut the -y and add -ier	heavier easier	we cut the -y and add - iest	the heaviest the easiest
irregular adj	adjective (+ than)	better worse	the + adjective	the ⁶ _____ the worst
regular adv	more + adverb	more slowly 3 _____	the most + adverb	the most slowly 7 _____

C Look at the sentences and answer the questions.

1 'My bag is a lot lighter than it used to be.'
Which two words make the comparative adjective *lighter* stronger?

2 'You can check words so much more quickly.'
Which two words make the comparative adverb *quickly* stronger?

3 'Mine is a bit heavier than some of the others because it has a camera.'
Which two words make the comparative adjective *heavy* weaker?

D Go to the **Grammar Hub** on page 140.

PRONUNCIATION
/ɪst/ and superlative adjectives

🔊 **A** Listen and repeat.
10.2
/ɪst/ heaviest, strongest, fastest

🔊 **B** Listen and <u>underline</u> the sound /ɪst/ in the sentences.
10.3 Then listen and repeat.

1 The cheapest devices aren't the best.
2 The lightest laptop is better than the rest.
3 It's the fastest phone in our product test.

SPEAKING

A Work in groups. Show and describe your mobile phone to the rest of the group. Use the questions to help you.

- When did you buy your phone? How old is it? How much was it? (If you don't mind saying!)
- How is it different from any other phones you have owned?
- What do you like about it?
- What don't you like about it?

B Use comparatives to compare your phones.

A: Jenny's phone is a bit heavier than Marvin's.
B: Carly's phone was a lot more expensive than Mohammed's.

C Talk to the other groups in the class. Use superlatives to tell them about your group's phones.

A: Lucia's phone is the newest.
B: Fa's phone is the most interesting.

○— **Describe and compare personal possessions**

V— using devices and the internet   G— more comparative structures   P— /əz/ in comparative structures

READING

A Complete the definitions (1–6) with the words in the box.

> advertise (v)   annoying (adj)   mix (n)
> rely on (phr verb)   security (n)   symbol (n)

1 _____ = making you feel slightly angry

2 _____ = to trust someone or something to do a job or task for you

3 _____ = a combination of different types of people who form a group, for example: *There was a good _____ of people at the party.*

4 _____ = to try to persuade people to buy a product or service by announcing it on television, on the internet, in newspapers, etc

5 _____ = a picture or shape used to represent something: &*+@

6 _____ = safety from attack, harm or damage

B Read the posts on the online forum *Is it just me?* Do you agree or disagree with the users' opinions?

	Agree	Disagree	Not sure
User 1			
User 2			
User 3			
User 4			

C Read again. Match the sentences to the users.

Which user …

1 says that other people might not have the same problem as they do?   *User 2*

2 often forgets important personal information? _____

3 feels that technology is often unreliable? _____

4 thinks that people waste money on technology? _____

5 feels that it is important to protect your money online? _____

6 gets annoyed when trying to communicate online? _____

7 finds it hard to concentrate when using the internet? _____

D **SPEAK** Work in groups. What would you post on the site? Are the other students in your group annoyed by the same thing?

Is it just me? **Tell the internet what annoys you and find out who agrees and who doesn't!**

You say: People say technology and the internet have made life better. Sure, there are benefits, but there are also lots of annoying things. Does anyone agree?

The internet says:

> **Glossary**
> **benefit (n)** an advantage you get from a situation
> **distracted (adj)** not able to concentrate on something
> **waste time (phrase)** to spend time doing things that aren't important

(User 1) Dancingmaggie
I agree! The worst thing is how often things go wrong. Many times, when I try to make a video call, for example, the screen freezes. Video calls seem to fail as often as they work! Other things, too – you connect a drive and your computer crashes. You install a new app and everything stops working. Technology is only good when it works.

(User 2) RossM8
We rely on the internet, but we also waste time because of it. I'm often searching for something online, but then I notice something interesting, click on a link and ten minutes later I'm reading about a cat that looks like Beyoncé or a man that married himself! Sometimes I forget what I was searching for in the first place. Some people are probably not as easily distracted as me.

(User 3) Aoneandatwo
The internet is amazing, and technology, too, in general. My problem is with the technology companies. They are always advertising new devices, so many people feel they have to own the latest model. If you ask me, the old models are usually just as good as the new ones, but, you know, 'your device is not as new as my device, so you're just not cool'. It annoys me that people stop using perfectly good phones and laptops.

(User 4) ABC123
I know online security is important, especially when it comes to your bank details, but trying to remember passwords is not as easy as it sounds. They usually have to be a mix of symbols, numbers and letters, and of course, you shouldn't write them down or use the same password on different websites. My memory is not reliable and I forget passwords as often as I remember them. I have blocked my accounts so many times!

VOCABULARY
Using devices and the internet

A Read *Is it just me?* again. Complete the collocations with verbs from the posts.

1 _____*make*_____ **a video call** – use the internet to talk to and see someone else

2 _____ **your account** – if a bank or a social media provider does this, they stop your account from working because you have done something wrong

3 _____ **your password** – keep in your mind the secret word you chose to keep your email, bank or social media account safe

4 _____ **a drive** – add a small device with extra memory to your computer

5 _____ **on a link** – press the button on your mouse to connect quickly to a website

6 **your computer** _____ – your computer stops working; often you see a blue screen and a warning

7 **the screen** _____ – there's a problem that means the screen on your device won't change

8 _____ **an app** – add a new application to your phone or tablet

B SPEAK Work in groups. Discuss the questions.

1 What was the last really good app you installed on a device? Why do you like it?

2 How do you remember passwords? Have you ever blocked an account by entering the wrong password?

GRAMMAR
More comparative structures

A WORK IT OUT Look at the sentences from *Is it just me?* and choose the correct words to complete the rules.

*If you ask me, the old models are usually **just as good as** the new ones.*

*Video calls seem to fail **as often as** they work!*

*Some people are probably **not as easily distracted as** me.*

Comparative structures

1 To say that two things or people are **the same / different** in some way, we use (*just*) *as* + adjective/adverb + *as*.

2 To say that two things or people are **the same / different** in some way, we use *not as* + adjective/adverb + *as*.

B Match the sentences (1–4) with the correct meanings (a–d).

1 I don't get as annoyed with technology as my boyfriend does.

2 I get just as annoyed with technology as my boyfriend does.

3 I don't forget my passwords as often as my girlfriend does.

4 I forget my passwords just as often as my girlfriend does.

a We get equally annoyed with technology.

b He gets more annoyed with technology than me.

c She forgets her passwords more often than me.

d There is no difference in how often we forget our passwords.

C Go to the **Grammar Hub** on **page 140**.

PRONUNCIATION
/əz/ in comparative structures

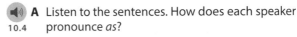

A Listen to the sentences. How does each speaker pronounce *as*?
10.4

1 I don't think online banking is as secure as personal banking.

2 Sending an email is not as thoughtful as making a phone call.

B Listen again and repeat the conversation.
10.4

C SPEAK Work in pairs. Make similar conversations about these topics. Use *as … as* in its weak form.

1 going to the cinema vs watching films online

2 paying in cash vs paying by credit or debit card

3 shopping online vs shopping in town

SPEAKING

Work in pairs. You are going to talk about different types of technology. Student A – go to the **Communication Hub** on **page 154**. Student B – go to the **Communication Hub** on **page 155**.

O— **Describe types of technology**

READING

A Work in pairs. Describe the picture. Try to use all the words in the box.

> astronaut   Earth   International Space Station (ISS)
> space   spacesuit   spacewalk   view

B **SPEAK** Work in groups. Discuss the questions.

1 What do you know about the history of human space travel?
2 What do you think would be the best and worst parts about visiting the ISS?

C **READ FOR GIST** Read the glossary and quickly read the article. Then choose the best subtitle.

1 A bridge to mars
2 The laboratory in the stars
3 Just another day in space

INTERNATIONAL SPACE STATION

There are more than seven billion human beings living on Earth, and then there are a very special group of people who live somewhere completely different. Four hundred kilometres above us and circling the planet at 7.7 km per second, there are between six and ten astronauts who call the International Space Station (ISS) home. Since the first crew members arrived in November 2000, records confirm that over 200 people from 18 countries have visited the ISS. Many only need to stay for a short time, but others need to spend several months there. So, what is the average zero-gravity day like on the ISS?

Living in space may seem exciting, but in fact, the daily routine is quite repetitive. The crew needs to follow a detailed schedule. Days begin each morning at 6 am when, instead of an alarm clock, a different song chosen by the crew's families back on Earth is played to wake them up. As on Earth, the first stop is the bathroom. Keeping clean is difficult because without gravity everything floats, including water. Residents of the ISS report that washing your hair is particularly difficult in space.

After a challenging start comes breakfast. Nearly all the food on the ISS is either dried or tinned. Most people would agree that the daily menu is not one of the highlights of life in space. Next, it's time to exercise. Research has shown that muscles and bones quickly become weak in space, so astronauts need to work out for at least two hours each day, using special zero-gravity gym equipment. The ISS is a large floating laboratory and astronauts spend much of the day doing research. Crew members work with scientists on Earth to do experiments and collect data, often about the effects of space travel on the mind and body. It is thought that one day humans will travel to Mars, so astronauts test new technologies and look for solutions to the challenges of spending large amounts of time in space.

ISS crews have made many important discoveries. For example, they have proved that it is possible to grow a range of different vegetables to provide food in space. They have also found new ways to develop drugs to help treat diseases.

Crews also need to repair equipment and solve any problems with the station itself. Sometimes this means going outside. Because of the obvious risks, the astronauts spend weeks making preparations. Incredibly, it takes four hours just to put on a spacesuit before going out for a 'spacewalk'.

When they don't need to do any other tasks, the astronauts usually use their free time to contact relatives, read or watch movies. However, there is no doubt that the most popular activity is simply looking out of the window at what is probably the best view in the universe.

Glossary

crew (n) the people who work on a ship, aircraft, space station, etc
float (v) to move slowly through air
gravity (n) the force that makes objects fall to the ground
laboratory (n) a building or large room where people do scientific research

D READ FOR DETAIL Read again. Are the sentences fact (F) or opinion (O)? Use the information in the box to help you decide.

Facts and opinions

With so much written information online these days, it is important to question what you read. To do this, you need to recognise the difference between facts and opinions. Facts are clearly true and often presented with support. Opinions are things that people believe, but may not be true.

Language often used to present facts

report, confirm, show, prove, find

There is no doubt that …

Language often used to present opinions

seem, think, believe, feel, hope

Most people would agree that …

1　There have been more than 200 visitors to the ISS.　*F / O*
2　Life in space is exciting.　*F / O*
3　It is hard to wash your hair when there is no gravity.　*F / O*
4　The food on the ISS is not particularly enjoyable.　*F / O*
5　The human body quickly loses strength in space.　*F / O*
6　People will travel to Mars in the future.　*F / O*
7　Plants can grow successfully in space.　*F / O*
8　Research on the ISS is helping people with serious illnesses.　*F / O*
9　The astronauts' favourite free time activity is looking down at Earth.　*F / O*
10　There is no better view than the one from the ISS.　*F / O*

E SPEAK Work in groups. Discuss the questions.

1　Would you visit the ISS if you had the chance? Why/Why not?
2　What would you miss most from Earth if you lived on the ISS for several months?

GRAMMAR
need to

A Look at the sentences from *International Space Station*. Choose the correct words to complete the rules.

The crew needs to follow a detailed schedule.

Crews also need to repair equipment and solve any problems with the station itself.

When they don't need to do any other tasks, the astronauts usually use their free time to contact relatives, read or watch movies.

need to

1　We use *need* to say something is *possible / necessary*.
2　When *need* is followed by a verb, we use *-ing / to + infinitive*.
3　We *add / don't add* -s to *need* when the subject is *he, she* or *it*.
4　We use the auxiliary *do / have* with negative and question forms of *need*.

B Go to the **Grammar Hub** on **page 140.**

VOCABULARY
Collocations: science and research

A Choose the correct verbs to complete the collocations in **bold** in the ISS schedule memo. Use *International Space Station* to help you.

ISS schedule memo 1174639 – Schedule number 4077

Good evening from Earth and the Control Centre. As always, please [1]***do / follow*** tomorrow's **schedule** carefully.
0900 – IMPORTANT [2]***repair / solve*** broken gym **equipment**. This must be fixed today. Exercise programme must return to normal.
1000 – Live link with University of Beijing – Give a presentation to students on Chinese astronauts who have [3]***made / found*** important **discoveries** on the ISS.
1100 – Continue [4]***testing / making*** new **technologies** for long-distance communication.
1300 – Meeting to [5]***look for / collect*** **solutions** to the recent computer problems.
1400 – Continue [6]***making / doing*** **research** into growing fruit in space. [7]***Do / Test*** **experiments** numbers 146 to 149 and [8]***collect / follow*** more **data** on water levels.
1700 – [9]***Make / Do*** more **preparations** for the next spacewalk. Try to [10]***test / solve*** the **problems** with spacesuit number 4.

B SPEAK Work in pairs. Go to the **Communication Hub** on **page 155** and complete the survey. Then compare your results. Which of you would be best at working in space?

PRONUNCIATION
/ʊ/ and /uː/

A Listen to the word pairs. How is the pronunciation of the vowel sounds different?
10.5

1　<u>foo</u>t　　<u>foo</u>d　　　　2　w<u>o</u>man　　ro<u>u</u>tine

B Listen again and repeat the word pairs.
10.5

C Write the words in the correct place in the table. Listen and check.
10.6

~~crew~~　group　look　move　room　would

/ʊ/	/uː/
	crew

D Listen again and repeat the words.
10.6

⃝ SPEAKING HUB

PREPARE You are going to talk about working in space. Go to the **Communication Hub** on **page 156** and follow the instructions.

◯– **Discuss the requirements for a job**

Café Hub

10.4 Locked out
F– make and receive formal and informal phone calls
P– word stress and intonation

COMPREHENSION

A ▶ Cover the video screen. Listen to the video and put the events (a–j) in the correct order (1–10).

a The front door closes and locks shut. ____

b Gaby phones Neena's work. ____

c The signal is bad. ____

d Gaby is put on hold. ____

e Gaby phones Zac's mobile. ____

f Gaby leaves a voice message for Neena. ____

g It starts raining. ____

h Neena's phone is switched off. ____

i Gaby phones Neena's mobile. ____

j Gaby opens the front door to take the rubbish out. ____

B ▶ SPEAK Work in pairs. Predict the answers to the questions. Then watch the video and check your answers.

1 Where is Gaby?

2 How does Gaby get locked out?

3 Where is Zac?

4 Where is Neena?

5 What is the music we hear three times?

6 How does the video end?

MILLY

SAM

NEENA

ZAC

GABY

FUNCTIONAL LANGUAGE
Make and receive formal and informal phone calls

A Write the words in the correct order to make useful phrases. Then write each phrase in the correct place.

1 up / breaking / You're / .

          You're breaking up.

2 you / hear / can't / I / .

_____

3 me / Can / you / hear / ?

_____

4 gone / You've / again / .

_____

5 that / What / was / ?

_____

6 very / The / isn't / signal / good / .

_____

Describe a phone problem	Ask for clarification
You're breaking up.	

B Complete the receptionist's replies with two of the words in the box.

just	over	soon	through

Receptionist: Good morning. You're
¹_____ to Jobs, Jobs, Jobs and Jobs. How can I help?

Gaby: Hello, is it possible to speak to Neena Patel?

Receptionist: Yes, of course. I'll ²_____ try to put you ³_____. I'm afraid the line is busy. Would you like to hold?

Gaby: Yes, please.

[MUSIC ON HOLD]

Receptionist: Thank you for calling.
⁴_____ putting you ⁵_____.

C **SPEAK** Work in pairs. Practise the conversation in Exercise B with your own ideas.

PRONUNCIATION
Word stress and intonation

🔊 **A** Listen and repeat Amelia's voicemail greeting. Copy the
10.7 word stress and intonation.

> **Amelia:** Hi, this is Amelia Jones. I can't take your call at the moment. Please leave a message after the beep.

B **SPEAK** Work in pairs. You are going to record your own voicemail greeting in English.

- Practise your voicemail greeting.
- Record your voicemail greeting on your phone.
- Call your partner and listen to his/her greeting.
- Leave a message for your partner.

SPEAKING

Work in groups. Choose a problem from the box or use your own ideas. Then roleplay calling two friends to ask for help. Use the Functional language box to help you.

> You've locked yourself out. You've lost your car keys.
> You've lost your house keys. You've missed the last
> bus home. You've forgotten your passport.

Student A: Call a friend (Student B). The signal is bad.

Student B: Answer Student A. The signal is bad.

Student A: Call another friend at Jones & Jones. You can't get through. You speak to Student C (the receptionist).

Student C: You are the receptionist at Jones & Jones. Answer Student A. The line is busy.

Student A: Answer Student C (the receptionist).

Glossary

trash (n) (American) rubbish
cell phone (n) (American) mobile phone

○ **Make and receive formal and informal phone calls**

➤ Turn to **page 167** to learn how to write a recommendation.

VOCABULARY

A Choose the correct words to complete the sentences.

1 My new *drone* / *fitness tracker* has arrived. Shall we go to the park and fly it?

2 I'm so bad at directions – this *USB drive* / *GPS* is really useful!

3 I think a *fitness tracker* / *tablet* would make me do more exercise.

4 I always take my *e-reader* / *power bank* on holiday with me. I love books.

5 My son wants a *drone* / *tablet* so he can watch his favourite TV programmes.

6 A *GPS* / *USB drive* is very useful when I go on business trips. I can take my work everywhere!

7 I don't know what I would do without my *power bank* / *e-reader* – my phone battery is always running out.

B Complete the information with the verbs in the box. You need to use one of the verbs twice.

> collect   do   look   make   test

Why study science at Higgerfield?

We asked three first-year students why they chose science subjects.

Sergei: I want to ¹_____ data and ²_____ for solutions to the problem of climate change.

Masha: I want to ³_____ research into space travel and ⁴_____ new technologies to help get us to other planets.

Melissa: I want to ⁵_____ discoveries and ⁶_____ experiments that will help save people's lives.

To find out more about studying Science at Higgerfield, join us at one of our open days.

GRAMMAR

A Complete the article with comparative and superlative forms of the missing adjectives and adverbs.

Hi-fi & Wi-fi Magazine **Awards**
Mobile phones
1ˢᵗ Chitchat 8
2ⁿᵈ Speakup 4   3ʳᵈ Talkabout 2

Overall

The Talkabout 2 is a good phone, but the Speakup 4 is ¹____*better*____. And this year, the Chitchat 8 is ²____*the best*____.

Is it reliable?

The Talkabout 2 is quite reliable, but the Speakup 4 is ³_____. Again, the Chitchat 8 is ⁴_____.

Is it easy to use?

The Talkabout 2 is quite easy to use, but the Speakup 4 is definitely ⁵_____ to use. However, the Chitchat 8 is ⁶_____ to use.

Does it charge quickly?

The Talkabout 2 charges quickly, but the Speakup 4 charges ⁷_____. Again, the Chitchat 8 wins this year because it charges ⁸_____.

B Add *as … as* to complete each sentence.

1 I get just ‿ᵃˢ annoyed with pop-up adverts ‿ᵃˢ anybody else.

2 That messaging service is not private this one.

3 My wife doesn't forget passwords easily I do.

4 My dad's phone is just old-fashioned my mum's.

5 I don't learn how to use new devices quickly I used to when I was young.

6 This game is just good the other football games on the market.

FUNCTIONAL LANGUAGE

Complete the words in the phone conversation. The first letter of each word has been given to help you.

Derek: Hello, this is Derek Lebarge. ¹Sorry, I can't t_____ your call at the m_____. ²Please leave a m_____ after the b_____.

Murray: Derek? Derek? It's Murray. ³Sorry, the s_____ isn't very g_____. ⁴What was t_____? ⁵You're b_____ up. Hello?

NATURAL WORLD

Everybody needs beauty as well
as bread, places to play in where
nature may heal and give strength
to body and soul alike.

John Muir

An urban fox begins his nightly hunt for food, Twickenham, United Kingdom.

OBJECTIVES

- talk about natural wonders
- read and talk about wildlife photography
- talk about the causes and effects of plastic pollution
- tell a story
- write an email giving suggestions and advice

Work with a partner. Discuss the questions.

1 Do you find the city or the countryside more relaxing? Why?

2 Read the quote. Do you agree with Muir?

3 Look at the picture. What wildlife is there in your city?

V— natural features   **P**— /e/ and /iː/   **G**— the passive (present and past simple)

1 ☐   2 ☐   3 ☐
4 ☐   5 ☐   6 ☐   7 ☐

VOCABULARY
Natural features

A Label the pictures (1–7) with the words in the box.

> canyon   harbour   lights   mountain
> reef   volcano   waterfall

B Go to the **Vocabulary Hub** on **page 151**.

C **SPEAK** Work in pairs. Name other examples of the natural features in Exercise A and in the Vocabulary Hub.

A: Well, there's Mount Fuji and The Great Barrier Reef. But I can't think of a famous canyon.

B: What about The Grand Canyon in Arizona?

PRONUNCIATION
/e/ and /iː/

A Listen to the vowel sounds /e/ and /iː/. What is the vowel sound in each word in the box? Write the words in the correct place.

11.1

> be   get   leave   met   reef   rest   see   ten

/e/	/iː/

B Listen and check your answers. Then listen again and repeat the words.

11.2

LISTENING

A The places in the pictures above have recently been named as the *Seven Natural Wonders of the World*. Match the names (a–g) with the pictures (1–7). What do you know about them?

a   Mount Everest _____4_____
b   Great Barrier Reef _____
c   Grand Canyon _____
d   Northern lights (aurora borealis) _____
e   Rio de Janeiro harbour _____
f   Victoria Falls _____
g   Paricutin volcano _____

B **LISTEN FOR KEY WORDS** Listen to a radio travel show about the *Seven Natural Wonders of the World*. In which order did the travel writer visit the places?

11.3

1 _____the Great Barrier Reef_____
2 _____
3 _____
4 _____
5 _____
6 _____
7 _____

Glossary

coral (n) a very small sea creature that lives in large groups that look like plants, in places where the water is warm
crater (n) the round hole at the top of a volcano
form (v) to make something exist
promote (v) to support something
unique (adj) not the same as anything else

C LISTEN FOR DETAIL Listen to the radio show again and answer the questions.

11.3

1 What is the aim of the Seven Natural Wonders organisation?

2 What three main factors were used to choose the Seven Natural Wonders?

3 Why did Mike decide to visit the Seven Natural Wonders?

4 Which of the seven natural wonders …

a is visible only at certain times of the year?

_____

b was formed the most recently?

_____

c is located in two countries?

_____

d is famous for its different colours?

_____

e is the highest?

_____

f is the most visited?

_____

D SPEAK Work in pairs. Which of the Seven Natural Wonders you would most like to visit and why?

GRAMMAR

The passive (present and past simple)

A WORK IT OUT Look at the sentences from the radio show about the seven natural wonders. Then complete the rules using the words in the box.

1 The decision **was based** on three main things.

2 The places **were chosen** according to how unique the place is …

3 It's **made** of over 400 different kinds of coral.

4 It **was** only **formed** in 1943.

5 The canyon **was created by** the Colorado River.

6 It's **visited by** about four-and-a-half million people a year.

| be | by | do not say | past participle |

The passive (present and past simple)

1 We make the passive with the auxiliary verb _____ + the _____ of the main verb.

2 We most commonly use the passive when we _____ who or what performs or causes the action. This is usually because the person or thing is not known, not important or obvious.

3 We sometimes use the passive with an agent (the person or thing that performs or causes the action). We use _____ to introduce the agent.

B Go to the **Grammar Hub** on **page 142**.

C SPEAK Work in pairs. Test your general knowledge! Make sentences about these natural wonders using a word from each column. Discuss what you know about each place.

Jeju Island is located off the coast of South Korea.

1	Jeju Island	form	around 30 million people a year
2	The White Cliffs of Dover	locate	40–50 million years ago
3	The Himalayas	visit	as Ayers Rock
4	The Niagara Falls	make	off the coast of South Korea
5	Uluru in Australia	discover	of chalk and similar minerals
6	The Galapagos Islands	also/know	the Bishop of Panama in 1535

SPEAKING

A Listen to a presentation about the Gullfoss Waterfall in Iceland and answer the questions.

11.4

- Where is it located?
- When was it formed or created?
- What is it surrounded by?
- How is it reached?
- Who and how many people visit it?
- Why are people attracted to it?

B Work in pairs. Choose a natural wonder in your country or continent to give a presentation about. Use the questions in Exercise A to help you.

C Give your presentation to the class.

◯ **Talk about natural wonders**

VOCABULARY
Animals

A SPEAK Work in pairs. Make a list of animals. You have one minute.

B Go to the **Vocabulary Hub** on **page 151**.

C SPEAK Work in pairs. Write down your three favourite animals. Tell your partner what you wrote. Explain your choices.

D SPEAK Work in pairs. Go to the **Communication Hub** on **page 157** to see what your answers to Exercise C mean. Do you agree or disagree?

My first animal is a dolphin. I think I'm like a dolphin because it's smart, moves quickly, is very sociable and always in groups.

READING

A Match the words and phrases (1–5) with the definitions (a–e).

1 habitat
2 wildlife
3 make eye contact
4 facial expression
5 life cycle

a the series of changes that happen to an animal or plant during its life
b the look on someone's face that shows what their thoughts or feelings are
c animals, birds and plants that live in natural conditions
d the type of place that a particular animal usually lives in or a particular plant usually grows in
e situation in which two people look at each other's eyes

Behind the lens:
Anthony Remy, wildlife photographer

You may not know Anthony Remy's name but you will almost certainly have seen one of his photos. He spoke to us about his 30-year career close-up with wildlife.

◉ Where did your interest in wildlife photography come from?
I grew up in Canada with nature right on my doorstep. I just had to step outside and I could see all manner of mammals, reptiles, birds and amphibians. One day my older cousin, Julian, took me to see a grizzly fishing with her cub … from a safe distance, of course. Julian passed me his camera so that I could zoom in. It was great to watch them so closely, I never wanted to forget it. I pressed the shutter and that's when I decided what I wanted to do for the rest of my life.

◉ Is it easy to find work? I imagine it's quite difficult.
It is at first when no one knows your name and you don't have any contacts at magazines. Over time your reputation grows. You ask local shops to put up framed photos or sell some of your cards … you know, anything to make a living!

◉ I guess you're asked this a lot but what's your favourite animal?
Well … I love dogs … I have four at home. In terms of photography though orang-utans without a doubt. Their name literally means 'person of the forest' in Malay and you can see why. It's not just their body language and facial expressions that are so like ours, but also their social interactions. Over my career I've also taken a lot of photos of spiders, which you may not understand! But most people come to realise, like me, that up close they are unexpectedly fascinating.

◉ And which animal don't you enjoy taking photos of?
Well some animals are so 'seen' there are hundreds of photographs of them … you know, elephants, eagles, tigers. It isn't easy to take something amazing that everyone would be interested in. Certain types of monkeys are challenging too as they don't want to make eye contact with people. Then there are lemurs which will look you in the eye, in fact they'll climb all over you, but they live deep in the Madagascan rainforest. Habitats like that are hard to get to, especially carrying camera equipment.

◉ So any top tips for future wildlife photographers out there?
Don't rush out and spend a fortune on a new camera. It really isn't the most important thing. An interest in animals is obvious but essential. Unless you are incredibly lucky, be prepared for uncomfortable hours or even weeks waiting for the perfect shot. Researching habitats and life cycles can certainly help this. If you watch an animal for long enough, you can predict its behaviour. For example, I always know when a grizzly will swipe for the salmon and so I am there ready to capture the moment.

Glossary
body language (n) the movements or positions of your body that show others what you are thinking or feeling
close-up (n) a picture of someone or something taken from a position very near them
make a living (phrase) to earn money from a job

B SCAN Read *Behind the lens* and answer the questions.

Which animal(s) …

1 did Anthony Remy first take pictures of?

2 is/are his favourite to photograph?

3 is/are difficult to get a good picture of?

4 does he think have predictable behaviour?

C READ FOR DETAIL Choose the correct answers, a, b or c.

1 Anthony Remy started taking pictures of bears …

   a to show his cousin what he had seen.

   b to help him remember them.

   c to capture the beauty of where he is from.

2 He thinks orang-utans are …

   a shy.   **b** dangerous.

   c similar to humans.

3 He thinks his pictures of spiders often …

   a surprise people.   **b** frighten people.

   c disappoint people.

4 He thinks some animals, such as elephants …

   a are not interesting to photograph.

   b don't do anything surprising.

   c have been photographed too much.

5 He says monkeys …

   a don't like to look at humans.

   b try to hide from humans.

   c behave like humans.

6 In Anthony's opinion, it is <u>not</u> necessary …

   a to know about the animals you are photographing.

   b to spend time watching and have a lot of patience.

   c to have a lot of expensive camera equipment.

D SPEAK Work in pairs. Discuss the skills and characteristics you need to be a wildlife photographer.

GRAMMAR
Adjective + to + infinitive

A WORK IT OUT Look at the sentences from *Behind the lens*. Add the missing adjective + *to* + infinitive. Then complete the rule.

1 It was _____ them so closely …

2 It isn't _____ something amazing that everyone would be interested in.

3 Habitats like that are _____ to, especially carrying camera equipment.

Adjective + *to* + infinitive
When a verb comes after an adjective, we use the _____ form of the verb.

B Go to the **Grammar Hub** on **page 142**.

C SPEAK Go to the **Communication Hub** on **page 153** and follow the instructions.

PRONUNCIATION
to /tə/

A Listen to the weak pronunciation of *to* /tə/ in the sentences. *11.5*

1 It's easy to take a good picture.

2 It's important to be patient.

3 Are you ready to leave?

B Listen again and repeat the sentences. *11.5*

SPEAKING

A Read the tips about what makes a good animal picture. Do you agree? Add a tip of your own.

> ✓ It's important to show the animal in its natural habitat.
>
> ✓ It's important to be able to see the animal's face and eyes. It gives an idea of how the animal is feeling or what it's thinking.
>
> ✓ It's good to photograph the animal doing something. It's even better to catch it doing something unusual or maybe something funny.
>
> ✓ A good animal picture shows detail and colour that you don't normally see.
>
> ✓ A good picture is one where you see something new. You learn something about the animal.

B Look at the pictures (a–f) above and answer the questions.

• Which of the features in the tips above does each picture have?

• Choose the best animal picture in your opinion.

• Put the others in order of second favourite, third favourite.

C Work in groups. Compare your ideas. In your group, decide on the best animal picture.

◯- **Read and talk about wildlife photography**

P – /r/ pronounced and silent   **G** – even   **V** – somewhere, nowhere, everywhere, anywhere
S – looking for ways of expressing cause and effect

READING

A Work in pairs. Discuss the questions.

1 Do you recycle? What kind of things do you recycle? Is it easy to recycle things where you live? What happens to things you throw away that are not recycled?

2 Look at the picture. What can you see on the beach? How do you think it got there?

B **READ FOR GIST** Read *The nightmare of Plastic Island* and decide which is the best summary.

a Plastic is often blown into the sea and is carried around the world by ocean currents. The pictures of Henderson Island show how we should clean the beaches before the plastic enters the sea.

b Plastic is carried to certain parts of the world by ocean currents, but it does not reach other parts of the world. The pictures of Henderson Island suggest that the situation is worse than it actually is.

c Plastic is carried around the world by ocean currents and reaches the most remote beaches and other places. The pictures of Henderson Island show how serious the problem is.

C **READ FOR DETAIL** Answer the questions. Use the information in the box to help you. Then read again and check your answers.

Looking for ways of expressing cause and effect

Look for verbs, linking words and nouns that express cause and effect:

• **verbs:** This **means** there are … This has **led** to …

• **linking words:** This is **because** … **Because of** this, … **If** we do this, …

• **nouns:** And as **a result**, …

1 Why is there plastic everywhere?

2 Why was plastic successful when it first appeared?

3 Scientists believe that there are five trillion pieces of plastic in the oceans. What is this number based on?

4 Some marine animals eat plastic. How can this affect humans?

5 Experts believe plastic pollution in the oceans is a serious problem. How have some governments responded to this?

6 What can individuals do to help reduce the amount of plastic pollution?

The nightmare of PLASTIC ISLAND

Plastic is everywhere. It is at the bottom of the oceans, on tropical beaches and at the top of Mount Everest. It is even on the surface of Mars. This is because each year, over 300 million tonnes of plastic is produced, used and then most of it is thrown away.

Plastic was invented over 100 years ago. When it first appeared, it was an instant success. It was cheap, convenient, had many uses and was long-lasting. And that is the problem. Plastic will not go away. It may break into smaller and smaller pieces, but every piece of plastic ever made still exists somewhere in the world.

Up to 12 million tonnes of plastic enters the world's oceans every year. This means there are around five trillion pieces of plastic currently in our oceans. Once there, it can be carried by the currents for many years and travel thousands of kilometres. Some of it is eaten by marine wildlife and enters the food chain. As a result, thousands of pieces of marine plastic are consumed by humans each year when they eat fish and other seafood. However, most of the plastic in the seas and oceans eventually washes up on beaches. Nowhere on Earth has as much plastic as the beaches of Henderson Island in the South Pacific. The remote island is the most polluted anywhere in the world, and 99.8 per cent of this pollution is plastic. The island's beaches contain around 38 million pieces of plastic; most of this is from everyday consumer goods.

Henderson Island is a UNESCO World Heritage site and it is an important habitat for wildlife. Jennifer Lavers, of the University of Tasmania, says that the situation on Henderson Island shows that 'nowhere is safe from plastic pollution'. She even believes that marine plastic pollution is 'as important as climate change'. Other experts describe the situation as 'a major ecological disaster' and 'an environmental emergency'.

Because of this, there is a global effort to reduce the amount of plastic pollution. For example, Indonesia has promised to spend up to $1 billion on reducing plastic and other waste products which pollute its waters. This has led to other governments making similar pledges.

However, the best way to prevent rubbish from washing up on beaches is for us as individuals to use less plastic, especially things that we don't even need. These are single-use and 'disposable' items, such as cutlery and even toothbrushes. We can also buy products with less packaging and recycle more. If we do this, we will reduce the amount of plastic that ends up in our oceans and on our beaches. We will also be less likely to find plastic returning to us on our dinner plates.

Glossary

consumer goods (n) things you buy for personal or home use, such as food and clothing
current (n) a strong movement of water in one direction
marine (adj) living or happening in the sea
remote (adj) far away from other cities, towns or people

PRONUNCIATION
/r/ pronounced and silent

A Listen to the words. Is the letter *r* pronounced in each word?

11.6

1	result	**3**	marine	**5**	large	**7**	consumer
2	remote	**4**	world	**6**	horrible	**8**	major

B Work in pairs. Write the words in the correct place. Listen and check.

11.6

r is pronounced	*r* is not pronounced

C **SPEAK** Work in pairs. Why is the letter *r* pronounced in some words and not in others?

GRAMMAR
even

A **WORK IT OUT** Look at the phrases from *The nightmare of Plastic Island*. Then choose the correct words to complete the rules.

It is even on the surface of Mars.

She even believes that marine plastic pollution is 'as important as climate change.'

… especially things that we don't even need.

These are single-use and 'disposable' items, such as cutlery and even toothbrushes.

---

even

1 We use *even* to suggest that something is *surprising / obvious*.

2 We use *even* **before / after** verbs, but **before / after** auxiliary verbs (*be, have, can, don't*).

3 We *can / cannot* use *even* before nouns.

B Go to the **Grammar Hub** on **page 142**.

C **SPEAK** Work in groups. Tell your group three things that you think are surprising. You can talk about natural wonders, animals or pollution. Use *even* and *don't even*.

VOCABULARY
somewhere, nowhere, everywhere, anywhere

A Complete the sentences from *The nightmare of Plastic Island* with *somewhere, nowhere, everywhere* or *anywhere*. Then read again and check your answers.

1 Plastic is _____.

2 Every piece of plastic ever made still exists _____ in the world.

3 _____ on Earth has as much plastic as the beaches of Henderson Island.

4 The remote island is the most polluted _____ in the world.

5 Jennifer Lavers says that '_____ is safe from plastic pollution'.

B Complete the sentences with *somewhere, nowhere, everywhere* or *anywhere*.

1 I'd like to live by the sea – ideally, _____ near a big sandy beach and without too many people.

2 There is _____ like India. It's unique. There's quite a lot of pollution and poverty, but it's an amazing place. _____ you go, you see something incredible.

3 If I could visit _____ in the world, I'd go to California. I've always wanted to go there. If not California, I'd like to go _____ similar with big cities, lots of beaches and warm weather.

4 I was very impressed by Singapore. _____ was so clean. There was no litter _____.

C **SPEAK** Rewrite the sentences in Exercise B using your own ideas. Then work in pairs and share your ideas. Ask questions to find out more information.

I'd like to live in a village – ideally, somewhere with a few shops and surrounded by nice countryside.

SPEAKING HUB

A You are going to do the Plastic Challenge. Read about the Plastic Challenge, which is organised by the Marine Conservation Society.

The Plastic Challenge asks people to stop using plastic items for as long as they can. This could be for a day, a week or a month. Our message is 'reduce, reuse, recycle'. We're challenging people to give up their single-use plastics, such as pre-packed sandwiches, ready meals, bottled drinks and so on. Do the Plastic Challenge and you'll never look at your shopping in the same way again!

B **PLAN** Spend a few minutes thinking about the following.

1 Make a list of all the plastic you have used …

  a today.

  b in the last week.

  c How much of this was single-use items?

2 Imagine you are going to do the Plastic Challenge.

  a Which items would be easier to stop using and which would be more difficult?

  b What changes would you need to make in your daily life to do the challenge?

  c How long do you think you could do the challenge for?

C **DISCUSS** Work in groups.

1 Compare and discuss your lists and your ideas about the Plastic Challenge.

2 Decide on a plan for doing the Plastic Challenge. You must agree to do the same things.

○— **Talk about the causes and effects of plastic pollution**

COMPREHENSION

A ▶ 00:00–03:33 Watch the first part of the video and answer the questions.

1 What is a 'power cut'?

2 What kind of story does Sam tell Neena and Gaby?

3 How do Neena and Gaby feel as Sam tells the story?

4 How do you think Sam's story ends?

B ▶ 03:33–04:29 Watch the second part of the video. Compare the end of Sam's story with your ideas in Exercise A. Is it a good story?

C ▶ Work in pairs. Put the events of Sam's story in the correct order (1–10). Then watch the video again and check your answers.

a After <u>that</u>, I tried to switch the lights on, but there was no power. ____

b I wasn't alone. ____

c It was <u>stormy</u>. Very stormy. ____

d I arrived back at my uncle's house, got out of the car and walked up to the front door. ____

e So <u>anyway</u>, I went inside and called out to see if my uncle was home. 'Uncle Mike' I shouted – there was no answer. ____

f It all <u>started</u> on a stormy night when I was in Cornwall staying with my uncle. ____

g I walked into the kitchen and sat down in the dark. My uncle was missing – I was <u>scared</u>. ____

h I pushed the door and the wind blew it open. ____

i In the <u>end</u>, I sat there alone in the dark. ____

j Then the front door slammed shut behind me. ____

D Match Sam's sentences (1–5) with the replies (a–e).

1 This reminds me of a very scary experience I once had.

2 It all started on a stormy night when I was in Cornwall staying with my uncle.

3 Can I continue my story now?

4 I was scared.

5 My phone was dead.

a Where is Cornwall?

b You <u>poor</u> thing!

c How <u>awful</u>!

d So, <u>tell</u> us. What happened?

e Sure. Go on.

MILLY

SAM

NEENA

ZAC

GABY

FUNCTIONAL LANGUAGE
Tell a story

A Look at the <u>underlined</u> words in Comprehension Exercises C and D. Complete the box with one of the words.

Tell a story and listen to a story
Give background information
It was ¹_____/windy/raining.
The sun was shining and it was hot.
Use linking phrases
Beginning: At first … / To start with … / It all ²_____ …
Middle: Then … / After ³_____ … / So ⁴_____, …
End: In the ⁵_____, …
Say how you felt
I was excited/surprised/worried/relieved/frightened/ ⁶_____.
Keep the story going
Go on. / So, ⁷_____ us. (Then) What happened?
Respond to dramatic events
You ⁸_____/lucky thing.
How ⁹_____/frightening/funny.
That's terrible/awful/funny.

B SPEAK Work in pairs. You are going to practise responding to events.

1 Look at the responses in the box. Choose three responses you want your partner to give. Circle them.

> How awful/frightening/funny.   That's terrible/awful/funny.
> You poor/lucky thing.

2 Write down three things you could tell your partner to get him/her to give those responses.

3 Tell your partner your ideas. How does he/she respond?

Student A wants Student B to say 'You lucky thing'.

A: I found €5 in the street this morning.
B: You lucky thing!

Glossary
power outage (n) (American) power cut – a period when the electricity supply stops
flashlight (n) (American) torch

PRONUNCIATION
Showing interest

 A Listen and write how the responses sound in the correct place.

11.7

Very interested	Not very interested
That's awful.	

B Listen again and repeat the responses.

11.7

C SPEAK Work in pairs. Practise saying the responses. Listen to your partner and say whether he/she sounds very interested or not very interested.

SPEAKING

A Work in pairs. You are going to tell your partner a story. Choose one of the topics or use your own ideas. Include background information, linking phrases and say how you felt.

A time when … you got lost / you lost your keys / you met an old friend / you won a prize / something happened on holiday.

B Tell each other your stories and react and respond appropriately.

A: I lost some car keys once.
B: That's awful!
A: I was on holiday with the family in Menorca …
B: Where is Menorca?

○— **Tell a story**

➤ Turn to **page 168** to learn how to write an email giving suggestions and advice.

Unit 11 Review

VOCABULARY

A Complete the sentences using a word from box a and box b.

> **a** Amazon Atlas Death Grand
> Lascaux Panama ~~Sahara~~ San Francisco

> **b** Bay Canal Canyon Caves
> ~~Desert~~ Mountains Rainforest Valley

1 The __Sahara Desert__ is 9.3 million square kilometres, which is almost the same size as China.

2 The _____ stretch for 2,500 km in Morocco, Algeria and Tunisia.

3 The Golden Gate Bridge is 2,737 metres long and crosses the _____.

4 The _____ is 446 km in length and 29 km across at its widest point.

5 The _____ is 9.3 million square kilometres and is located in nine countries in South America.

6 In 1913, a temperature of 56.7°C was recorded in _____ in eastern California.

7 The _____ connects the Atlantic Ocean with the Pacific Ocean.

8 The walls of the _____ in south-western France are decorated with 17,000-year-old paintings of animals, such as cows, horses and deer.

B Find 17 animals and write them in the correct place.

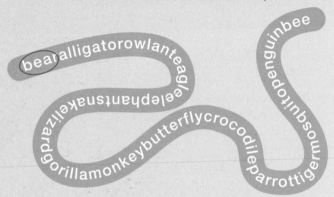

Mammals	Birds	Reptiles	Insects	Fish
bear				

C Choose the correct words to complete the sentences.

1 Plastic is *anywhere / everywhere*. It has more forms and uses than any other material on the planet.

2 About 30 per cent of all the plastic ever made is still in use *anywhere / somewhere* in the world today.

3 Recycling rates of plastic are not the same *somewhere / everywhere* in the world. For example, in Europe about 30 per cent is recycled, in China around 25 per cent and in the USA the figure is just 10 per cent.

4 There is almost *anywhere / nowhere* on Earth that does not have plastic pollution.

GRAMMAR

A Complete the text with the correct passive form of the verbs in brackets. Add *by* where it is needed.

Ayers Rock ¹_____ (*locate*) in the Uluru-Kata Tjuta National Park in central Australia. It ²_____ (*also / know*) as Uluru, which is its original Aboriginal name. The rock ³_____ (*form*) over 600 million years ago and it ⁴_____ (*originally / locate*) under the sea. The summit is generally flat but, there are valleys and caves that ⁵_____ (*create*) the wind and rain over millions of years.

B Complete the conversations with the words in the box.

> easy/use lucky/see necessary/have safe/drink unusual/see

1 A: Is your camera _____?
   B: Yes, it's very easy. Anyone can use it.

2 A: It isn't _____ the water here.
   B: OK, I'll get some bottled water.

3 A: It isn't _____ expensive equipment to take good pictures.
   B: I agree. A creative eye is all you need.

4 A: It's _____ the northern lights at this time of year.
   B: Yes, we were very _____ them.

C Rewrite the sentences with the correct form of *even / don't even*.

1 I use plastic bags. (*not even*)

   _____

2 Ella does a lot of recycling; she recycles clothes. (*even*)

   _____

3 I never buy plastic. I let my children play with plastic toys. (*not even*)

FUNCTIONAL LANGUAGE

Add the missing words to complete the conversation.

A: It all ¹s__ __ __ __ __ __ when we decided to walk along the Samaria Gorge in Crete.

B: ²G__ on.

A: Well, Sandy, my friend, didn't want to do it. It's quite a long and steep walk to get down in the gorge. But she finally agreed to it.

B: So, what ³h__ __ __ __ __ __ __ __?

A: After about two hours, Sandy fell over and hurt her leg.

B: Oh, no! ⁴H__ __ awful! ⁵P__ __ __ thing!

A: So, ⁶a__ __ __ __ __ __, she took some painkillers and decided to go back to the hotel.

B: ⁷T__ __ __ what happened?

A: Well her leg was broken …

B: ⁸T__ __ __ __' __ terrible.

A: Yes, but in the ⁹e__ __ __, everything was OK.

MEDIA

I do not take a single newspaper,
nor read one a month, and I feel
happier for it.

Thomas Jefferson

A printer works through the night to get out the news on time.

OBJECTIVES

○— talk about the pros and cons of online news

○— talk and debate about different TV viewing habits

○— talk about advertising and what makes a good advert

○— give and respond to opinions

○— write a story

Work with a partner. Discuss the questions.

1 How often do you read the news?

2 Look at the picture. Do you think
   newspapers will exist in the future?

3 Do you think 24-hour news on TV and the
   internet is a positive thing? Why/Why not?

VOCABULARY
News expressions

A Replace the words in **bold** with the words and phrases with the same meaning in the box.

> breaking news   follow   ~~get~~   journalist
> news headlines   report   share

1 How do you generally ~~watch / listen to~~
_____*get*_____ the news? TV? Radio? Online?

2 How closely do you **pay attention to** _____ the news?

3 What are the current **biggest news stories** _____?

4 How do you usually find out about **the very latest news** _____?

5 How often do you **repost** _____ news stories on social media?

6 What characteristics and qualities do you need to be a **person who writes about the news** _____?

7 Do different news organisations **communicate** _____ the news in different ways? How?

B Work in pairs. Ask and answer the questions in Exercise A.

READING

A READ FOR GIST Read the article and choose the best subtitle. Give reasons.

a here and now   b good or bad?

c past and present   d truth or lies?

B READ FOR DETAIL Read again and answer the questions.

1 Today, what are the main ways we get our news?

2 Do people trust newspapers, radio and TV news more or less than online news sites?

3 Why is there less control over the quality of journalism today than in the past?

4 What is fake news and what is the main reason for it?

5 Why is it often difficult to know if something is fake news or not?

6 What can help us to decide if a news story is fake or not?

C SPEAK Work in pairs. Discuss the questions.

1 What are the pros and cons of online news?

2 Do you think fake news is a problem? Why/Why not?

The news: _____

Not long ago, television, radio and newspapers were the main ways of receiving the latest news. But the way we get our news today is very different. Most of us have mobile devices and the internet is available almost everywhere. As a result, online news sites and social media give us quick and easy access to what is going on in the world. Headlines change constantly, we get breaking news as it happens and we can follow the latest developments minute by minute.

Most people still believe traditional media more than news found online – stating that online articles tend to have a very one-sided view. When questioned further one person said they thought the news was often unreliable or that they did not trust it. In contrast, those who get their news from the TV, radio or paper said that 'fake' or biased news was not really a concern. This lack of trust in online news is mostly because it is so easy for anyone to set up a website and report the news. This means there is less control over online journalism, and separating fact from fiction is becoming more difficult.

'Fake news' has become a familiar term. It describes invented news stories that are designed to seem real. Fake stories are often used for political reasons or to support some other way of thinking. There were a number of famous fake news stories, for example, during the 2016 United States presidential election. Some fake news websites are designed to look like genuine news sites and

have similar web addresses, for example ABCnews.nett. Also, the fake news stories are often mixed in with real stories, which makes it difficult to notice them.

So, how do we know if a story is fake or not? First, check the source of the story. If the story comes from an unfamiliar organisation, check the 'about' section to learn more. Look closely at the website address. When you are reading, notice how much information there is to support the story. Genuine stories will have a lot of supporting facts. Also, look carefully at the pictures – false news stories often contain fake images. Finally, check to see if other reliable organisations are reporting the story. If not, it may mean that the story is false. Also most important of all, use your own common sense and think critically about the stories being reported – don't believe everything you read!

Glossary

balanced (adj) considering all arguments and opinions fairly and equally

fake (adj) made to look like something real in order to trick people

genuine (adj) real rather than false

source (n) someone who provides information for a journalist

GRAMMAR
Reported speech

A **WORK IT OUT** Look at the sentences from *The news*. Do they show direct speech or are they reporting speech and ideas? What tense are the verbs in **bold**? Why is this?

*When questioned further one person said they **thought** the news **was** often unreliable or that they **did not trust** it.*

In contrast, those who get their news from the TV, radio or paper said that "fake" or biased news was not really a concern.

B Read the rules and complete the example sentences (1–4) with the correct form of the verbs.

> **Reported speech**
>
> When we report what people say or report their thoughts or ideas, we use a reporting verb (*said, told, asked*) and we usually change the tense of the verb(s) in the sentence (present simple → past simple, present continuous → past continuous, *will* → *would*).
>
> - *65 per cent of people said they had a preferred news website.*
> - *The survey asked how often people checked the news.*
> - *Most people said they would think more carefully about the news stories.*
>
> We also do this when we report someone's words directly. We also change the pronoun (*I* → *he/she, you* → *me*)
>
> - *'Do you like your job?'* → *She asked me if I* [1]_____ *my job.*
> - *'I'm doing some work.'* → *He said he* [2]_____ *some work.*
> - *'I don't think there's a lot of fake news.'* → *She said she* [3]_____ *there* [4]_____ *a lot of fake news.*
> - *'I'll get back to you later.'* → *He said he* [5]_____ *back to me later.*

C Go to the **Grammar Hub** on **page 144**.

D **SPEAK** Complete the questions with your own ideas. Then work in pairs and ask and answer each other's questions. Then work with another person and tell them what your partner's answers were.

1 What's your favourite …?

2 How often do you …?

3 Do you think you'll …?

Sara said her favourite TV show was Game of Thrones.

PRONUNCIATION
/ɒ/, /ɔː/ and /əʊ/

A Listen to the sounds /ɒ/, /ɔː/ and /əʊ/. They are easily confused.
12.1

　　1 /ɒ/ hot　　　2 /ɔː/ report　　　3 /əʊ/ hope

B Listen again and repeat.
12.1

C **SPEAK** Write the words in the correct place in the column. Be careful! One word contains two of the sounds. Listen and check.
12.2

> box　caught　episode　follow
> honest　more　online　short　show

/ɒ/	/ɔː/	/əʊ/

SPEAKING

A Work in groups. You are going to conduct a short survey about people's attitudes to the news. Write at least four survey questions to ask your classmates.

Where do you get most of your news?
Do you always use the same news source?
Do you think that news on the internet is generally reliable?

B Each of you interview one or two classmates and write down their answers.

C Work in groups. Discuss your findings and prepare a report of your results.

D Present your results to the class.

First, we asked where people got their news. Four people said they got it mostly from the internet, including social media. And two said they got it mostly from TV.

○─ **Talk about the pros and cons of online news**

VOCABULARY
Television

A SPEAK Work in groups. Check you understand the words in **bold**. Discuss the questions.

1 Which TV **channels** do you watch the most often? What kind of **programmes** do you generally watch?

2 Do you own any box sets? Do you watch on-demand TV or online streaming services?

3 Are there any **series** that you always try to watch on TV or online? How long is each **episode**? How many **seasons** of this programme are there? Have there been any exciting **season finales**?

HOW BINGE-WATCHING HAS CHANGED TV FOREVER

Once upon a time

Not long ago, once a week, people regularly discussed what had happened in the previous night's episode of a certain television show. They knew that they had to wait seven long days to find out what happened next. If it was a season finale, the wait was even longer. Those days are gone.

What changed?

It all started with the DVD box set. And now, thanks to on-demand TV and internet streaming services such as Netflix (which actually started as a mail-order DVD rental service) and Amazon Prime, the way we watch television has changed forever. At the heart of this is binge-watching.

The 'now' generation

Thirty to sixty minutes of our favourite series is no longer enough. Instead, people spend hours and even whole weekends watching episode after episode. As a result, audiences are now watching more TV than ever, and around 75 per cent admit to binge-watching. It is now the 'new normal'.

People want new content and they want it now. They don't want to wait to find out what happens next. Because of this, TV companies now release a complete series at one time, rather than releasing the shows episode by episode as they have done in the past.

Some of the most popular shows of all time became so successful because they could be binge-watched. As a result, a whole industry has built up around binge-watching and TV has been changed forever.

A new kind of show

Today, programmes are made differently. Now, there is no need for a whole story to be contained in one episode. There is also less need for the traditional end-of-episode 'cliffhanger'. This is changing the familiar format of TV series, and programme-makers now can be much more creative. For example, shows often include actual real-world events that are happening at the same time.

TV is the new cinema

Budgets for this new generation of TV shows are high and the shows have huge international audiences. Consequently, a lot of Hollywood stars are moving away from making traditional cinema films and appearing more on TV. At the same time, binge-watching is replacing going to the cinema as a social occasion, with friends getting together for an evening of television. You don't actually need to be in the same physical place. Thanks to social media sites such as Twitter and Facebook, even watching alone can be a social event.

Is binge-watching here to stay?

In today's online world, people are becoming more demanding and more impatient. They want and expect everything to be immediately available. TV companies will therefore need to make more and more shows that meet this demand. As other media companies are starting to make their own TV programmes, too, binge-watching will continue to be big business.

> ### Glossary
>
> **binge-watching (n)** the activity of watching TV for an extended period of time, for example, several episodes of a series
>
> **budget (n)** the amount of money a person or organisation has to spend on something
>
> **cliffhanger (n)** an exciting end to a television programme that makes you want to watch the next part
>
> **format (n)** the arrangement, design or organisation of something
>
> **release (v)** to make a film, TV show, etc. available for people to see or buy

READING

A Look at the title of the article and the glossary. How do you think binge-watching has changed TV? Read the article and check your answer.

B **READ FOR DETAIL** Read *How binge-watching has changed TV forever*. Are the sentences true (T) or false (F)? Correct the false sentences.

1 Netflix was originally a DVD manufacturer. *T / F*
2 We are now watching less TV than in the past. *T / F*
3 People binge-watch because they want to find out what happens next. *T / F*
4 Many shows have become successful because people could binge-watch them. *T / F*
5 Today, TV shows need to have a complete story in one episode. *T / F*
6 More and more famous film actors are starring in TV shows. *T / F*

C **SPEAK** Work in pairs. Are you a binge-watcher? Are you addicted to TV? Go to the **Communication Hub** on **page 154** and do the quiz! Compare your answers.

GRAMMAR
Past perfect

A **WORK IT OUT** Look at the verbs in **bold** in this sentence from *How binge-watching has changed TV forever*. Which action was first, 1 or 2?

Not long ago, once a week, people regularly ¹discussed what ²had happened in the previous night's episode of a certain television show.

B Choose the correct words to complete the rules.

Past perfect

1 We make the past perfect with *had / have* + past participle.
2 When we are talking about two events in the past, we use the past perfect to show that one event happened *after / before* the other.
  • *I found a ticket that someone had dropped.*
  • *I'd seen a couple of episodes before the one last night.*
  • *I was late, but the film hadn't started.*
3 We often use the past perfect with *already* and *just*.
  • *The bus had already left when we got to the station.*
  • *The meeting had just finished when we arrived.*
  • *Had you already seen the film?*

C Go to the **Grammar Hub** on **page 144**.

PRONUNCIATION
Word stress in past perfect sentences

A Listen and underline the stressed words. What happens to words which are not stressed? *12.3*

1 I was late, but the film hadn't started.
2 I found a ticket that someone had dropped.

B Listen and repeat. *12.3*

C **SPEAK** Work in pairs. Underline the stressed words in the sentences. Practise saying them.

1 I'd seen a couple of episodes before the one last night.
2 The meeting had just finished when we arrived.
3 Had you already seen the film?

D **SPEAK** Complete the sentences using the past perfect. Then work in groups and compare your sentences. Who has the most interesting or unusual idea for each sentence?

1 We arrived late because …
2 We didn't watch any more TV because …
3 We talked for ages because …

SPEAKING

A Work in groups. You are going to hold a debate about which is better, box sets and on-demand viewing or more traditional weekly TV shows.

• Decide who will be in Group A and Group B.
• Group A are going to argue that box sets and on-demand viewing is better, and Group B are going to argue that more traditional weekly TV shows are better.
• Group A – go to the **Communication Hub** on **page 153**. Group B – go to the **Communication Hub** on **page 154**.

B Using the ideas in the **Communication Hub** and your own ideas, plan what you are going to say and prepare your argument. Also, think about what the other group's arguments might be and prepare to argue against this.

C Hold the debate. Can you convince the other group to agree with you or to agree with some of your points?

Debating language

Building an argument
• *First, …*
• *Also, …*
• *Furthermore, …*
• *On top of that, …*

Agreeing and disagreeing
• *I (don't) agree.*
• *Yes, but …*
• *I see what you mean, but …*
• *You have a point, but …*

◯– **Talk and debate about different TV viewing habits**

G— *shall*   **V**— advertising   **P**— /æ/ and /e/   **S**— identifying opinion and attitudes of speakers

LISTENING

A SPEAK Work in pairs. What do you think makes a successful advert?

B Look at the pictures of two different advertising campaigns. What is the product? How do you think each campaign works?

🔊 **C LISTEN FOR MAIN IDEA** Listen to two people discussing the
12.4 advertising campaigns and check your answers to Exercise B.

Glossary

ad (n) an advertisement on television or radio, on the internet, in a newspaper or magazine, etc
billboard (n) a large board for advertisements in an outside public place
suck (v) to pull air or liquid somewhere

Campaign 1

Campaign 2

D Listen again. Match the sentences to *Alex*, *Kerry* or *both*. Use the information in the box to help you.

12.4

Identifying opinion and attitudes of speakers

Listen for expressions that people use to express their opinions and attitude and to agree or disagree.

Expressing opinion or attitude

I (don't) think …

In my opinion, …

… to be honest.

To agree

I agree.

Yes, … / Yes, and … / And yes, … / Yes, but …

To disagree

I don't agree. / I disagree.

Actually, …

I'm not (so) sure …

Which person (Alex, Kelly or both) think(s) …

1 the Reebok advert campaign is clever?   ____

2 Alex is a fast runner?   ____

3 the vacuum advert was a real billboard?   ____

4 the best adverts are simple and original?   ____

5 an advert needs a clear message that you can connect with?   ____

6 the most important thing about an advert is that you notice it?   ____

E **SPEAK** Work in pairs. Discuss your opinion of the two adverts. Which do you think is the more creative, clever or original? Why?

GRAMMAR
shall

A Look at the sentences from the conversation between Alex and Kerry. Choose the correct words to complete the rules.

*You know what, I think I might have a go at it. **Shall** I?*

shall

1 We often use *shall* to **ask permission / make suggestions** or offers.

2 *Shall* has **a different meaning from / the same meaning as** will.

3 We use *shall* with **I and we / he, she, they and** it.

B Go to the **Grammar Hub** on page 144.

C **SPEAK** Work in pairs. Make two questions with *shall*. Ask and answer the questions with your partner.

VOCABULARY
Advertising

A Complete the advice about adverts with the words in the box.

attention   brand   connect   eye   logo   message   slogan

What makes a good advert?

A good advertisement must catch your [1]_____.
It needs to be original and needs to grab your
[2]_____. It needs to make you stop and look
at it. The image should also be something the viewer can
[3]_____ with on a personal level. A good advert also
needs to have a clear and simple [4]_____ and also
have a catchy [5]_____, such as Nike's 'Just do it'
or Microsoft's 'Where do you want to go today?' It should also
have the company name or [6]_____ on the advert
somewhere. But above all, the advert needs to tell you that the
product or [7]_____ is the best there is and it needs
to make you go and buy it.

B **SPEAK** Work in pairs. Discuss the questions.

1 How many famous logos and slogans can you think of?

2 What famous adverts or advertising campaigns do you know? Do you have any favourites?

PRONUNCIATION
/æ/ and /e/

A Listen to the sounds /æ/ and /e/. Then underline the letters that represent /æ/ and circle the letters that represent /e/.

12.5

best   brand   can   connect   grab   message

B Listen and check.

12.6

C Listen again and repeat the words.

12.6

◯ SPEAKING HUB

A Work in groups. You are going to plan an advertising campaign for an everyday item. Go to **page 155** and choose the product for your campaign.

B **PLAN** Decide if your campaign will be an online, billboard, magazine or 'live' (like the Reebok) campaign. You may want to have a mix of these.

- Think about what makes a good advertising campaign. Consider all the points in the article *What makes a good advert?*

- Plan your campaign in detail. Think of a name, logo and slogan.

C **PRESENT** Present your advertising campaign to the class.

D **REFLECT** Have a class vote for the best advertising campaign.

◯– Talk about advertising and what makes a good advert

COMPREHENSION

A SPEAK Work in pairs. Make a list of ten different types of programme you can watch on TV. Then discuss how often you watch them.

I never watch …   I often watch …

A: *I watch dramas and films, but I never watch documentaries. How about you?*

B: *I like documentaries, but most of the time I watch series.*

B ▶ 00:00–01:04 Watch the first part of the video. What do Zac, Neena and Gaby want to watch?

C SPEAK Work in pairs. The housemates argue about the pros and cons of football. Predict some of the arguments.

In favour of football	Against football
	Players are paid far too much money

D ▶ 01:04–04:15 Watch the second part of the video. Do the housemates use any of your arguments in Exercise C? What do they watch in the end?

MILLY

SAM

NEENA

ZAC

GABY

FUNCTIONAL LANGUAGE
Give and respond to opinions

A Write the phrases in the correct place.

> I don't have a strong opinion.   I'm not so sure about that.
> It seems to me that …   That's a good idea.

Give an opinion

Personally, I think …
1 _____

In my view, …
Look, all I'm saying is (that) …

Agree

I completely agree!
Exactly!
Yeah, that's true.
That's fair enough.
2 _____

Neutral

3 _____
I don't mind.

Disagree

I totally disagree, I think …
Oh please! I mean, what about …
I'm sorry, Gaby, but I think …
4 _____

I see what you mean, but …
I see what you're saying about … but …

B Highlight the phrases that show *strong* agreement or disagreement.

Glossary

you've seen it already! (phrase) (American) you've already seen it!

PRONUNCIATION
Agreeing and disagreeing

🔊 **A** Listen to and read a conversation about agreeing and
12.7   disagreeing. Then work in groups and practice the
conversation copying the word stress and intonation.

Tim: <u>Pers</u>onally, I think football's pretty <u>bor</u>ing.

Sarah: It seems to <u>me</u> that football these days is just all about the <u>mon</u>ey.

Tim: In <u>my</u> view, it's just some <u>guys</u> running around a field kicking a <u>ball</u>.

Beth: I com<u>plete</u>ly agree.

Sarah: <u>Ex</u>actly.

Andy: I totally <u>dis</u>agree.

Sarah: Oh, <u>please</u>!

B SPEAK Work in pairs. Practise agreeing or disagreeing
with each other. Talk about other professional sports, for
example basketball, golf, rugby, tennis or your own ideas.

A: Personally, I think tennis players earn far too much money.

B: I see what you mean, but it's a very popular sport.

SPEAKING

A Complete the sentences with your own opinions.

1 I think _____ is the greatest band of all time.

2 In my view, _____ food is the best food in the world.

3 I think the safest way to travel is _____.

4 It seems to me that most celebrities are
_____.

5 Personally, I think money makes people
_____.

B Work in pairs. Student A – read one of your sentences in
Exercise A. Student B – agree or disagree. Take turns.

◯ **Give and respond to opinions**

➤ Turn to **page 169** to learn how to write a story.

VOCABULARY

A Complete the sentences with the words in the box.

> breaking   follow   headlines   report   share

1 I generally _____ the news quite closely and check it every hour or so.

2 I always check the news _____ as soon as I get up in the morning.

3 I have an alert on my phone that gives me any _____ news.

4 I sometimes _____ news stories on social media.

5 I think different news channels _____ the news in different ways.

B Complete the crossword.

Across

4 The last episode of a season (6, 5)

5 One show in a TV series (7)

7 For example, BBC, HBO, Cartoon Network, MTV, al Jazeera (7)

8 A show that is broadcast on television or radio (9)

Down

1 A collection of DVDs or Blu-rays of the same series (3, 3)

2 You can watch at any time (2, 6)

3 A set of shows that have the same main characters or the same topic (6)

6 A set of shows as part of a series, traditionally broadcast a year before the next one (6)

C Complete the sentences with the words in the box.

> attention   brands   connect
> eye   logos   message   slogan

1 In recent years, the world's most powerful _____ have included Lego, Google and Visa.

2 A recent survey has shown that the world's most recognisable _____ that don't contain the company name are Nike, Apple and McDonald's.

3 A good _____ gives a clear _____ that people can _____ with. One of the most successful is MacDonald's 'I'm loving it'.

4 A good advert needs to catch your _____ and grab your _____.

GRAMMAR

A Dasha was interviewed about her attitude to online news. Read the questions and her answers. Complete what Dasha says when she reports the questions and her answers.

Q Do you have a favourite news website?

1 She asked me if ___*I had a favourite news website.*___

A There are two or three I usually look at.

2 I said _____

Q What kind of news stories are you interested in?

3 She asked me _____

A I don't have a preference.

4 I said _____

Q Are you following a news story at the moment?

5 She asked me _____

A I'm following the election.

6 I told her _____

B Complete the fact file with the verbs in brackets. Use past simple or past perfect.

THE INVENTION OF THE TELEVISION

Before it [1]_____ (*become*) a reality, television [2]_____ (*be*) a dream of inventors for over 100 years. And by the time it was finally invented there [3]_____ (*be*) many different ideas for television. Despite the many scientists and inventors who [4]_____ (*each / play*) an important part in the development of the television, it was the British inventor John Logie Baird who on 26th January 1926 [5]_____ (*give*) the world's first demonstration of true television.

C Choose the correct words to complete the questions.

1 *Shall / Will* I give you some help?

2 Who do you think *shall / will* be interested in this?

3 *Shall / Will* we meet at six?

4 *Shall / Will* everyone understand this advert's message?

5 Who *shall / will* I invite to the meeting?

FUNCTIONAL LANGUAGE

Complete the conversation with the words in the box.

> disagree   see   seems   strong   true   view

A: It [1]_____ to me that things are getting more and more expensive all the time.

B: Yeah, that's [2]_____ . Each time I go to the supermarket, things have gone up in price.

A: In my [3]_____, footballers' pay is disgusting!

B: I [4]_____ what you're saying, but they do give pleasure to millions of people.

A: I'm sorry, but I totally [5]_____. What do you think, Chris?

C: I don't have a [6]_____ opinion either way, to be honest. I'm not at all interested in football.

Irregular Verbs

Infinitive	Past simple	Past participle
be	was/were	been
become	became	become
begin	began	begun
break	broke	broken
bring	brought	brought
build	built	built
buy	bought	bought
can	could	been able to
catch	caught	caught
choose	chose	chosen
come	came	come
cost	cost	cost
cut	cut	cut
drink	drank	drunk
eat	ate	eaten
fall	fell	fallen
feel	felt	felt
find	found	found
forget	forgot	forgotten
get	got	got
give	gave	given
go	went	gone / been
grow	grew	grown
have	had	had
hear	heard	heard
hit	hit	hit
hold	held	held
hurt	hurt	hurt
keep	kept	kept
know	knew	known
leave	left	left
lend	lent	lent
let	let	let

Infinitive	Past simple	Past participle
lose	lost	lost
make	made	made
mean	meant	meant
meet	met	met
must	had to	had to
pay	paid	paid
put	put	put
read	read	read
ride	rode	ridden
run	ran	run
say	said	said
see	saw	seen
sell	sold	sold
send	sent	sent
set	set	set
shut	shut	shut
sing	sang	sung
sit	sat	sat
sleep	slept	slept
speak	spoke	spoken
spell	spelt / spelled	spelt / spelled
spend	spent	spent
stand	stood	stood
steal	stole	stolen
take	took	taken
teach	taught	taught
tell	told	told
think	thought	thought
throw	threw	thrown
understand	understood	understood
wear	wore	worn
win	won	won
write	wrote	written

PHONETIC SYMBOLS

Single vowels			Diphthongs			Consonants					
/ɪ/	fish	/fɪʃ/	/ɪə/	**ear**	/ɪə/	/p/	**p**en	/pen/	/s/	**s**nake	/sneɪk/
/iː/	b**ea**n	/biːn/	/eɪ/	f**a**ce	/feɪs/	/b/	**b**ag	/bæg/	/z/	**z**oo	/zuː/
/ʊ/	f**oo**t	/fʊt/	/ʊə/	t**ou**rist	/ˈtʊərɪst/	/t/	**t**ea	/tiː/	/ʃ/	**sh**op	/ʃɒp/
/uː/	sh**oe**	/ʃuː/	/ɔɪ/	b**oy**	/bɔɪ/	/d/	**d**og	/dɒg/	/ʒ/	televi**si**on	/ˈtelɪvɪʒən/
/e/	**e**gg	/eg/	/əʊ/	n**o**se	/nəʊz/	/tʃ/	**ch**ip	/tʃɪp/	/m/	**m**ap	/mæp/
/ə/	moth**er**	/ˈmʌðə/	/eə/	h**air**	/heə/	/dʒ/	**j**azz	/dʒæz/	/n/	**n**ame	/neɪm/
/ɜː/	w**or**d	/wɜːd/	/aɪ/	**eye**	/aɪ/	/k/	**c**ake	/keɪk/	/ŋ/	ri**ng**	/rɪŋ/
/ɔː/	t**al**k	/tɔːk/	/aʊ/	m**ou**th	/maʊθ/	/g/	**g**irl	/gɜːl/	/h/	**h**ouse	/haʊs/
/æ/	b**a**ck	/bæk/				/f/	**f**ilm	/fɪlm/	/l/	**l**eg	/leg/
/ʌ/	b**u**s	/bʌs/				/v/	**v**erb	/vɜːb/	/r/	**r**oad	/rəʊd/
/ɑː/	**ar**m	/ɑːm/				/θ/	**th**ing	/θɪŋ/	/w/	**w**ine	/waɪn/
/ɒ/	t**o**p	/tɒp/				/ð/	**th**ese	/ðiːz/	/j/	**y**es	/jes/

Grammar Hub

1.1 Question forms

Questions with *do / does / did*

Do/Does/Did + subject + infinitive
Do you have children?
Does he go to English classes?
Did she write a blog post?
Did they do their homework?

- We use the auxiliary verb (*do, does, did*), without a question word, to ask yes/no questions.

Question words

Question word + *do/does/did* + subject + infinitive
What do you say to a stranger?
Where does he come from?
What did you say to your colleague?
Where did she study psychology?

- We use *What* to ask about things and *Where* to ask about places.

Questions with *be*

Am/Is/Are + subject
Am I in this class?
Are they strangers?

Am/Is/Are + subject + *-ing*
Is she doing her homework now?
Are you having fun?

Was/Were + subject
Was he a sensible person?
Were they good at English?

- We use questions with *be*, without a question word, to ask yes/no questions.
- We can also ask questions with *What, Where, When, Why* and *Who* before the verb *be*.

Questions with the present perfect

Have/Has + subject + past participle
Have you visited that website?
Has he written a bucket list?

- We use present perfect questions, without a question word, to ask yes/no questions.
- We use *ever* to ask about life experiences.

  *Have you **ever** met a famous person?*
- We can also ask question with *What, Where, When, Why* and *Who* before the verb *have*.

1.2 Frequency words and phrases

0% ⟵ ⟶ 100%

never   rarely   occasionally   sometimes   often   normally   always

- We use frequency words after *be* and *can*.

  *He **is normally** very sensible.*
  *I **can never** read your handwriting!*
- We use frequency words before other verbs.

  *I **sometimes watch** vlogs online.*

once twice three times	a	day week month year
every so often	now and again	most of the time

- We usually use frequency phrases at the beginning or end of the sentence.

  *I take my dog for a walk **twice a day**.*
  ***Every so often**, I travel to another country.*

1.3 Indefinite pronouns

	-one	*-body*	*-thing*	*-where*
every-	everyone	everybody	everything	everywhere
any-	anyone	anybody	anything	anywhere
some-	someone	somebody	something	somewhere
no-	no one	nobody	nothing	nowhere

- We use the ending *-body* or *-one* with people. They have the same meaning.

  Everybody loved the party. OR Everyone loved the party.
- We use the ending *-thing* with objects.

  I always take something to read on the train.
- We use the ending *-where* with places.

  They live somewhere in Italy.
- We use *any-* in negative sentences.

  I don't know anything.
- We also use *any-* in questions.

  Is there anything unusual about her handwriting?

> **Be careful!**
>
> - With offers, we can also use *some-* in questions.
>
>   *Do you want **something** to eat?*
> - We use indefinite pronouns with singular verbs.
>
>   *Everyone **is** interested. NOT ~~Everyone are interested.~~*
> - We use *'s* with indefinite pronouns for possessives.
>
>   *Is this **anybody's** mobile phone?*

1.1 Question forms

A Put the words in order to make questions.

1 you / do / go / skiing / want / to

_____ *Do you want to go skiing?* _____

2 does / what / do / he / weekends / at

_____

3 did / you / meet / where / for coffee

_____

4 you / tea / are / coffee / or / drinking

_____

5 your / new colleagues / were / at the office

_____

6 you / been / have / ever / Mexico / to

_____

7 tried / that / she / has / new restaurant

_____

B Correct the mistakes in each sentence.

did you

1 Why ~~you did~~ choose that topic?

2 Have you ever meet a graphologist?

3 What you are talking about?

4 Did they went to the cinema last night?

5 Where you did put the new keyboard?

6 What your best friend's name is?

7 Did you anything nice last weekend?

➤ Go back to page 3.

1.2 Frequency words and phrases

A Write the missing letters.

1 I n _e_ _v_ _e_ r get bored writing my blog.

2 She's s___ __ __ __ __ __ __s late for work.

3 They a___ __ __ __ __ __ watch vlogs in their free time.

4 We're n___ __ __ __ __ __y home before 11.

5 He o___ __ __ __ __ __ __ __ __ __ __y checks his social media accounts at work.

6 I r___ __ __ __ __ go online before starting work.

7 He o___ __ __ __ __ visits his relatives in Italy.

B Put the words and phrases of frequency in the correct place in each sentence. Sometimes more than one answer is possible.

1 We go on holiday. (*once a year*)

_____ *We go on holiday once a year.* _____

2 They comment on online articles. (*now and again*)

_____

3 I read online tips. (*every so often*)

_____

4 She writes for popular magazines. (*most of the time*)

_____

5 He takes his dog to the park. (*three times a week*)

_____

6 We play computer games on Saturdays. (*always*)

_____

7 We meet up for a coffee on Sunday. (*usually*)

_____

➤ Go back to page 5.

1.3 Indefinite pronouns

A Choose the correct option.

1 I need *something's* / *somebody's* help.

2 I want to go *somewhere* / *something* new.

3 There is *nobody* / *nothing* I can do.

4 We don't need *everything* / *anything* else.

5 We go *everywhere* / *anywhere* together.

6 *Someone* / *Anyone* broke the ice.

7 *No one* / *Someone* came to Vant's party.

B Complete the sentences with the correct indefinite pronouns.

1 _Somebody/Someone_ left a comment.

2 _____ could get online – there was no internet connection.

3 Do you know _____ at this party?

4 I don't want to speak to you. I have _____ to say to you.

5 Did you write _____ on her Facebook page?

6 There is _____ unusual about this signature. It's strange!

7 They live _____ in Romania.

➤ Go back to page 7.

Grammar Hub

2.1 Adverbs of degree

almost	= *nearly*	She **almost** fell from the balcony.
completely	= 100%	This is a **completely** new idea.
extremely	= stronger than *very*	Life here is **extremely** expensive.
very		The city centre is **very** lively at night.
so	= *very*	Living here is **so** convenient.
really	= *very*	This building is a **really** clever design.
quite	= weaker than *very*	The town is **quite** crowded at weekends.

- We use adverbs of degree to make something stronger or weaker.
- Adverbs of degree usually come **before** the adjective.
- We can also use *very*, *really*, *extremely* and *completely* before adjective + noun.

Be careful!

- We don't use *so* or *almost* before adjective + noun.
  It's so noisy. NOT ~~It's a so noisy area.~~
- We can use *quite* + *a/an* before adjective + noun.
  It's quite a noisy area. NOT ~~It's a quite noisy area.~~
- We can also use adverbs of degree before adverbs.
  The pollution problem is improving very slowly.
- We can also use adverbs of degree before verbs.
- When a verb has an auxiliary verb (*have*, *be*, *do*), we usually put the adverb between the auxiliary verb and the main verb.

2.2 Present simple and present continuous

	Positive	Negative
I/you/we/they	**They love** their house.	**I don't live** in a big city.
he/she/it	**She loves** her family.	**He doesn't cook** every evening.

	Positive	Negative
I	**I'm studying** at the moment.	**I'm not studying** at the moment.
he/she/it	**She's living** with her parents.	**She isn't living** with her parents.
you/we/they	**We're moving** to the city.	**We aren't moving** to the city.

Question	Positive short answer	Negative short answer
Does he love cooking?	Yes, **he does**.	No, **he doesn't**.
Are they working?	Yes, **they are**.	No, **they aren't**.

- We use the present simple to talk about routines and things which are always or generally true.
- We use the present continuous to talk about temporary actions happening now or around now.
- We also use the present continuous to talk about trends.

2.3 Past simple – regular and irregular verbs

Subject	Positive	Negative
I/you/he/she/it/we/they	**He talked** to Jim yesterday.	**He didn't talk** to Jim yesterday.

Question	Positive short answer	Negative short answer
Did you talk to Jim yesterday?	Yes, **I did**.	No, **I didn't**.

- We use the past simple to talk about finished actions in the past.
- We often use the time phrases *yesterday*, *an hour ago*, *on Monday*, *in 2015*, etc. with the past simple.

	Infinitive	Past simple positive
Add -*ed*.	ask	asked
Add -*d* after verbs ending -*e*.	decide	decided
Add -*ed* after verbs ending in a vowel + -*y*.	play	played
Change -*y* after a consonant to -*ied*.	study	studied
For verbs ending in a vowel and a consonant, double the consonant before adding -*ed*.	stop	stopped
For verbs ending -*l*, double the *l* and add -*ed*.	travel	travelled

2.1 Adverbs of degree

A Put the words in order to make sentences.

1 have / they / completely / new / a / designed / building / apartment

   They have designed a completely new
   apartment building.

2 this / extremely / area / expensive / an / is

   _____

3 is / park / on / Sundays / crowded / so / the

   _____

4 cars / move / slowly / city / the / in / very

   _____

5 polluted / is / in / it / places / some / quite

   _____

6 ready / am / move / to / I / almost

   _____

7 is / really / there / beautiful / park / a / here / near

   _____

B Choose the correct option.

1 I'm (so) / almost happy to be living in London!

2 Cleaning up the city is almost / extremely expensive.

3 Our new apartment is almost / really nice. I love it!

4 Architects used a so / completely new design.

5 In the summer, it gets extremely / completely hot here.

6 It is almost / very impossible to get to know everyone in your neighbourhood.

7 My last house was quite a / quite big, but I didn't have enough space.

➤ Go back to page 13.

2.2 Present simple and present continuous

A Correct the mistakes in each sentence. Use contractions where possible.

   _We're_
1 ~~We be~~ living in Rome at the moment.

2 I stay at my parents' house this week.

3 She's liking doing the washing very much.

4 They're usually helping with the housework on Sundays.

5 Paul's doing the cooking most of the time.

6 I travel a lot for work at the moment.

7 We both look for a permanent job right now.

B Complete the sentences with the correct form of the verb in brackets. Use contractions where possible.

1 I ___'m studying___ (study) French history this year.

2 My mum still _____ (do) all my washing.

3 I _____ (not / need) you to help me look for a new place.

4 What _____ (you / argue) about now?

5 They _____ (save) money to buy a house.

6 She _____ (not / always / cook) for herself.

7 He _____ (talk) to his cousin right now.

➤ Go back to page 15.

2.3 Past simple – regular and irregular verbs

A Put the verbs into the past simple. Use contractions where possible.

1 They (go) to Amsterdam yesterday.   ___went___

2 She (not / visit) her parents at the weekend.   _____

3 I (buy) a new laptop.   _____

4 (you / bring) your bag with you?   _____

5 Dan (take) the train to work this morning.   _____

6 I (not / leave) work until 10 last night.   _____

7 We (not / be) worried when we took our exams.   _____

B Complete the conversation with the past simple form of the verbs.

Will   (1) _____ (you / enjoy) your childhood?

Rebecca Yes, my friends and I (2) _____ (go) to the cinema a lot, and we played on our bikes. What sort of things (3) _____ (you / do)?

Will   I (4) _____ (not / have) a good time. My school (5) _____ (be) terrible. I (6) _____ (take) my exams three times before I passed.

Rebecca Oh dear! So you didn't have much free time, I imagine.

Will   Exactly!

➤ Go back to page 17.

Grammar Hub

3.1 all / some / most / no / none

- We use *all*, *some*, *most* and *no* before nouns.

  Give him all the money.

  There are no taxis.

- We can use *all*, *some*, *most* and *none* with *of* + pronoun or *the/this/that/these/those*.

  I've stayed in many hotels and I liked most of them.

  I like all of the Greek islands.

  Some of her journeys were by bus.

  None of the countries were in Africa.

- With *all*, we don't have to use *of* before a pronoun + noun or *the/this/that/these/those*.

  Did you spend all your dollars? OR Did you spend all of your dollars?

- With *all*, we must use *of* before a pronoun without a noun.

  Did you spend all of it? NOT Did you spend all it?

- We cannot use *no* with *of* + pronoun or *the/this/that/these/those*.

  None of us want to leave. NOT No of us want to leave.

3.2 Past continuous and past simple

	Positive	Negative
I/you/he/she/it/we/they	**They travelled** by train all night.	We **didn't go** by ferry.

Question	Positive short answer	Negative short answer
Did they enjoy the holiday?	Yes, **they did**.	No, **they didn't**.

- We use the past simple to talk about finished actions or situations, and things that happened one after another.
- See Grammar Reference 2.3 for more information about the past simple.

	Positive	Negative
I/he/she/it	**He was riding** the bus when his phone rang.	**She wasn't cycling** to work when the rain started.
you/we/they	**They were sleeping** when I arrived.	**We weren't driving** when the car crashed.

Question	Positive short answer	Negative short answer
Was it snowing outside?	Yes, **it was**.	No, **it wasn't**.

- We use the past continuous for actions or situations that were unfinished at a past time.
- The past continuous describes a longer action and the past simple describes a shorter action.

  They were sailing (=long action) from Portsmouth to Caen when the storm hit (=short action).

- We use *when/while* before the past continuous to describe an action that was in progress when something else happened.

3.3 Verb + -ing and to + infinitive

- After some verbs (e.g. *agree*), we use *to* + infinitive.
- After some verbs (e.g. *enjoy*), we use *-ing*.
- After some verbs (e.g. *hate*), we can use either *to* + infinitive or *-ing*.

Verb	+ *to* + infinitive
can't afford	I **can't afford to buy** a new car.
hope	They **hope to meet** again soon.
learn	When did you **learn to drive**?
would like	We **would like to travel** the world.
would prefer	He **would prefer to go** to France.
Other verbs: agree / choose / decide / expect / manage / need / plan / refuse / seem / want	They **decided to go** by plane.

Verb	+ *-ing*
consider	She **considered saying** yes.
enjoy	We **enjoy reading** guide books.
avoid	He **avoided getting** wet on his journey.
spend time	Tina **spent time researching** the Andes.
Other verbs: advise / allow / begin / can't help / continue / finish / keep / mind / regret / stand	I **keep making** mistakes.

Verb	+ *to* + infinitive or *-ing*
hate	I **hate driving** in bad weather. OR I **hate to drive** in bad weather.
love	We **love visiting** Italy. OR We **love to visit** Italy.
prefer	I **prefer staying** in a hotel. OR I **prefer to stay** in a hotel.
like	They **like going** surfing. OR They **like to go** surfing.
Other verbs: begin / start	It **started to rain**. OR It **started raining**.

3.1 all / some / most / no / none

A Put the words in order to make sentences.

1 his / none / journeys / were / by / of / train
   _____None of his journeys were by train._____

2 dry / the / of / some / were / seats
   _____

3 all / the / unhappy / passengers / were
   _____

4 trip / us / none / wanted / end / of / to / the
   _____

5 kinds / most / don't / I / like / of / resorts / beach
   _____

6 have / money / no / left / wallets / our / we / in
   _____

7 Dilly / problems / airport / some / had / also / the / in
   _____

B Choose the correct option.

1 *No / None* of the tourists were paying attention.

2 All of *the people / people* were shouting.

3 Most *of taxis / taxis* in London are black.

4 I met *some of / some* nice people on my holiday.

5 How was your holiday? Did you enjoy *all / all of* it?

6 *No / None* visitors can go in this area.

➤ Go back to page 22.

3.2 Past continuous and past simple

A Correct the mistakes in each sentence.

1 We were living in London when the London Eye ~~was opening~~. *opened*

2 Jan was having an accident while she was sailing in the Pacific.

3 While they asking for directions, I looked at a guide book.

4 She travelled through China when she first met Clive.

5 The pilot was landing the plane when the crash was happening.

6 When the ferry crossed the sea, we saw some dolphins.

7 She swam in the lake when something was biting her leg.

B Match to make sentences.

1 We were sailing round the island
2 While I was taking photographs,
3 They were not paying attention
4 Someone stole her bag
5 He met Rob
6 Some birds hit the plane

a I dropped my phone.
b while she was lying by the pool.
c while he was cycling across Italy.
d while it was taking off.
e when they got on the wrong bus.
f when I started to feel sick.

➤ Go back to page 25.

3.3 Verb + -ing and to + infinitive

A Choose the correct option.

1 Avoid *to book / booking* a room at this hotel.

2 Consider *to write / writing* your own travel blog.

3 Refuse *to take / taking* no for an answer.

4 Spend time *to try / trying* different foods.

5 Learn *to enjoy / enjoying* life.

6 Don't agree *to get / getting* in the car with a stranger.

B Complete the text messages with the correct forms of the verbs.

Fay: I would like (**1**) _____ (stay) somewhere fun for a weekend trip. Any ideas?

Joy: What about a campsite?

Fay: I can't stand (**2**) _____ (sleep) outdoors. Maybe a hostel or a guest house?

Joy: I don't mind (**3**) _____ (go) to either. Which would you prefer?

Fay: I'd prefer (**4**) _____ (stay) at a hostel. Sound OK?

Joy: Yes, I enjoy (**5**) _____ (meet) new people.

Fay: Great! I can't afford (**6**) _____ (spend) much money.

Joy: Then a hostel is a good choice – they usually have low prices.

➤ Go back to page 27.

Grammar Hub

4.1 *be going to* + infinitive and present continuous for the future

	Positive	Negative
I	**I'm going to meet** my friends.	**I'm not going to have** a night out.
he/she/it	**He's going to play** snooker.	**She isn't going to relax** at home.
you/we/they	**They're going to spend** the evening at home.	**We aren't going to see** a play at the weekend.

Question	Positive short answer	Negative short answer
Is he going to hang out with us?	Yes, **he is.**	No, **he isn't.**
Are they going to have a party to celebrate?	Yes, **they are.**	No, **they aren't.**

- We use *be going to* to talk about intentions.

	Positive	Negative
I	**I'm meeting** Steff at 6.	**I'm not having** dinner with Steve tonight.
he/she/it	**She's going** to the cinema on Saturday.	**She isn't visiting** her grandparents this weekend.
you/we/they	**We're visiting** Tina tomorrow.	**We aren't playing** in the concert next week.

Question	Positive short answer	Negative short answer
Am I meeting you at 8?	Yes, **you are.**	No, **you aren't.**
Are you watching a film tonight?	Yes, **we are.**	No, **we aren't.**

- We use the present continuous to talk about arrangements in the future.

> **Be careful!**
>
> - We don't use the present continuous for intentions.
>   *I'm going to open my own restaurant when I'm older.* NOT ~~I'm opening my own restaurant when I'm older.~~

4.2 Making predictions

	Positive	Negative
I/you/he/she/it/we/they	**He will go** on a virtual date.	**It won't be** very romantic.
	They may/might fall in love.	**It may/might not be** easy to meet people.

Question	Positive short answer	Negative short answer
Will they go out for dinner?	Yes, **they will.**	No, **they won't.**

- We use *will*, *may* and *might* to make predictions about the future. We use *will* when we are certain. We use *may* or *might* when we are less certain. There is little difference in meaning between *may* and *might*.

- Because *will*, *may* and *might* are modals, they only have one form.
  She might bring her VR headset. NOT ~~She mights bring her VR headset.~~

- We use adverbs of probability with *will* to make predictions more or less certain.
  100% We'll **definitely/certainly** need to bring a warm blanket.
  75% She'll **probably** stay at home with her family.
  50% **Maybe** they'll go on holiday to Denmark.
  25% I **probably** won't cook a meal.
  0% You **definitely** won't forget the experience.

> **Be careful!**
>
> - *Maybe* goes at the beginning of the sentence.
>   *Maybe you'll play board games.* NOT ~~You'll maybe play board games.~~

4.3 Subject and object questions

- We ask subject questions when we don't know what/who/which/whose something (or someone) is.
  What is hygge?
- We ask object questions when we want to know more information about something (or someone).
  How do you pronounce hygge?
- Subject questions don't include an auxiliary verb. Object questions do.
  Subject question: Whose is this blanket?
  *Object question: Which restaurant **did** you go to?*

- With subject questions, we don't change the word order in the answer.
  Who is your best friend? *Friya is my best friend.*
- In object questions, the question word is the object of the sentence.
  ***What** do you do to relax?* *I play **computer games** to relax.*

4.1 *be going to* and + infinitive and present continuous for the future

A Correct the mistakes in each sentence.

1 I'm going to ~~introducing~~ *introduce* you to my friends.
2 She going to the theatre with Alice tonight.
3 We meet Pamela at 4 pm this afternoon.
4 They going to cook pizza for everyone.
5 She's going buy a cake for his birthday.
6 What time we meeting for lunch?

B Put the words in order to make sentences.

1 to / invite / my colleagues / I'm / to the party / going / all
   I'm going to invite all my colleagues to the party.
2 to / I / going / tonight / think / at home / I'm / stay
   _____
3 are / that new sushi place / to / Karl and Inge / going / try
   _____
4 sister / seeing / you / again / when / are / your / ?
   _____
5 on Friday night / having / Tom's / a birthday party
   _____
6 at five o'clock / meeting / we're / in the central square
   _____

➤ Go back to page 33.

4.2 Making predictions

A Choose the correct option.

1 I (definitely) / *maybe* won't go to the concert because it's raining.
2 *Maybe you will* / *You maybe will* be home early on Friday.
3 They *will* / *might* definitely go sailing tonight.
4 Robots *might* / *definitely* won't understand human feelings in the future. I don't believe that's possible.
5 I *may* / *will* not have enough money for the tickets. Let's see how much they are.
6 We probably *mightn't* / *won't* have the party next week.
7 I'll definitely *going* / *go* to university when I leave school.

B Make sentences with *will* or *might*.

1 Robots _____ (*definitely* / *do*) all the work in the future.
2 We _____ (*control*) computers with our minds in the future. It's possible.
3 It _____ (*not* / *be*) a good idea to sell my car. I need to think about it.
4 They _____ (*probably* / *not* / *go*) to the party.
5 I don't think robots _____ (*have*) feelings.
6 It _____ (*not* / *cost*) more than 20 euros. That's for sure.

➤ Go back to page 35.

4.3 Subject and object questions

A Complete the sentences with the question words in the box. Then select the correct question type: subject (S) or object (O).

| how   what   when   where   who   why |

1 _____ is going on the trip to Denmark? *S / O*
2 _____ do you leave for Copenhagen? *S / O*
3 _____ is your favourite board game? *S / O*
4 _____ do you want to meet? *S / O*
5 _____ do you say 'hello' in French? *S / O*
6 _____ is our English class cancelled? *S / O*

B Put the words in order to make questions. Then match the answers (a–f).

1 you / have / do / when / lessons / English
   When do you have English lessons?   *f*
2 favourite / place / where / your / relaxing / is / for
   _____
3 does / do / she / free / time / what / her / in
   _____
4 feeling / Sara / is / how / driving test / about / the
   _____
5 they / for / when / leaving / are / Bucharest / for
   _____
6 best / the / is / who / cook / the / in / family
   _____

a the bath   d Fred
b worried   e She goes to the gym.
c next weekend   f on Thursdays

➤ Go back to page 37.

Grammar Hub

5.1 *can, could, be able to*

- We use *can* to talk about general possibility and ability in the present.

  I can choose when I work.

  They can't come to the meeting.

  Can I speak to you for a moment? Yes, you can. / No, you can't.

- We use *could* to talk about general possibility and ability in the past.

  She could work shifts when she was younger.

  They couldn't come to the meeting last Saturday.

  Could you take long holidays in your last job? Yes, I could. / No, I couldn't.

- We use *be able to* to talk about possibility and ability in the present, often at a particular time or for a particular reason.

  I'm able to work with different people.

  He isn't able to work late tonight.

  Are they able to work nights? Yes, they are. / No, they aren't.

- We use *be able to* directly after another verb because *can* has no *-ing* or *to* + infinitive form.

  I like being able to work nights. NOT ~~I like can work nights.~~

- We use *was/were able to* to talk about possibility and ability in the past, often at a particular time or for a particular reason.

  She was able to find a new job.

  They weren't able to get the bus to work.

  Was he able to find the office? Yes, he was. / No, he wasn't.

5.2 Obligation, necessity and permission: *must, have to* and *can*

	Positive	Negative
I/you/he/she/it/we/they	**You can wear** casual clothes in the office. **You must get** to work before 9 am.	**You can't wear** jewellery. **You mustn't be** late.
I/you/we/they	**You have to get** to work before 9 am.	**They don't have to use** English at work.
he/she/it	**He has to get** to work before 9 am.	**She doesn't have to work** on Sundays.

Question	Positive short answer	Negative short answer
Can she wear earrings?	Yes, **she can.**	No, **she can't.**
Do we have to wear a tie?	Yes, **you do.**	No, **you don't.**
Does he have to have special training?	Yes, **he does.**	No, **he doesn't.**

- We use *can* for something that is allowed.
- We use *can't* for something that is not allowed.
- We use *must* and *have to* for something that is necessary or a rule.

Be careful!

- *Mustn't* has a different meaning to *don't have to*.

  mustn't = not allowed

  *You **mustn't** wear sportswear in the office.*

  don't have to = not necessary (but possible)

  *You **don't have to** dress really smartly for work, but you can if you want.*

- In questions, we usually use *have to* and not *must*.

  Do you have to wear boots? NOT ~~Must you wear boots?~~

5.3 Present perfect with *for* and *since*

	Positive	Negative
I/you/we/they	**I've worked** here for 12 years.	**They haven't called** since last week.
he/she/it	**She's worked** in telemarketing since 2017.	**She hasn't checked** her messages for two days.

Question	Positive short answer	Negative short answer
Have you worked in a restaurant before?	Yes, **I have.**	No, **I haven't.**
Has he finished the project?	Yes, **he has.**	No, **he hasn't.**

- We use the present perfect to talk about actions and situations that started in the past but are unfinished and so continue until the present time.

  *I **have worked** here for three weeks. (= and I am still working here now)*

- We use *for* to show the amount of time, and *since* to show when the action or situation started.

  *She has been at this company **since** January.*

  *She has been at this company **for** six months.*

- We use *How long* plus the present perfect to ask about the length of time until the present.

  How long has Maria worked there?

- We also use the present perfect to talk about things that happened in the past at an unspecified time and our experiences up to now.

  I've done lots of different jobs.

Be careful!

- The verb *go* has two past participles: *been* and *gone*.
- We use *been* when someone has gone somewhere and come back.

  Bill has been to a lot of job interviews.

- We use *gone* when someone has gone somewhere and not come back yet.

  Jeff has gone for an interview and he'll be back later.

5.1 *can, could, be able to*

A Complete the sentences with the words in the box.

> able   can (x2)   can't   could   to   were

1 As a manager, you _____**can**_____ have a company car!
2 I _____ do this. Can you help me?
3 She's not _____ to work on Saturday.
4 _____ you do the night shift tomorrow?
5 We _____ able to get a lot of work done yesterday.
6 In my last job, I _____ start late on Fridays.
7 Brenda's self-employed so she's able _____ choose when she works.

B Put the words in order to make sentences.

1 hate / not / make / decisions / I / being / to / able
   _____*I hate not being able to make decisions.*_____
2 wants / able / she / buy / to / house / be / to / a
   _____
3 last / in / finish / job / my / could / at / four / I
   _____
4 wants / able / to / she / take / be / long / holiday / a / to
   _____
5 training / he / do / the / can't / because / involves / special / job / it
   _____
6 they / being / like / from / work / able / home / to
   _____

➤ Go back to page 43.

5.2 Obligation, necessity and permission: *must, have to* and *can*

A Choose the correct option.

1 You **can't** / *can* do this job unless you have training.
2 You *mustn't* / ***don't have to*** do this work today. Next week's fine.
3 We *can* / *must* wear casual clothes on a Monday. It's our choice.
4 You *can* / *have to* believe in your idea for it to be a success.
5 Simon *mustn't* / *doesn't have to* be rude to the manager. He'll lose his job!
6 I *can* / *don't have to* get the bus. It's easy to walk there.
7 Everyone *can* / *must* start work at 9. It's a rule.

B Complete the text messages with the words in the box.

> can   can't   don't have to   has to   have to

Hannah: (1) _____ you meet me and Lily for a coffee after work – at five thirty?

Fatima: No, I (2) _____. We (3) _____ work late today, remember?

Hannah: Oh, yeah. Well, I (4) _____ work late because I did all my work this morning. Have you asked Lily?

Fatima: She (5) _____ stay too. She told me this morning.

Hannah: OK. Another time then.

➤ Go back to page 45.

5.3 Present perfect with *for* and *since*

A Choose the correct option.

1 I have wanted to work there **for** / *since* a long time.
2 I have worked here *for* / *since* 2014.
3 We haven't had a day off *for* / *since* a long time.
4 They've worked in recruitment *for* / *since* the last 10 years.
5 She hasn't spoken to the manager *for* / *since* months.
6 Giles hasn't worked *for* / *since* he lost his job in accounts.
7 Things have changed *for* / *since* we did our research.

B Make sentences with the present perfect.

1 she / do / a lot of charity work
   _____*She's done a lot of charity work.*_____
2 they / be / in your office / for an hour
   _____
3 you / change / your appointment / three times
   _____
4 we / not have / a pay rise / for a while
   _____
5 How long / she / be / the owner of the company / ?
   _____

➤ Go back to page 47.

Grammar Hub

6.1 Quantifiers *too* and *enough*

- We use *too* + adjective or adverb, *too much* and *too many* to mean more than the right amount.

  *I am **too tired**.*

  *You drink **too much** cola and you eat **too many** sweets.*

Be careful!

- We use *too many* with countable nouns.

  *They buy **too many** snacks.*
- We use *too much* with uncountable nouns.

  *We eat **too much** sugar.*
- We use *enough* + noun to mean the right amount.

  *We have **enough** drinks for everyone.*
- We use *not enough* + noun to mean less than the right amount.

  *She **doesn't have enough** time to cook.*

Be careful!

- When we use *too* and *enough* with adjectives or adverbs, we put *too* **before** the adjective or adverb and *enough* **after** the adjective or adverb.

  *I feel **too ill** to have dinner.*

  *I don't feel **well enough** to have dinner.*

  *You exercise **too hard**.*

  *You don't exercise **hard enough**.*

6.2 *-ing* forms

- We use the present participle *-ing* form to talk about things that are happening now or around now and that are not finished. This is the present continuous.

  *You're **doing** really well at yoga.*
- We use the *-ing* form as an adjective to describe a noun.

  *He has developed a **growing** interest in Nordic walking.*
- We use the *-ing* form as a gerund to make a noun.

  *They like **working out** at the gym twice a week.*

6.3 Present perfect with *just*, *already* and *yet*

	Positive	Negative
I/you/we/they	I**'ve** just **seen** the doctor.	I **haven't seen** the doctor yet.
he/she/it	She**'s** already **left** the hospital.	He **hasn't gone** to the gym yet.

Question	Positive short answer	Negative short answer
Have you taken your painkillers yet?	Yes, **I have**.	No, **I haven't**.
Has the nurse just **given** you some medicine?	Yes, **he has**.	No, **he hasn't**.

- We use the present perfect with *just* in positive statements to say that something happened very recently.

  *I have **just** passed my fitness test.*
- We use the present perfect with *already* in positive statements to say that something happened before now, or earlier than expected.

  *We have **already** been to the supermarket twice today.*

- We use the present perfect with *yet* in negative statements to say that something hasn't happened, but it still might.

  *You haven't finished your vegetables **yet**.*
- We use the present perfect with *yet* in questions to ask if something has happened.

  *Have you cleared the dinner table **yet**?*

Be careful!

- *Just* goes before the past participle.

  *I've **just** eaten some fruit. NOT ~~I've eaten some fruit just.~~*
- *Yet* goes at the end of the sentence.

  *Have you gone vegetarian **yet**? NOT ~~Have you yet gone vegetarian?~~*
- *Already* goes before the past participle. In American English, *already* often goes at the end of the sentence.

  *I've **already** stopped eating meat. OR I've stopped eating meat **already**.*
- See Grammar Reference 5.3 for more information about the present perfect.

6.1 Quantifiers *too* and *enough*

A Choose the correct option.

1 Don't eat too *much* / (*many*) eggs.
2 I am *enough* / *too* tired to jog.
3 Make sure you are getting *enough* / *too much* sleep.
4 You don't drink *enough* / *too much* water.
5 I have eaten too *many* / *much* sweets.
6 The gym closes *too* / *enough* early.
7 We haven't got *enough* / *too much* food in the fridge.

B Match to make sentences.

1	We've got too	___	**a** enough exercise.
2	You don't do	___	**b** sick for football practice.
3	We haven't got	___	**c** people in this yoga class.
4	There are too many	___	**d** enough milk.
5	She has too much	___	**e** many cups on the table.
6	He's too	___	**f** energy to sit still.

➤ Go back to page 53.

6.2 *-ing* forms

A Correct the mistakes in each sentence.

1 We both enjoy ~~go~~ *going* for walks.
2 To jog is my favourite form of exercise.
3 I'm watch a good TV programme about superfoods.
4 She doesn't like swim in the sea.
5 Recently, there has been an increase number of accidents in the home.
6 My next-door neighbour isn't to do very well at the moment.
7 A rise number of people can't afford to buy medicine.

B Put the words in order to make sentences. Then choose gerund (*G*), adjective (*A*) or present participle (*PP*) for the words in **bold**.

1 doesn't / **being** / her / on / like / she / own   (G)/ A / PP
   She doesn't like being on her own.

2 love / doctor / **visiting** / we / family / our   G / A / PP
   _____

3 now / **growing** / in / there / is / interest / a / pilates   G / A / PP
   _____

4 **studying** / food / we're / health / in / class / groups   G / A / PP
   _____

5 my / **cooking** / free time / activity / favourite / is   G / A / PP
   _____

6 now / people / vitamins / in / taking / **increasing** / are / numbers   G / A / PP
   _____

➤ Go back to page 55.

6.3 Present perfect with *just*, *already* and *yet*

A Write *just*, *already* or *yet*.

1 Have you had anything to eat _____?
2 He hasn't asked her to work out with him _____.
3 I've _____ run two marathons this year.
4 She's _____ finished her workout – she's showering now.
5 It's only 11 a.m., but Jack's _____ eaten his lunch.
6 **A:** Who was on the phone?
   B: Frida. She's _____ got back from hospital.

B Make sentences with the present perfect and *just*, *already* and *yet*.

1 you / get / your exam results / ?
   Have you got your exam results yet?

2 they / lose / 5 kilos / from their diet
   _____

3 I / have / a phone call / from the nurse
   _____

4 we / not use / our new cooker
   _____

5 she / take / her medicine / today
   _____

6 you / buy / the food / for tonight / ?
   _____

7 I / see / Pamela / in the supermarket
   _____

➤ Go back to page 57.

Grammar Hub

7.1 Articles

- We use *a/an* to refer to something indefinite when it is one example of many. We often use it when we refer to something for the first time.

  Petros told me a funny joke.
- We use *the* to refer to something definite, which we know. This is often because it has already been mentioned.

  Petros told me a funny joke. The joke was about …
- We use *the* when there is only one of something.

  Do you often use the internet?
- We use – (no article) to refer to a plural or uncountable noun or something in a general sense.

  I love finding bargains when I go shopping.

Be careful!

- We don't use *the* before meals, days, streets, and singular place names.

  I eat dinner at 6 every evening. NOT I eat the dinner at 6 every evening.
- We use *the* before the names of seas and rivers and countries whose names are plural.

  the Atlantic Ocean / the River Nile / the United States / the Philippines
- We use *an* before a vowel sound. We use *a* before a consonant sound, even if the word begins with *a, e, i, o* or *u.*

  an article, an old friend
  a university, a euro

7.2 used to

	Positive	Negative
I/you/he/she/it/we/they	**I used to be** able to speak French.	**They didn't use to have** the internet in the 80s.

Question	Positive short answer	Negative short answer
Did you use to work hard at school?	Yes, **I did**.	No, **I didn't**.

- We use *used to* to talk about past situations that do not exist now. These include past habits and past states.

  Past habit: *We used to watch more TV before we had the internet.*

  Past state: *He used to be quite anxious but he's more relaxed these days.*

Be careful!

- We use *use to* with the auxiliary verb *did*.

  I didn't use to chat online for hours. NOT I didn't used to chat online for hours.
  Did you use to be addicted to video games? NOT Did you used to be addicted to video games?
- In the negative, we can also say *never used to*.

  I didn't use to chat online for hours. OR I never used to chat online for hours.

7.3 No article (*school, the school*)

- When we are referring to a place in terms of the **activity** associated with a place, we use **no** article.

  He studied Maths at university. NOT He studied Maths at the university.
  My grandfather never went to secondary school. NOT My grandfather never went to the secondary school.
- When we are referring to the **physical place**, we use an article.

  The university I go to is called Cambridge. NOT University I go to is called Cambridge.
  This is a good school. NOT This is good school.

7.1 Articles

A Choose the correct option

1 (The)/ A / – way you feel about life can affect your health.
2 I heard a great saying. *The / A / –* saying goes: 'Smile and the world smiles with you'.
3 George wasn't in *the / a / –* very good mood this morning.
4 What did you have for *the / a / –* lunch today?
5 *The / A / –* research they did into the effects of laughter was very interesting.
6 Sarah put *the / an / –* angry face at the end of her text message.
7 We usually have a lot of *the / a / –* fun at parties.

B Complete the text messages with *the, a, an* or –.

Emma: Do you want to see (**1**) _____ film at the weekend?

Ian: Great! (**2**) _____ cinema in Orwell Street has four screens. I'll see what's on.

Emma: Maybe try to find (**3**) _____ comedy because (**4**) _____ horror films and thrillers make me too scared!

Ian: Sure! I need (**5**) _____ good laugh! I'll find out and let you know.

Emma: OK. 😃

➤ Go back to page 63.

7.2 *used to*

A Correct the mistakes in each sentence.

　　to work
1 I used ~~working~~ in a restaurant.
2 Did you used to live here?
3 They didn't used to be friends.
4 She use to study all the time.
5 We used live in Germany.
6 He used surfing the internet for hours every day.
7 You used to being good at remembering names.

B Make sentences with *used to*.

1 your school / give you / all your books / ?
　　Did your school use to give you all your books?
2 in the past, / people / not have / things like the internet
　　_____
3 in the 1990s, / mobile phones / be / much bigger
　　_____
4 in the early days, / the internet / be / very unreliable
　　_____
5 you / find / it hard / to study at school / ?
　　_____

➤ Go back to page 65.

7.3 No article (*school, the school*)

A Complete the sentences with the words in the box. Use the definite article *the* if necessary.

> hospital　hospital　prison　school
> school　university　~~university~~

1 I started studying Maths at _____*university*_____ but I soon dropped out.
2 They brought the child up badly and he ended up in _____ for robbery.
3 The _____ beside my house is called Gregory's. It's for talented children.
4 It's easy to make friends at _____. I had lots as a kid.
5 His illness meant he was in _____ for months and he had to give up his job.
6 Anna also went to _____ where I studied Law.
7 The best place to see a doctor is at _____ in the city centre.

B Complete the text with *the* or – (no article)

(1) ___*The*___ hospital I work at is called St Anne's. I'm a nurse there. When I was a kid, I used to hate (2) _____ hospitals. I had to go to (3) _____ hospital twice then; once for a broken leg and the other time for a bad back. Another thing I hated was (4) _____ school. (5) _____ school I went to was very bad and it didn't have good facilities. I loved it when I went to (6) _____ university, though, because (7) _____ university I studied at was very modern, and it's also where I met my best friend, Jillian.

➤ Go back to page 67.

Grammar Hub

8.1 Reflexive pronouns

Subject pronoun	Reflexive pronoun	
I	myself	I see **myself** performing in this band for two more years.
you (singular)	yourself	You know **yourself** better than anyone else does.
him	himself	He works for **himself** as a photographer.
her	herself	She's the only actress I know who likes watching **herself** on TV.
it	itself	This problem won't fix **itself**. We need to do something.
we	ourselves	We are going to treat **ourselves** to front-row seats at the theatre.
you (plural)	yourselves	I hope you all enjoyed **yourselves** at the show.
they	themselves	They bought **themselves** an expensive sculpture.

- We use a reflexive pronoun as the object of a verb when the subject and the object are the same person or thing.

  *I taught **myself** how to play the guitar.*
- We can use a reflexive pronoun after the object of a verb. This is to emphasise the person or thing that does the action.

  *She chose the costumes for the play **herself**.*
- We use *by* + reflexive pronoun to say we do something alone or with no help.

  *He worked out what had happened **by himself**.*
- For emphasis, we can also use *all by* + reflexive pronoun.

  *I can't believe you did it **all by** yourself!*
- We use *each other* when two or more people or things perform the same action to the other person/people.

  *Eric and Patricia sang **each other** a song. NOT Eric and Patricia sang **themselves** a song.*

Be careful!

- We don't use reflexive pronouns after prepositions of place. We use object pronouns.

  *I took my camera with **me**. NOT I took my camera with **myself**.*

8.2 Infinitive of purpose

- We can use *to* + infinitive when we express the purpose or reason for doing something.

  *I went to the art shop **to get** some paint.*
  *We went to the ticket office early **to avoid** the queues.*

Be careful!

*Trine went to the concert **to see** her favourite band perform. NOT Trine went to the concert **seeing** her favourite band perform.*

8.3

First conditional

Condition	Result
If + present simple,	*will/won't*
If **you go** to the festival,	**you'll have** a great time.
If **it doesn't rain**,	**we'll go** to the street fair.
If **it's** busy,	**we won't go** to the theatre.
If **you don't ask** for help,	**you won't get** any.

Result	Condition
will/won't	*if + present simple*
You'll meet the artist	**if you visit** the gallery tonight.
She won't go to the concert	if **it's** expensive.

Question	Positive short answer	Negative short answer
If Star Wars **is** on at the cinema, **will you go**?	Yes, **I will**.	No, **I won't**.
Will you go if Star Wars **is** on at the cinema?		

- We use the first conditional to talk about possible situations in the future.
- The *if*-clause describes the action or condition.

  If he sells all his art, he'll get a bigger studio.
  The result clause says what will happen.

  *If he sells all his art, **he'll get** a bigger studio.*
- We can use other modal verbs (e.g. *can*, *could*, *might*, *should*) instead of *will*.

  *If you sing really well, you **can** become famous.*
  *If it's open, we **might** go to the museum.*
  *If you win an award, we **should** celebrate.*
- We can use *shall* to ask questions and make suggestions.

  ***Shall** we work on our paintings if you're not too tired?*

Be careful!

- We use a comma (,) when the *if*-clause comes first.

  If you go, I'll come too. NOT If you go I'll come too.
  I'll buy your ticket if you get the popcorn. NOT I'll buy your ticket, if you get the popcorn.

8.1 Reflexive pronouns

A Correct the mistakes in each sentence.

1 I got ~~me~~ *myself* a membership to a book club.
2 We didn't give ourself enough time to set up the exhibition.
3 Paul, be careful! Please don't hurt himself climbing over those seats.
4 He wrote the songs for his album all by itself.
5 You look tired, Eleni. You should look after yourselves and get more sleep.
6 I wish our friends Pete and Lynne could be ourselves around strangers.
7 The show I organised ran myself – it didn't take a lot of work.

B Write the missing reflexive pronoun.

1 We got ___ourselves___ a new piano.
2 Jane, please don't compare _____ to other people.
3 Rachel hurt _____ singing on stage.
4 The problem with my music player fixed _____.
5 They bought _____ tickets to see Adele in concert.
6 He asked _____ if he was happy as a writer.
7 We must learn to love _____ before we can love others.

➤ Go back to page 73.

8.2 Infinitive of purpose

A Make sentences with *to* + infinitive.

1 I / play / the violin / relax
 I play the violin to relax.

2 she / attend / drawing classes / spend / time / with other artists

 _____

3 we / go / to the cinema / early / get / good seats

 _____

4 some people / visit / Paris / just / see / the Louvre

 _____

5 they / sell / their art / on the street / last weekend / make / money

 _____

6 she / go / to voice lessons / every evening / improve / her singing

 _____

7 we / travel / to Florence / next year / do / some photography

 _____

➤ Go back to page 75.

8.3 First conditional

A Tick the sentences that are correct. Correct the mistakes in the others.

1 She will give you an autograph if you ~~will~~ ask her.
2 If I have time, I will paint your portrait tomorrow. ✓
3 He stars in the film if they pay him well.
4 I go with you to the cinema if we can watch a comedy.
5 The audience will love us, if we play our best songs.
6 If we all join the book club, it will be lots of fun.

B Complete the sentences with the correct form of the verbs in the box.

> ask   buy   go   have   like   ~~ring~~

1 I ___'ll ring___ Claire if you call Simon.
2 If you get the cinema tickets, I _____ the snacks.
3 If it rains tomorrow, we _____ a concert in the park.
4 I _____ to the audition if you come with me.
5 You'll love *Wicked* if you _____ musicals.
6 If she _____ for my help, I'll give it to her.

C Complete the conversation with the correct form of the verbs in brackets.

Wes: (1) What about next week's gallery opening? If you ___organise___ (*organise*) the food, I ___'ll look after___ (*look after*) the drinks.

Trisha: (2) OK. What about setting up the artwork? If I _____ (*do*) that, _____ (*you / send*) out the invites?

Wes: (3) Sure. Should I invite students from the university? If they _____ (*come*), we _____ (*not have*) enough food and drinks.

Trisha: (4) I know … It's a problem. If we _____ (*invite*) all of them, the gallery _____ (*get*) too full!

Wes: (5) If everyone _____ (*show*) up, there _____ (*probably / not be*) enough space.

Trisha: (6) If that _____ (*happen*), people _____ (*might damage*) the art.

Wes: You're right. Let's not invite them, then.

➤ Go back to page 77.

Grammar Hub

9.1 Second conditional

Condition *If + past simple,*	Result *would/wouldn't*
If **you spent** less money,	**you would be** happier.
If **I didn't work** all the time,	**I'd make** more friends.
If **it were** expensive,	**I wouldn't buy** it.
If **they didn't travel** a lot,	**they wouldn't gain** new experiences.

Result *would/wouldn't*	Condition *if + past simple*
You'd discover your interests	if **you travelled** more.
She wouldn't do it	if **she didn't want** to.

Question	Positive short answer	Negative short answer
If **you had** a lot of money, **would you give** it to charity? **Would you give** money to charity if **you had** a lot?	Yes, **I would**.	No, **I wouldn't**.

- We use the second conditional to talk about hypothetical situations in the present or future. The *if*-clauses can be an unlikely or impossible situation.

  Unlikely: *If I won the London marathon, I would be so happy!*

  Impossible: *If I were you, I wouldn't lend him the money.*
- We only use a comma (,) when the *if*-clause comes first.
- We can use other modal verbs (e.g. *could, might*) as an alternative to *would* in the main clause.

  If she tried something new, it could open her mind.

  If you had more free time, you might feel happier.
- When the *if*-clause is clear or is implied, we often only state the result clause.

  What would you do if you won a million dollars?

  I'd leave my job! And I might buy a new house.

Be careful!

- With *I, he, she* and *it*, we usually use *were* in the *if*-clause, not *was*.

  If I were rich, I would give money to my favourite charity.
- We only use *would* in the result clause.

  If we had children, we'd buy a bigger house. NOT If we would have a family, we'd buy a bigger house.

9.2 Defining relative clauses

	Relative pronoun	
Person	who	The friend **who** lent me the money is called Jack.
	that	The person **that** gave away the money is a billionaire.
Thing	which	The salary **which** I earn is too small.
	that	The donation **that** he made is very large.
Possession	whose	The man **whose** wallet I found thanked me.
Place	where	The company **where** I work supports many charities.
Time	when	The year **when** Rockefeller died was 1937.

- We use a defining relative clause to give information about and identify a noun (person or thing).
- We can use *who* or *that* for people, and *which* or *that* for things.

  The person who lent me the money is called Jack. OR The person that lent me the money is called Jack.

  The donation which he made is very large. OR The donation that he made is very large.
- We can leave out the relative pronoun when it is followed by a subject and verb, rather than just a verb.

  Relative pronoun + subject and verb: *The charity that she supports helps animals. OR The charity she supports helps animals.*

  Relative pronoun + verb: *The person that lent me the money is called Jack. NOT The person lent me the money is called Jack.*

9.3 Gerunds

- Gerunds are a type of noun.

  Noun: *He likes clothes.*

  Gerund: *He likes shopping.*

  Noun: *Money doesn't bring happiness.*

  Gerund: *Owning things doesn't bring happiness.*
- We use gerunds after prepositions.

  I dream about setting up my own business.

  He's good at trading things online.
- We can use gerunds directly after some verbs. See Grammar Reference 3.3 for more information.

  They like making a profit.

  We love doing online research.

- We can use gerunds as either subjects or objects.

  Subject: *Cleaning the house is boring.*

  Object: *She hates cleaning the house.*
- Gerunds can act like verbs and take an object.

  She hates doing the ironing.

Be careful!

- If the verb ends in *-e*, remove the final *-e* before adding *-ing*.

  make → making   *give → giving*

  He enjoys making money.   *She likes giving money to charity.*

9.1 Second conditional

A Correct the mistakes in each sentence. Make second conditionals.

would

1 If I could travel, I discover more about myself.

2 If people aren't obsessed with money, the world would be a better place.

3 If I had the choice, I will buy experiences, not possessions.

4 Carol would travel more if she have not children.

5 You would inspire other people if you would do something amazing.

6 Did you throw away your all possessions if I asked you?

7 If I could take two months off work, I travelled around India.

B Complete the conversation with the correct form of the verbs in brackets.

Molly: I just did the lotto. It's £10 million tonight. Imagine what (1) ___would happen___ (happen) if I (2) _____ (win)!

Nelly: Well, you (3) _____ (be) rich – that's for sure! What (4) _____ (you / do) with the money?

Molly: If I (5) _____ (have) £10 million, I (6) _____ (give) most of it to my family, or to charity, you know?

Nelly: Really? I (7) _____ (not / do) that. I'd buy a big house, and some expensive artworks.

➤ Go back to page 83.

9.2 Defining relative clauses

A Choose the correct option.

1 I know many people *which* / *who* would love to travel.

2 The student *who* / *whose* father is a well-known philanthropist has plenty of money.

3 The charity *who* / *that* I often donate to is *Help the Children*.

4 This is the city *where* / *which* I went to university.

5 Wealthy people *that* / *which* join the Giving Pledge can inspire others.

6 That was the time *when* / *where* Rockefeller gave away most of his fortune.

7 He started his own charity *which* / *whose* helps protect the environment.

B Match to make sentences.

1 My smartphone is the possession _b_

2 The London Marathon is an event ___

3 Andrew Carnegie was another person who ___

4 The money ___

5 She's the woman ___

6 South America is where ___

7 She gained a lot of experience ___

a gave away most of his wealth.

b which I could never give away!

c she travelled as a student.

d which raises millions of pounds for charity.

e that he left will be given to charity.

f when she was travelling in India.

g who set up the charity.

➤ Go back to page 85.

9.3 Gerunds

A Complete the sentences with the gerund form of the verbs in the box.

| do | give | have | make | ~~save~~ | set up | spend |

1 He isn't very good at ___saving___ money.

2 She often dreams of _____ a family of her own.

3 Gareth is looking forward to _____ his own business.

4 Andrew Carnegie was famous for _____ away nearly all his money.

5 _____ research is one of the most enjoyable things about my course.

6 We really need to stop _____ so much money on entertainment.

7 We hope that our business will start _____ a profit.

B Complete the sentences with the gerund form of the verb in brackets. Then choose subject gerund (*S*) or object gerund (*O*).

1 They aren't good at ___making___ (make) a living.   *S* / *O*

2 _____ (dream) of new places to visit is my favourite way to pass the time.   *S* / *O*

3 _____ (spend) money on designer clothing is a total waste.   *S* / *O*

4 The most important thing to practise and be good at is _____ (be) yourself.   *S* / *O*

5 Saving money may involve _____ (do) without certain luxuries.   *S* / *O*

6 _____ (be) a successful trader is harder than it sounds.   *S* / *O*

7 You cannot enjoy life unless you spend it _____ (live) for today.   *S* / *O*

➤ Go back to page 87.

Grammar Hub

10.1 Comparatives and superlatives

	Comparative	Superlative
One syllable adjective	adj + -er (+ than) slow → slower	the + adj + -est cheap → the cheapest
Short adjectives ending in -e	adj + -r (+ than) late → later	the + adj + -st late → the latest
Short adjectives ending in one vowel + one consonant	double the consonant + -er (+ than) big → bigger	the + double the consonant + -est big → the biggest
Adjectives ending in -y	adj without -y + -ier (+ than) easy → easier	the + adj without -y + -iest heavy → the heaviest
Longer adjectives (two + syllables)	more + adj (+ than) expensive → more expensive	the most + adj useful → the most useful
Irregular adjectives	good → better	good → the best
Regular adverbs	more + adv (+ than) quickly → more quickly	the most + adv efficiently → the most efficiently
Irregular adverbs	badly → worse far → farther/further fast → faster hard → harder well → better	badly → the worst far → the farthest/furthest fast → the fastest hard → the hardest well → the best

- We use comparatives to say how two or more things are different.
- We use superlatives to say that something is top or bottom of a group.
- To make a negative comparative, we use *less* instead of *more*.

  *My e-reader was **less** expensive than yours.*

- To make a negative superlative, we use *the least* instead of *the most*.

  *This phone works **the least** efficiently of them all.*

- We use the pattern *get/become* + comparative adjective + *and* + the same comparative adjective to talk about change over time.

  *Computers are **getting smaller and smaller**.*

- For longer adjectives, we use *get/become* + *more and more* + comparative adjective.

  *Computer games are **becoming more and more realistic**.*

Be careful!

- We only use *than* when it is followed by the thing we are comparing.

  This phone is good but this one is better.
  NOT ~~This phone is good but this one is better than.~~

- We don't put *the* before a superlative when we use a possessive adjective.

  *What was your **biggest** mistake when buying gadgets? NOT* ~~What was your the biggest mistake when buying gadgets?~~

10.2 More comparative structures

- We use *as* + adjective/adverb + *as* to say that two things are the same in some way.

  *Your phone is **as good as** mine.*
  *My drone flies **as quickly as** yours.*

- For emphasis, we use *just as … as*.

  *You are **just as good as** I am at this video game.*

- We use *not as* + adjective/adverb + *as* to say that two things are different in some way.

  *Your computer isn't **as fast as** mine.*
  *I don't use technology **as often as** you do.*

10.3 need to

	Positive	Negative
I/you/we/they	**You need to prove** what you're saying.	**We don't need to do** any more research.
he/she/it	**He needs to make** preparations.	**She doesn't need to wear** a spacesuit.

Question	Positive short answer	Negative short answer
Do you need to prepare for the test?	Yes, **I do.**	No, **I don't.**
Does she need to report her findings?	Yes, **she does.**	No, **she doesn't.**

- We use *need to* like *have to* to say that something is or isn't necessary.

  *Astronauts **need to** be fit. OR Astronauts **have to** be fit.*
  *Astronauts **don't need** to be young. OR Astronauts **don't have to** be young.*

- The verb *need* is followed by *to* + infinitive.

  *Astronauts need **to** be fit. NOT* ~~Astronauts need being fit.~~

10.1 Comparatives and superlatives

A Correct the mistakes in each sentence.

              interesting

1 Exercising is a lot more ~~interested~~ with a fitness tracker.
2 This is the better device I've ever owned.
3 You got the more expensive phone in the shop.
4 This laptop is worst than my old one.
5 Your tablet is more light than mine.
6 This tablet starts the more quickly than my other devices.
7 Technology is getting more the more advanced.

B Complete the sentences with the correct form of the adjectives and adverbs in brackets.

1 This new mobile phone is _____*lighter*_____ (light) than my old one.
2 My computer is _____ (expensive) thing I own.
3 An e-reader is _____ (good) for reading books than a laptop.
4 Computers are getting _____ and _____ (cheap) every year.
5 You can check spelling _____ (quick) online than you can by using a dictionary.
6 Although my phone was _____ (heavy) one in the shop, I bought it for all its features.

➤ Go back to page 93.

10.2 More comparative structures

A Choose the correct option.

1 When my computer crashes, I get *just* / (*as*) annoyed as everyone else does.
2 My tablet is *as not* / *not as* useful as I thought it would be.
3 Is your drone *as much fun* / *fun as much* as you expected it to be?
4 Getting more computer memory is *just as simple as* / *simple as just* connecting a USB.
5 Video calls are as cheap *than* / *as* normal calls on a computer.
6 This GPS is not *as reliable as* / *reliable as* it should be.
7 Your internet connection is just *as fast as* / *fast as* mine.

B Make sentences. Use contractions where possible.

1 tablets … = useful … laptops
      Tablets are just as useful as laptops.
2 tablets … > useful … laptops
      Laptops aren't as useful as tablets.
3 TV advertising … > effective … advertising on the radio
      _____
4 the GPS on my phone … = good … the GPS in the car
      _____
5 4G … > fast … 3G internet
      _____
6 new models … > reliable … old models
      _____

➤ Go back to page 95.

10.3 *need to*

A Make questions with *need to*. Then write short answers.

1 you / need / find / a solution ✔
      Do you need to find a solution? Yes, I/we do.
2 astronauts / need / wear / spacesuits all the time ✘
      _____
3 she / need / follow / a schedule ✘
      _____
4 the food / need / be / tinned ✔
      _____
5 astronauts / need / be / fit ✔
      _____
6 I / need / repair / this computer ✘
      _____

B Make sentences with *need to*.

1 You / not / use a telescope to see the ISS
      You don't need to use a telescope to see the ISS.
2 the scientists / do / more research on the subject
      _____
3 people / think / about the future
      _____
4 you / find / a solution
      _____
5 he / confirm / what he believes
      _____
6 they / not / install / an app
      _____

➤ Go back to page 97.

Grammar Hub

11.1 The passive (present and past simple)

	Positive	Negative
I	**I am told** the desert is beautiful.	**I'm not expected** to be an expert on the environment.
he/she/it	It **is visited** by lots of people.	**It is not understood** by many people. **It isn't understood** by many people.
you/we/they	**You are advised** to stay away from the volcano.	**They aren't studied** by scientists.

Question	Positive short answer	Negative short answer
Am I allowed to take photographs?	Yes, **you are.**	No, **you aren't.**
Are we permitted to get close to the waterfall?	Yes, **we/you are.**	No, **we/you aren't.**

	Positive	Negative
I/he/she/it	**I was told** to read the article.	**She wasn't asked** to help.
you/we/they	They **were invited** to the island.	The clothes **weren't needed** on the journey.

Question	Positive short answer	Negative short answer
Was she joined by her friends?	Yes, **she was.**	No, **she wasn't.**
Were they told what to do?	Yes, **they were.**	No, **they weren't.**

- We use the passive when we don't say who or what causes the action (usually because the person or thing is not known, not important or obvious).

  *The new road to the site **was opened** last year.*

- We also use the passive with *by* when we know who does/did an action and we want to emphasise it.

  *This report was produced **by** scientists from Cambridge University.*

- We can sometimes say the same thing in the active or passive voice. The choice often depends on the topic we are talking about.

  Active: *Many tourists **visit** the site.* (The topic is tourists.)

  Passive: *The site **is visited** by many tourists.* (The topic is the site.)

Be careful!

- We don't use *by* + the agent unless it is important, useful information.

  The research is paid for by the World Wildlife Fund. NOT ~~The research is paid for by someone.~~

11.2 Adjective + *to* + infinitive

- When we want to use an adjective to describe an action, we can use adjective + *to* + infinitive.

  *It's **interesting to study** the life cycle of a mammal.*

  *It was **nice to watch** animals in their natural habitat.*

- When we want to say that an adjective doesn't describe an action, we use the negative form of the verb.

  *It **wasn't** easy to make a living as a scientist.*

- When we want to say that an adjective describes the opposite of an action, we use *not* + *to* + infinitive.

  *It's important **not to do** any damage to the environment.*

11.3 *even*

- We use *even* as an adverb to suggest that something is surprising.

  *Recycling is not difficult – there is **even** a recycling bin at the office.*

  *You don't **even** have to leave your room to find things made of plastic.*

  *She doesn't **even** know where the Pacific Ocean is!*

- We use *even* before main verbs and after auxiliary verbs and modals.

  *We **even found** waste plastic on Mount Everest.*
  NOT ~~We found even waste plastic on Mount Everest.~~
  *Plastic **can even** be found on Mars NOT ~~Plastic even can be found on Mars.~~*

- We can also use *even* before nouns.

  ***Even** experts make mistakes sometimes.*

11.1 The passive (present and past simple)

A Correct the mistakes in each sentence.

1 The volcano _is_ located in the middle of a jungle.
2 The cliffs were form 200 million years ago.
3 The museum opened by the President last night.
4 The mountain is make of a strong type of rock.
5 The village doesn't known for its art.
6 The new park wasn't open by anyone famous.
7 She attracted to Africa because of the wildlife.

B Complete the text messages with the correct passive form of the verbs in brackets.

Gloria: How was your trip to Uluru?

Toby: Great! I learnt a lot. I (1) _was helped_ (help) by all the tourist information there.

Gloria: Like what?

Toby: Well, it (2) _____ (make) of sandstone and it's nearly 350m high.

Gloria: Cool. What else did you learn?

Toby: It (3) _____ (create) over 600 million years ago.

Gloria: Wow, that's really old!

Toby: I know! Also, it (4) _____ (own) by the native Australian people.

Gloria: I thought the government owned it.

Toby: It's (5) _____ (not own) by them. They just manage it.

➤ Go back to page 103.

11.2 Adjective + *to* + infinitive

A Put the words in order to make sentences.

1 easy / understand / a person's / it's / to / body language
   It's easy to understand a person's body language.
2 necessary / be / it's / quiet / to / near / wild animals
   _____
3 fascinating / take / was / photos of insects / to / it
   _____
4 good / live / green / a / it's / to / lifestyle
   _____
5 to / is / educational / it / wildlife programmes / watch / ?
   _____

B Choose the correct option.

1 It's **good not** / **not good** to feed the animals in the zoo.
2 It's **important not** / **not important** to make wild animals angry or upset.
3 It's **not easy** / **easy not** to take the perfect photo.
4 It's **necessary not** / **not necessary** to be an expert to enjoy studying animals.
5 It's **not essential** / **essential not** to go near crocodiles.
6 It's **not safe** / **safe not** to go travelling in the wild on your own.
7 It's **essential not** / **not essential** to have top quality equipment in order to take great photos.

➤ Go back to page 105.

11.3 *even*

A Choose the correct place to put *even*, A or B.

1 Most (A) people haven't (B) thought about it before.
2 (A) some experts are surprised (B) that the problem is so serious.
3 A lot of people (A) don't (B) realise that plastic lasts so long.
4 There (A) is (B) a place to recycle glass in my street.
5 You (A) can't (B) walk 100 metres without seeing some plastic that has been thrown away.

B Put *even* in the correct place in each sentence.

1 A lot of people don't _even_ notice the pollution.
2 The base camp for Mount Aconcagua is very high.
3 There are many solutions – we can stop using plastic.
4 There are a lot of organisations in my town – there's a bird-watchers' club.
5 I love all animals, and I like spiders.
6 I know some adults who don't know the difference between a lion and a tiger.

➤ Go back to page 107.

Grammar Hub

12.1 Reported speech

Direct speech	Reported speech
present simple **'We like** Channel 4 News best.' **'Do you like** Channel 4 News best?'	past simple Most people said (that) **they liked** Channel 4 News best. She asked them if **they liked** Channel 4 News best.
present continuous **'We are watching** the news.'	past continuous They said (that) **they were watching** the news.
will **'I will** watch TV later.'	would She said (that) **she would** watch TV later.
may **'Elle may** buy the box set.'	might He said (that) **Elle might** buy the box set.
can **'We can** record the episode.'	could They said (that) **they could** record the episode.

- We use reported speech to report what people say or report their thoughts or ideas.
- We use a reporting verb in the past simple.

  He said … They told me … She asked him if …
- We usually go back one tense from the tense the speaker used, but we often don't go back one tense with the past simple.

  'I'm watching TV.' → *He said he was watching TV.*
  'We often went to the cinema.' → *He said they often went to the cinema.*

- We also need to change some pronouns (*I* to *he/she*, *my* to *his/her*, *your* to *my*, etc).

  'I like your radio show,' said Lola. →
  Lola told me that she liked my radio show.
- We sometimes also need to change other words.

Direct speech	Reported speech
now 'We're going to watch the news **now**.'	then / at that moment They said they were going to watch the news **then / at that moment**.
tonight 'I will be on social media **tonight**.'	that night He said he would be on social media **that night**.
tomorrow 'We'll set the budget **tomorrow**.'	the next day / the following day She said they would set the budget **the next day**.
today 'That new show is on TV **today**.'	that day He said that new show was on TV **that day**.
here 'There are some reporters **here**.'	there She said there were some reporters **there**.

12.2 Past perfect

	Positive	Negative
I/you/he/she/it/we/they	**I'd heard** the story before you read it.	**She hadn't seen** the ad before yesterday.

Question	Positive short answer	Negative short answer
Had you visited the news website before?	Yes, **I had**.	No, **I hadn't**.

- When we are talking about two events in the past, we use the past perfect to show that one event happened before the other.

past ⟶ present
↑   ↑
I saw you on the news.   You told me about it.

I had seen you on the news before you told me about it.

- We often use *just* and *already* with the past perfect.

  The film had just started when we arrived at the cinema.
  Had they already seen the show?

Be careful!

- If we use the past simple with *when*, the meaning is different to when we use the past perfect.

  I checked the news when I left. (= I checked the news after I left.)
  I had checked the news when I left. (= I checked the news before I left.)

12.3 shall

Subject	Question
I/we	**Shall I buy** tickets for the cinema?

- We use *shall* to make offers and suggestions.

  offer: *Shall I turn the TV on?*
  suggestion: *Shall we go to the cinema tonight?*
  suggestion: *Let's go to the cinema tonight, shall we?*
- We also use *shall* to ask for suggestions.

  Which episode shall we watch this evening?

Be careful!

- We only use *shall* with *I* and *we*.

  Which episode shall we watch this evening? NOT
  ~~*Which episode shall you watch this evening?*~~

- We use *will* to ask questions about the future.

  Will you binge-watch the show this weekend?

12.1 Reported speech

A Report the statements.

1 Paul and James: 'We're going shopping tonight.'
   They said *(that) they were going shopping that night.*

2 Tina: 'I'll post it online later.'
   She said _____

3 Roy: 'I can't help with the budget.'
   He said _____

4 James: 'Don't watch the show without me!'
   He told me _____

5 Helen: 'Can I borrow your box set?'
   She asked me if _____

6 Alan: 'Are they going to show the ad tonight?'
   He asked me if _____

7 Nora: 'You may need to speak to a journalist today.'
   She told me that _____

D Complete the text messages with the correct form of the verbs in brackets.

> **Pat:** Fred said you (1) _____ *went* _____ (*go*) to the cinema with him the other night.

> **Nuala:** Yeah. He told me he (2) _____ (*want*) to watch a new sci-fi film, but I asked him if we (3) _____ (*can*) see a comedy instead. I said I (4) _____ (*not feel*) like seeing a serious film.

> **Pat:** He said you (5) _____ (*see*) *Ride Away* in the end. Was it good?

> **Nuala:** That's right. We (6) _____ (*be going to*) choose *Hideout*, but it was on too late. *Ride Away* was the best option.

➤ Go back to page 113.

12.2 Past perfect

A Correct the mistakes in each sentence.

1 Someone had ~~drop~~ *dropped* a newspaper on the ground.

2 I was late, but the film wasn't starting, so it was OK.

3 The show have just begun when we arrived.

4 They had already saw the film twice.

5 The journalist has already left when she got to the meeting.

6 Had you just seen the show before last night?

7 **A:** Had she posted it before?
   B: Yes, she did.

B Complete each sentence with the correct form of the verb in brackets.

1 The film _had already begun_ (*already begin*) when I arrived.

2 I didn't watch the film because I _____ (*already see*) it.

3 They didn't want to watch the news because they _____ (*already read*) the newspaper.

4 We _____ (*just start*) the journey home when the accident happened.

5 I _____ (*find*) the DVD that my girlfriend had dropped behind the sofa.

➤ Go back to page 115.

12.3 *shall*

A Choose the correct option.

1 (Shall) / *Will* we see what's on TV?

2 *Shall* / *Will* I invite Amy round to watch the show?

3 *Shall* / *Will* they release the show on DVD soon?

4 *Shall* / *Will* we binge-watch the show this weekend?

5 *Shall* / *Will* this catch people's attention?

6 What film *shall* / *will* we see at the cinema?

7 What *shall* / *will* you say to the journalist?

B Write questions using *shall* or *will*.

1 we / share / our photos online tonight
   Shall we share our photos online tonight?

2 they / release / the new film / this weekend
   _____

3 I / pay / for the cinema tickets
   _____

4 she / finish / her journalism course this year
   _____

5 we / watch / something exciting this weekend
   _____

➤ Go back to page 117.

Vocabulary Hub

1.1 People

A **SPEAK** Work in pairs. Look at the pictures. Describe the people and their relationships. Use the words in the box to help you.

> children colleagues friends grandparents parents
> relatives strangers students teacher

B Choose the correct words to complete the sentences.

1 Sally and Nicole are good *friends / strangers* and they go to the same college.

2 Jamal is a photography *colleague / teacher*. He knows a lot about cameras.

3 Every weekend, I go to stay at my *grandparents' / couple's* house.

4 I never know what to say to *strangers / parents* when I meet them for the first time.

5 Janelle and Carla are *colleagues / students*, and they work together in the office very well.

6 All of my *relatives / teachers* live in the same town – we're a very close family.

➤ Go back to page 3.

1.2 Types of people

A Match the descriptions (1–10) with the types of people in **bold** in *Three of the best*.

1 a person who likes animals ___*animal lover*___

2 a woman who has three children _____

3 a person who is very interested in food

_____

4 a person who enjoys seeing other places

_____

5 a person who watches or takes part in sports

_____

6 a person who plays computer games _____

7 a person who enjoys spending time with others

_____

8 a person who loves reading _____

9 a person who writes online regularly _____

10 a person who listens to music regularly

_____

B Complete the sentences with the words in the box.

> coffee   dog   father   football   positive

1 I'm a _____ owner. I take it for a walk twice a day.

2 I'm a big _____ drinker. Cappuccino is my favourite, but I also like espresso.

3 I'm a _____ of two. My wife and I have two daughters.

4 I'm a _____ person. I try not to worry or complain.

5 I'm a _____ fan. My favourite team is Manchester United.

keen on

We say *keen on* + verb + *-ing* or *keen on* + noun.

- I'm keen on travelling.
- I'm keen on tennis.

We can also say *a keen* + noun.

- I'm a keen traveller.

➤ Go back to page 4.

2.3 Life events

Match the life events (1–10) with the pictures (a–j).

1 have a baby / children   6 fall in love

2 go to university   7 get your own place

3 get a job   8 retire

4 get married   9 learn to swim

5 leave home   10 leave school

➤ Go back to page 17.

3.3 Accommodation and facilities

A Label the pictures with the words in the box. Which types of accommodation have you stayed in?

> beach resort   apartment   campsite   hostel
> chalet   cruise ship   five-star hotel   guest house

1 _____

2 _____

3 _____

4 _____

5 _____

6 _____

7 _____

8 _____

B **SPEAK** Work in pairs. What do the words in **bold** mean? Explain them. Then decide who would say each sentence. Write guest (*G*) or receptionist (*R*).

1 **Reception** is open 24 hours. Just dial nine on the phone in your room.

2 We don't have any **double** or **twin rooms** for tonight, I'm afraid, but there are two **single rooms** available.

3 I understand the **dorms** in the hostel are non-smoking, but can I smoke on the **balcony**?

4 All our rooms have **safes** for your valuables, quiet **air con** and beautiful **sea views**.

5 Hello, is that **room service**? I'd like to order some food, please. It's room 442.

6 If you'd like to exercise or have a massage, our **gym**, pool and **spa** are on the fourth floor.

7 We're **checking out** tomorrow and we'd like to book an **airport transfer** for 10 am, please.

8 You have booked a **self-catering** apartment, but there is a restaurant by the pool if you'd like to eat there.

➤ Go back to page 27.

4.2 Suffixes

A Complete the diagrams with the verbs in the box. Check your answers in the *Macmillan English Dictionary*.

> agree   ~~develop~~   ~~discuss~~   improve   invent   predict

discuss _____   _____

-ION

_____

          develop _____

-MENT

_____   _____

B Complete the diagrams with the adjectives in the box. You need to change the spelling in some of the words when you add a suffix. Which ones? Check your answers in the *Macmillan English Dictionary*.

> ~~able~~   active   ~~happy~~   kind   possible   sad

happi _____   _____

-NESS

_____

          abil _____

-ITY

_____   _____

➤ Go back to page 35.

Vocabulary Hub

4.3 Relaxing

A Complete the gaps in blue in the survey with the words in the box. Read *Make yourself at home* on page 36 again to help you.

> a good book   board games   by the fire
> friends or family   get together   homemade food
> hot bath   quiet night   relaxed atmosphere
> simple things   some candles   some time out

How *hygge* is your lifestyle?

1 It's a rainy Sunday afternoon. Do you prefer to …

   a go to a shopping centre and spend some money?

   b order delivery food and switch on the games console?

   c sit down with [1]_____ and read all afternoon under a cosy blanket?

2 How would you rather celebrate your birthday?

   a Go out with friends and stay out until late.

   b Meet friends in the [2]_____ of a café or restaurant and have a nice meal.

   c Have [3]_____ over to eat [4]_____ and play [5]_____.

3 What makes you happiest?

   a Money, shopping, holidays, etc.

   b A chance to [6]_____ with family and friends.

   c The [7]_____ in life, like a [8]_____ in or a long walk in the countryside.

4 It's Friday night and your working week is over. Would you rather …

   a go out with your colleagues?

   b go home, watch TV and have an early night?

   c go home, have a nice, [9]_____ and then sit [10]_____ and dry off?

5 How do you create the perfect atmosphere at home?

   a Turn on the lights, turn up the music and dance round the living room.

   b Close the curtains, switch on the TV and lie on the sofa.

   c Light [11]_____, play some soft music and take [12]_____ to relax.

Finished? Work out your score: a = 0, b = 1, c = 2

B **SPEAK** Work in pairs. Ask and answer the questions in Exercise A. Make a note of your partner's answers. Go to the **Communication Hub** on **page 155** and check your scores. Who has more *hygge* in their lives?

➤ Go back to page 37.

5.3 *work* + proposition

A Complete the diagram with the words in the box.

> a design firm   a hospital   accounts   Volkswagen

+ *at/for* + a named company, for example, [1]_____

+ *for* + type of company, for example, [2]_____

work

+ *in* + area of business or department, for example, [3]_____

+ *at/in* + place, for example, [4]_____

B Write the correct prepositions to complete the sentences.

   1 He works _____ Base One IT Services.

   2 We work _____ a law firm.

   3 They work _____ a restaurant.

   4 She works _____ a telemarketing company.

   5 He works _____ the IT department.

   6 They work _____ Human Resources.

➤ Go back to page 47.

6.2 Exercise

A Label the pictures of sports and activities with the words in the box.

> cycling   hockey   jogging   marathon running
> Nordic walking   squash   working out at the gym   yoga

1 _____
2 _____
3 _____
4 _____
5 _____
6 _____
7 _____
8 _____

D Complete the instructions with the correct form of the verbs in the box. You will need to use some of the verbs more than once.

| burn   do   go   keep   lose   play   run   ~~work out~~ |

Find someone who …

1 hates ___working out___ at the gym.

2 can give a tip on how to _____ weight in a healthy way.

3 _____ jogging or running regularly.

4 knows someone who has _____ a marathon, a half-marathon or a 10 km race.

5 knows how to _____ squash.

6 _____ fit by walking or cycling to school or work.

7 knows how many calories an average person _____ in a day.

8 _____ yoga or goes to an exercise class.

9 has a parent or grandparent who _____ Nordic walking.

10 regularly _____ a team sport such as hockey or football when they were at school.

➤ Go back to page 54.

6.3 Food groups

A Write the food words in the box in the correct place.

| avocado   banana   cod   lettuce   lobster   oats   rice   shrimp   tomato   tuna   wheat |

Fruit and vegetables	Grains	Seafood

B Complete the lists with words from Exercise A.

1 Foods that are mostly used in salads: cucumber, _____, _____

2 Foods that are used in breakfast cereals: nuts, _____, _____, _____.

3 Examples of shellfish: crab, _____, _____.

C Complete the sentences with words from Exercise A.

1 I think I'll have a _____ mayonnaise sandwich.

2 The _____ is ground into flour, and this is the main ingredient of bread.

3 A prawn looks very much like a _____, but is smaller.

4 Sushi is made with raw fish, rice and sometimes _____ and _____.

5 I prefer white fish, like haddock and _____.

➤ Go back to page 57.

7.1 Feelings

A Match the adjectives (1–6) with their meanings (a–f).

1 pleased   a frightened or worried
2 cheerful   b calm and not worried
3 confused   c worried because you think something bad might happen
4 anxious   d happy and satisfied
5 relaxed   e behaving in a happy, friendly way
6 scared   f unable to understand something or think clearly about it

B Which words in Exercise A have similar meanings to these words? Are the words positive or negative?

glad: _____, _____

nervous: _____, _____

C Complete the sentences with adjectives from Exercise A. More than one answer may be possible.

1 I'm feeling _____ because I have an exam tomorrow.

2 Olaf's finished all of his work, so he's in a _____ mood.

3 That was a hard day, but now it's over I can feel _____ .

4 I'm not going anywhere near that spider – I'm too _____ .

5 I don't understand these questions – they just make me feel _____ .

6 Jordi's really _____ now that he has passed his driving test.

➤ Go back to page 63.

7.2 Shortened words

A Work in pairs. How do you shorten these words? Circle the parts of the words that can be shortened.

internet   introduction
website   information
university   newspaper
suitcase   aeroplane
mobile phone
microphone

B Complete the sentences with shortened words from Exercise A.

1 We need more _____ before we can make a final decision.

2 The singer dropped the _____ halfway through the song.

3 So many of the _____ on the _____ are basically just full of pictures of people's cats.

4 I asked the staff to let me take my _____ on to the _____ as carry-on luggage.

5 Read the _____ to this article in the _____ and see if you can understand it.

6 My parents are going to buy me a new _____ when I start _____ so they can call me at any time.

➤ Go back to page 65.

8.1 Music

Label the pictures (1–2) with the words in the box. You will need to use some words more than once.

> audience   drummer   drums   guitar
> guitarist   keyboard player   keyboards
> light show   microphone   singer   stage

➤ Go back to page 73.

8.2 Types of art

Look at the pictures (1–8). Label them with the words in the box.

> abstract art   exhibition   gallery   landscape
> photograph   portrait   sculpture   still life

The Hay Wain by John Constable

1 _____

Sunflowers by Vincent van Gogh

2 _____

Mona Lisa by Leonardo da Vinci

3 _____

Guitar on a Chair by Juan Gris

4 _____

David by Michelangelo

5 _____

Lunch atop a Skyscraper by Charles C Ebbets

6 _____

A collection of landscapes

7 _____

The Louvre, Paris

8 _____

➤ Go back to page 74.

9.3 *make* and *do* expressions

Match the expressions (1–6) with the pictures (a–f).

1 make a mess
2 make a mistake
3 do some damage
4 make a decision
5 do your homework
6 make a complaint

➤ Go back to page 87.

10.1 Electronic devices

A Label the pictures of electronic devices (1–6) with the words in the box.

> drone   e-reader   fitness tracker
> power bank   tablet   USB drive

1 _____   2 _____

3 _____   4 _____

5 _____   6 _____

B Complete the sentences with the devices in Exercise A. There is one word you do not need.

1 A _____ is great when you are not at home and your phone battery runs out.

2 He always uses his _____ to transfer large files.

3 I wear my _____ 24 hours a day. I love it because it tells me how many steps I take.

4 Tina got a _____ for her birthday, but she was flying it in the back garden and it got stuck up in a tree!

5 My husband won't buy an _____ because he says he loves the feel and smell of paper books.

➤ Go back to page 92.

11.1 Natural features

Label the pictures (1–8) with the words in the box.

> bay   canal   cave   cliff   desert   ocean   rainforest   valley

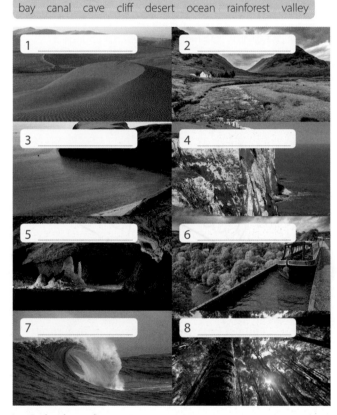

1 _____   2 _____
3 _____   4 _____
5 _____   6 _____
7 _____   8 _____

➤ Go back to page 102.

11.2 Animals

Write the animal words in the box in the correct place.

> alligator   ant   ~~bear~~   bee   butterfly   crocodile   duck
> eagle   elephant   fly   frog   gorilla   lion   lizard
> monkey   mosquito   moth   owl   panda   parrot
> penguin   shark   snake   tiger   toad   tuna

Mammals	Birds	Insects
bear		

Reptiles	Amphibians	Fish

➤ Go back to page 104.

Communication Hub

7.3 Student A

MICHAEL KEARNEY: the world's youngest university graduate

1984: born and grew up in Honolulu, Hawaii

4 months: spoke his first words

6 months: told his doctor, 'I have a left ear infection'

10 months: learnt to read

School: didn't go to school; his parents taught him at home; went to high school for one year; graduated and received his high school diploma when he was six

University: went to university to study anthropology; graduated from university aged ten; *The Guinness Book of Records* lists him as the world's youngest university graduate; appeared on TV chat shows; received a master's degree in biochemistry when he was 14, a master's degree in computer science when he was 18 and a doctorate in chemistry aged 22

Career: started teaching at university, aged seventeen

Other information
2006 and 2008: competed in several TV quiz shows and won over $1,000,000

➤ Go back to page 67.

9.2 Student A

A Write a definition for each word. Start your sentences with '*This is …*' and use a relative clause.

1 a philanthropist

   This is someone who gives money to help people.

2 a course book

3 a vegetarian

4 a hashtag

5 a mobile phone

6 money

B Read your definitions to Student B. Can he/she guess what you are describing?

➤ Go back to page 85.

4.2 Student C

ROBOT RELATIONSHIPS

Meet Pepper, the world's friendliest robot. Pepper's Japanese makers say the cute little robot can understand 70–80 per cent of conversations with a human. They even say Pepper can understand when someone is happy or sad. And this is just the beginning. Experts predict that in the future, humans will probably develop close relationships with robots.

At the moment, most of the robots in Japan look like Pepper, but it definitely won't be long until robots look, sound and move like humans. Erica, a robot developed by Professor Hiroshi Ishiguro of Osaka University, can show basic feelings on her face and gives us a better idea of what is already possible.

Experts such as Ishiguro think that developments in technology might help scientists to make machines that really understand human feelings. This means your robot might be able to work out if you are happy or sad and use this information to talk and behave like a friend. That could make it possible for robots to look after people. Some experts even believe that one day it may be possible for robots to feel love.

> **Glossary**
>
> **expert (n)** someone who knows a lot about a particular subject

➤ Go back to page 34.

3.2 Students C and D

Work in pairs. Look at the pictures to tell a story. Think about:

1 What happened during the journey?

2 What decisions did people make?

3 How did the people feel at the end of the journey?

➤ Go back to page 25.

11.2 Students A and B

Work in pairs. Choose one of the hobbies or activities and give suggestions and advice to improve. Use the phrases in the box.

> It's better (not)   It's easy   It's essential   It's good
> It's important   It's (not) necessary   It's useful   It's sensible

learn a musical instrument	live a 'green' lifestyle
do a sport	keep an animal as a pet
learn a language	have a job interview
keep fit and healthy	host a party

➤ Go back to page 105.

7.1 Student B

A Listen to Student A and write down the sentences he/she says.

B Read these sentences to Student A, who will write them down. Be careful to pronounce *a* and *an* using the weak sound /ə/ (schwa). Check Student A's sentences are correct.

1 It's **a** great idea.
2 We had **a** fun day.
3 It was **an** amazing time.
4 It was **a** total surprise.
5 He told **a** funny story.

C Tell your partner about events or situations that the sentences in Exercise B describe.

➤ Go back to page 63.

9.1 Group B

A SPEAK Look at questions 1–3 in Exercise B. What would you do in each situation? Why?

B Think of two more questions. Write them down. Use the second conditional.

1 If you had to choose between a luxury break for two in your country's capital and the very latest smart television with cinema sound, which would you choose?

2 If you had to choose between a well-paid job in a city you don't like and a slightly lower-paid job in a city you like, what would you do?

3 If you won €500, what would you spend it on? What about if you won €5000 or €50,000?

4 _____

5 _____

➤ Go back to page 83.

4.2 Student B

Social media 🐦 💬 👍

Social media is everywhere and is a normal part of many people's lives. However, experts agree that the way we use social media will change in the future.

Ten years ago, people used social media to share messages. Then everyone got cameras on their phones and began sharing pictures and video. But if Mark Zuckerberg of Facebook is right, you and your friends will soon put on your VR (Virtual Reality) headsets and meet in amazing 3D virtual worlds. Zuckerberg and Facebook are spending a lot of money on developing VR social media.

With VR social media, it will be possible to meet your friends 'inside' pictures and videos. This means, for example, that you will be able to spend time together at the top of mountains or the bottom of oceans! It will also be possible to hang out in virtual versions of real clubs or museums, or just about anywhere in the world (or the universe) you can imagine.

There is still a lot of work to do on the technology, so you might have to wait a while before you can share your selfies from the far side of the moon! However, experts agree that VR is the future of social media.

Glossary

expert (n) someone who knows a lot about a particular subject
virtual (adj) almost the same as the real thing

➤ Go back to page 34.

12.2 Group A

Box sets and on-demand viewing are better.

Here are some ideas for your argument. Add some ideas of your own.

- You can watch episodes when you want to and when is convenient for you.
- You will never miss an episode.
- It is easier to find a time to watch an episode or several episodes with other people, which can …

  be a fun social event.

  bring people closer together because of shared interest.

  help people to get to know each other.

➤ Go back to page 115.

Communication Hub

12.2 Group B

Traditional weekly TV shows are better.

Here are some ideas for your argument. Add some ideas of your own.

- You look forward to the show more.
- You don't become too obsessed with the show.
- There is no danger of binge-watching, which can …

  be bad for your health or eyesight.

  make your brain too active and cause sleeplessness.

  waste time.

➤ Go back to page 115.

10.2 Student A

A Look at the pictures. Think about how you will answer the questions. Make notes.

1 Can you describe the two pictures?

2 Which of these two ways of managing your money do you prefer and why?

3 What computer skills and knowledge about the internet does someone need to manage an online bank account?

B DISCUSS Your partner will ask you the questions in Exercise A.

C CHANGE Now ask your partner the following questions.

1 Can you describe the two pictures?

2 Which of these ways of communicating with other people do you prefer and why?

3 What computer skills and knowledge about the internet does someone need to make video calls?

D Can you think of one more question to ask?

➤ Go back to page 95.

9.2 Student B

A Write a definition for each word. Start your sentences with 'This is …' and use a relative clause.

1 a businessman or businesswoman

This is someone who works in business, especially in a top position.

2 a magazine

3 a professor

4 an emoji

5 the internet

6 food

B Read your definitions to Student A. Can he or she guess what you are describing?

➤ Go back to page 85.

12.2 Students A and B

Are you a binge-watcher? Are you addicted to TV? Do the quiz! Tick (✓) the sentences that are true for you. Then read what it means below.

You know you're a binge-watcher and addicted to TV if …

- you have ever said or thought 'Just one more episode'. ☐
- you dream, or daydream, about the show you're currently watching. ☐
- you feel that you know the show's characters as well as your actual friends. ☐
- when the series ends, you feel depressed (for around ten seconds until you start the next one). ☐
- you've stayed up all night, or at least until 3 am, watching episodes of a show. ☐
- the show is your favourite topic of conversation. ☐
- you want other people to watch the show and love it as much as you do. ☐
- watching the show, or even thinking about watching the show, is the best part of your day. ☐

What it means:

1–3 ticks: You enjoy watching TV shows. You are not addicted to TV, yet, but you are perhaps an occasional binge-watcher.

4–6 ticks: You are addicted to TV and probably a frequent binge-watcher. Be careful this doesn't take over your life.

7–8 ticks: You need to get a life!

➤ Go back to page 115.

3.3 Student A

The central three-star Hotel Rambla Park is 50 m from Barcelona's famous Las Ramblas walking street and close to some of its best shops, markets and restaurants. This attractive hotel has a good restaurant with room service and a small pool. All rooms are non-smoking and have air con, free wi-fi and a TV. One-way airport transfers are available for 15 euros per person. Reception is open 24 hours.

Room type: Double or twin room (extra bed available) – 40 euros per person, per night including breakfast.
Single room: 60 euros per night including breakfast.

⚹ Share   👍 Like   💬 Comment

➤ Go back to page 27.

10.2 Student B

A Look at the pictures. Think about how you will answer the questions. Make notes.

1 Can you describe the two pictures?
2 Which of these ways of communicating with other people do you prefer and why?
3 What computer skills and knowledge about the internet does someone need to make video calls?

B DISCUSS Your partner will ask you the questions in Exercise A.

C CHANGE Now ask your partner the questions below.

1 Can you describe the two pictures?
2 Which of these two ways of managing your money do you prefer and why?
3 What computer skills and knowledge about the internet does someone need to manage an online bank account?

D Can you think of one more question to ask?

➤ Go back to page 95.

12.3 Groups

Choose one of the products for your advertising campaign.

a   b   c

➤ Go back to page 117.

4.3 *Hygge* scores

What does your score mean?

7–10 points: Your lifestyle is already very *hygge*. Have you thought about moving to Denmark?!

4–6 points: Your lifestyle is quite *hygge*, but you could still learn a thing or two from the Danes.

0–3 points: Your lifestyle is not *hygge* at all. Be kind to yourself and let some more *hygge* into your life!

➤ Go back to page 148.

10.3 Students A and B

Do you have what it takes to work in space? Complete our survey to find out.

Tick (✓) the things you do or would like to do in your job.

Follow a detailed schedule	◯
Do research and collect data	◯
Do experiments and make discoveries	◯
Test or work with new technologies	◯
Solve problems	◯
Repair equipment	◯
Work away from home	◯
Study the mind or body	◯
Do dangerous work	◯
Work alone	◯
Work in a team	◯

Results

1–4 ticks: Space is probably not your place.
5–8 ticks: You could try a job in the sky.
9+ ticks: You'd be great for work on Mars or in the stars.

➤ Go back to page 97.

Communication Hub

3.3 Student B

Gaudí House Hostel is a half-hour walk or ten-minute bus journey from the centre of Barcelona and is perfect for travellers on a budget. The eight-person dorms (choose between male only, female only or mixed) are comfortable, the bathrooms are clean and the kitchen area has everything you need to cook for yourself. Guests can leave their valuables in the safe at reception. Wi-fi is available in the reception area. (Note: air con is not available in dorm rooms.)

Room type: Dorm bed 25 euros per person, per night. (Add breakfast for only 5 euros per person, per day!)

⚹ Share   👍 Like   💬 Comment

➤ Go back to page 27.

10.3 Groups

SPEAK Work in groups. Read the fact file and discuss the questions.

Mission to Mars

Distance: When Earth and Mars are closest, the distance between them is 57.6 million kilometres.

Journey time: 6–8 months one-way. Crew will be away from Earth for around two years.

Communication: As the ship moves further away from Earth, it will take up to 40 minutes to send and receive messages to and from Earth.

Mission: To visit and land on Mars and look for life. Crew will do research and experiments and collect data about the red planet.

1 What will be the biggest challenges for the crew on the mission to Mars?
2 What are the five most important skills and personal qualities crew members will need?
3 What kind of problems might they have to solve on the journey?
4 What will an average day be like on the space ship?

➤ Go back to page 97.

7.1 Student A

A Read the sentences to Student B who will write them down. Be careful to pronounce *a* and *an* using the weak sound /ə/ (schwa). Check Student B's sentences are correct.

1 It was **a** great party.
2 It's **a** really funny film.
3 It was **an** amazing view.
4 We had **a** lot of fun.
5 It put **a** smile on my face.

B Listen to Student B and write down the sentences he/she says.

C Tell your partner about events or situations that the sentences in Exercise B describe.

A: *My sister's 18th birthday was a great party. It was an amazing time and we had a lot of fun. We …*

B: *It was an amazing view from the top of the Eiffel Tower. I went there last year with …*

➤ Go back to page 63.

4.2 Student A

Work–life balance

Everybody loves long weekends, so why do they happen so rarely? When we have three full days off work, there is more time to relax and spend time with friends and family. The good news is that some people think it might not be long until *every* weekend is a long weekend.

Experts and business leaders predict that better technology will do more of our work for us. This will allow us to have shorter working weeks in the future. In fact, it is already beginning to happen. Carlos Slim, the famous Mexican telecoms billionaire, has introduced a shorter week for some of his older, more experienced employees. In Japan, companies such as car maker Toyota have found that working shorter hours leads to happier employees, and higher profits.

A better work–life balance won't be the only good thing about shorter working weeks. Offices will use less energy for lighting, computers and air conditioning. Also, there will be fewer car journeys to work, which is better for the environment.

Glossary

expert (n) someone who knows a lot about a particular subject
profit (n) money you make by selling something or from your business

➤ Go back to page 34.

9.1 Group A

A SPEAK Look at questions 1–3 in Exercise B. What would you do in each situation? Why?

B Think of two more questions. Write them down. Use the second conditional.

1 If you had to choose between having a new mobile phone and seeing your favourite band, which would you choose?
2 If you had to choose between a meal for two and an item of clothing, which would you choose?
3 If you could have a weekend break anywhere in the world, where would you go?

4 _____
5 _____

➤ Go back to page 83.

3.3 Student C

The Olympic Apartments are close to Barcelona's beaches and have beautiful sea views. The famous Las Ramblas walking street is a 20-minute walk away. The two- and three-bedroom self-catering apartments are simple and clean. Guests can pay to use the gym and spa on the first floor. Shops, public transport and restaurants are all very close. All apartments have a balcony and air con. Wi-fi is available for an extra 5 euros per day.

Room type: Two-bedroom self-catering apartment – 100 euros per night for up to four people.

➤ Go back to page 27.

5.1 Groups

Group A jobs: banker, nanny, professional footballer, politician

Group B jobs: doctor, pilot, social worker, actor

Group C jobs: lawyer, nurse, soldier, teacher

➤ Go back to page 43.

11.2 Students A and B

According to psychologists, the first animal you chose is how you like to see yourself. The second animal is how other people see you. And your third choice is what you are really like.

➤ Go back to page 104.

7.3 Student B

Judit Polgár: chess Grandmaster

1976: born in Hungary

Education: did not go to school; her parents brought her and her two sisters up as part of an 'educational experiment'; chess was the subject her parents chose

6 years: started playing in international tournaments

9 years: won her first international tournament

15 years: became the youngest person ever to become a chess Grandmaster

Career: was the world's number one female chess player for 20 years; has beaten 11 current or former male world champions

Other information

2012: started the Judit Polgár Chess Foundation; the aim is to introduce children around the world to chess

2014: retired from competitive chess; became head coach of the Hungarian National Men's Chess Team

➤ Go back to page 67.

3.2 Students A and B

Work in pairs. Look at the pictures and tell a story. Think about:

• what happened during the journey.
• what decisions the people made.
• how the people felt at the end of the journey.

➤ Go back to page 25.

Write information about yourself

W— checking your writing

Use it or lose it

Welcome. This is a blog for language learners written by … a language learner!

My favourite tip for people interested in learning languages is 'use it or lose it'. It means 'practise the language and you won't forget it'. I started this blog to practise my English. Would you like to practise your English? Send me a message in English and I'll reply. Twice a week, I'll post the most interesting messages on the blog.

About me

I'm Karolina. Tea drinker, [1]bloger and hard-working [2]langage learner. [3]I've 20 years old and I'm Polish. I study law at university, and English in my free time. I go to English lessons [4]three times week and I practise for half an hour every day. I have to be [5]wel organised to get everything done! Of course, I'm [6]serious with learning, but I also really enjoy it.

My blog [7]aren't my only hobby. I'm a book lover and I'm also [8]keen at old black and white films. I read and watch in Polish and English.

I'm a curious, sociable person and [9]I like talk to people who ask questions. I'm interested in creative types and I love meeting new people – especially other language learners (in the real world and online). I think that makes me a [10]person people. I hope you enjoy the blog. Remember … use it or lose it!

A Read the home page of Karolina's blog and answer the questions.

1 What is her blog about and who is it for?

2 How can you help Karolina?

B Work in pairs. Read the *About me* section of Karolina's blog. Then cover the blog and discuss what you remember about:

1 her work or studies   3 the type of person she is

2 her likes and dislikes

C Work in pairs. In Karolina's *About me* section there are ten mistakes with grammar, vocabulary and spelling. Correct them. Use the information in the box to help you.

Checking your writing

Follow these tips to help make your writing better.

- Always read your writing slowly and carefully before you finish.
- Try and find and correct any mistakes.
- Check your grammar.
- Check the vocabulary and spelling and be careful with any new language.

D Which colours are the different types of mistakes in Karolina's writing?

1 grammar mistakes   _____

2 vocabulary mistakes   _____

3 spelling mistakes   _____

E Find and correct one mistake in each sentence. Then decide what type of mistake it is. Write grammar (*G*), vocabulary (*V*) or spelling (*S*).

1 I'm a keen travller and I study tourism.   _____

2 Why you did start this blog?   _____

3 I try to learn a new word ever day.   _____

4 I usually am online during the evenings.   _____

5 I guess I'm an independant type.   _____

6 I'm responsible with updating the website.   _____

7 Are you want to know more about our group?   _____

8 I've never write a blog before.   _____

WRITING

A **PLAN** You are going to write an *About me* section for your own blog, website or social media page. Make notes about your work or studies, your likes and dislikes and the type of person you are.

B **WRITE** Use your notes and Writing Exercise A to help you write your blog. Then check your writing using the list below and the strategies in the Writing skills box.

- ☐ I have mentioned my work or studies.
- ☐ I have mentioned some of my likes and dislikes.
- ☐ I have described my personality and the type of person I am.
- ☐ I have checked my work for mistakes with grammar, vocabulary and spelling.

C **REVIEW** Work in groups. Read the group's profiles. Can you recommend any blogs, websites, magazines, books, TV shows or films the people in your group might be interested in?

A Read Emma's email about a problem in her neighbourhood. What is she complaining about?

To: Mr Black

Re: Road safety complaint

Dear Mr Black,

I'm writing to complain about the dangerous roads outside my block of flats.

My main complaint is that the roads are dangerous **because** there are no crossing points **or** traffic lights outside my block of flats. This is a problem for a number of reasons.

First of all, the traffic is very fast on the main road **and** this makes crossing difficult for older people and mothers with young children. The second problem is that there is a popular children's play area opposite the main road, **but** the children have no way to cross the road to use the play area. The last problem is that the supermarket car park entrance is on the corner of two busy roads, **so** it makes it more difficult to cross the road.

I would like to offer you two solutions for this problem. First of all, I think you should make a crossing point on the busy road between the supermarket and the children's play area. I also think you need to make a second crossing point across the main road from the block of flats to the play area. You could put traffic lights on this crossing to make it safe for children to use.

I hope you will make this dangerous road safer for the older people and children in our neighbourhood.

I'm looking forward to hearing from you.

Yours sincerely,

Emma Lopez

B Read again and answer the questions.

1 How many problems and solutions does Emma mention?

2 Do you think Mr Black will do what Emma wants him to do?

3 What tense does she use to begin and end her email?

C Look at the words in **bold** in Emma's email. Then complete the rules in the box with *and*, *but*, *or*, *so*, or *because*.

Linking words

We can join sentences and link ideas with *and*, *but*, *or*, *so* and *because*. This helps you to write longer and more interesting sentences.

We use [1]_____ to add more information.

We use [2]_____ to give contrasting information.

We use [3]_____ to give a negative alternative.

We use [4]_____ to give a result.

We use [5]_____ to explain why.

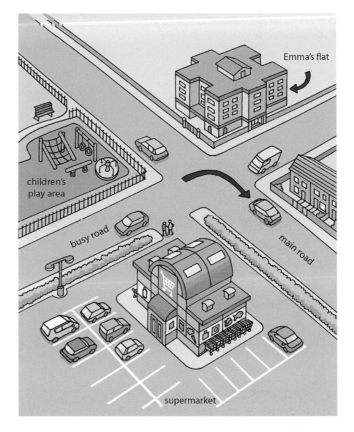

D Complete the sentences with *and*, *but*, *or*, *so* or *because*.

1 The air is dirty _____ there are too many cars.

2 There should be more green spaces for children _____ teenagers.

3 We shouldn't drop litter _____ play loud music.

4 We like the play area, _____ it's too small.

5 More children are living here, _____ the neighbourhood should be safer.

WRITING

A **PLAN** You are going to write an email of complaint. Think of a problem in your neighbourhood and two or more solutions to your problem.

B **WRITE** Write your email of complaint.

• Use Emma's email and the Writing skills box to help you.

• Check your writing for mistakes with grammar, vocabulary and spelling.

C **REVIEW** Work in groups. Read your emails and decide which one will be the most successful.

W— **ordering events**

A Work in pairs. Discuss the questions.

1 Why do some people feel it is important to have a holiday?

2 What kind of problems do people have on holiday?

B Read Amal's email. Underline any of the problems you thought of in Exercise A.

To: Cleo

Subject: We're back!

Hi Cleo,

How are you? Thanks for feeding the cat. We're home, but there's no electricity, so I'm writing this on my phone. We had a terrible holiday. Scott broke his leg!

First, bad weather delayed our flight. We arrived at the chalet in the middle of the night, so the next morning we were really tired. After breakfast, we went to the ski lifts, but they were closed because it was too windy.

The following day, it wasn't so windy and we had a great time on the slopes in the morning. Then, we stopped for some lunch, but when I wanted to pay I couldn't find my wallet!

Two days later, the real disaster happened. We were skiing down a busy slope when Scott fell over and broke his leg. We had to fly to the local hospital in a helicopter. His leg is in plaster for the next six weeks.

I'll call you tomorrow.

Amal

C Read again and number the events in the order they happened (1–6).

___ Scott had an accident.

___ There was a problem at Amal's home.

_1_ The flight left the airport late.

___ It wasn't possible to go up the mountain.

___ Amal lost something.

___ The weather was better.

D Find and underline the words that helped you order the events. There are six words or phrases.

E Complete the sentences with the words in the box. Use the information in the box to help you.

> **Ordering events**
>
> When you write about an experience, use sequencing words and phrases like the ones you underlined in Amal's email to help readers follow the order of events.

| after | ~~first~~ | hours | morning | next | then |

1 ___First___ , we missed the coach, so we had to take a taxi.

2 The following _____, I got the correct visa and crossed the border on foot.

3 The _____ day, we woke up to the sound of the sea.

4 We drove for four hours, and _____ stopped for some lunch.

5 Two _____ later, my friend found her mobile phone behind the sofa.

6 _____ a quick lunch, we set off walking again in the rain.

F Work in pairs. Cover Amal's email and retell the story using sequencing words and the events in Exercise C.

WRITING

A **PLAN** You are going to write an email to a friend about a good or bad travel experience. Think about the following:

1 Was it a good or bad experience?

2 Where were you and who were you with?

3 What happened?

4 How did the experience end?

B **WRITE** Write an email to a friend. Use the checklist to help you.

☐ I have written to a friend.

☐ I have started with an informal greeting and finished with an informal sign-off.

☐ I have used sequencing words and phrases to order the events.

☐ I have checked my spelling, vocabulary and grammar.

C **REVIEW** Work in pairs. Read your partner's email and ask questions about his/her experience.

W— informal emails

A Read Marta's message and answer the questions.

1 Why is Marta messaging her friends?
2 What kind of evening is she planning on Saturday?
3 What should her guests bring?

To: elviraandjan, ravi.gupta, stuart.jackson

Subject: Hygge Evening

Hi guys,

[1]How are things? Hope you're OK. [2]Life's good, but as usual, I'm looking forward to the weekend.

Actually, that is why I'm writing. [3]Are you doing anything on Saturday night? I'm planning a *hygge* evening round at my place from about 7 pm. [4]Can you make it?

I'm going to bake some cookies, light lots of candles and we could play a board game or watch a film – or both! 😃

Anyway, [5]let me know whether you can come. All you need to bring is yourself, some warm socks and a wool jumper 😉

[6]It would be lovely to see you.

Marta

B Look at Marta's message again. Match the underlined phrases (1–6) with the phrases with a similar meaning (a–f).

a Let me know if you're coming.
b Would you like to come?
c Everything is fine.
d Have you got any plans for …?
e How's life?
f I hope you can make it.

C Read two replies to Marta's message. Who is and is not coming to her *hygge* evening?

Dear Marta,

Lovely to hear from you!

Thanks for inviting us on Saturday. We'd love to come, but we're going to Jan's parents' house for dinner, so I'm afraid we can't make it. I'm meeting them for the first time! I'm sure it will be fine, but I am a bit nervous. Your *hygge* evening sounds much more relaxing!

Anyway, I'll let you know how it goes. Let's get together soon. I've got so much to tell you.

See you soon,

Elvira

Hi Marta,

Long time no see. I hope you're well!

Thanks for the invitation for Saturday. A *hygge* evening sounds like just what I need, and I'd love to come. Who else will be there? Are Elvira and Jan coming?

Are you sure I can't bring any food? I could do some homemade snacks or something.

Let me know. It'll be gr8 to see you.

Love,

Ravi

D Read again and underline the phrases Marta's friends use to:

1 say thank you
2 say yes to the invitation
3 say no to the invitation
4 give a reason for saying no
5 mention the next time they'll meet

E Complete the box with words from the emails in Exercises A and C.

Informal emails

Start informal emails with a friendly greeting.

• *Dear Marta,*
• *Hi/Hello Marta,*
• *Hi* [1]_____ (to a group; men, women or mixed)

Mention your last contact with other person.

• *Lovely to hear from you.*
• *Long time no* [2]_____ (when you haven't seen the person for a long time)

Use emoticons and abbreviations, but don't overuse them.

• *It'll be* [3]_____ *to see you.*

Don't use full forms. Use contractions.

• *I hope* ~~you are~~ *you're well.*
• *We* ~~would~~ [4]_____ *love to come.*

Finish with a friendly goodbye.

• *Bye for now,*
• [5]_____ *soon,*
• *Love,*

WRITING

A WRITE Work in pairs. You are organising a party at your place. Write a message inviting another pair of students. Use Exercise E above to help you. Write 100–150 words.

B WRITE Swap messages with another pair of students and reply to their invitation. Use the Writing skills box to help you. Write 50–100 words. Include the following information:

• say thank you for the invitation
• say yes or no to the invitation (if no, give a reason)
• mention the next time you'll meet

W – beginning and ending emails and letters

English-speaking holiday nannies and mannies (job s632)

Holiday Hands agency is looking for English-speaking nannies and mannies (male nannies) to travel with families on their summer and winter holidays. You will take care of the children during the day and babysit in the evenings. Experience is an advantage. Good pay, plus all travel, accommodation and food included. Reply with a CV and a copy of your passport to Olga Zatorska at ol.zator@holidayhands.nett

A Work in pairs. Read the advert. Would you or anyone you know be interested in this job? Why/Why not?

B Read Maurice's covering email. Do you think Maurice will be offered an interview? Why?

To: Ms Zatorska
Subject: Holiday manny job

¹Dear Ms Zatorska,

²I am writing to apply for the job of holiday manny with the Holiday Hands agency. ³I attach a copy of my CV.

⁴At the moment, I am studying at the University of Edinburgh and am available to work from 1ˢᵗ July to 30ᵗʰ September.

⁵I speak fluent English and Spanish and enjoy working with children. Last summer, I was an activities supervisor at a summer camp for 6–12-year-olds. My energy and creativity made me popular with the children. I believe this experience will be very useful. ⁶A job with the Holiday Hands agency would be an exciting opportunity to learn new skills and work in an international environment.

⁷I look forward to hearing from you.

⁸Yours sincerely,

Maurice Garcia

C Read again. Put the different parts of a covering email in the correct order (1–7).

___ why you want this job

___ what you are doing now and when you are available

___ polite ending

___ reason for writing

_1_ a formal greeting

___ details about your experience and character

___ attachments, for example, your CV

D Look at the box. Which beginnings and endings are formal (F)? Which are informal (I)?

Beginning and ending emails and letters

Beginning		Ending	
1 Hello,	_I_	7 See you soon,	___
2 Dear Sir/Madam,	___	8 Bye for now,	___
3 Dear all,	___	9 Lots of love,	___
4 Hi everyone,	___	10 Yours sincerely,	___
5 Dear Mr Cox,	___	11 Yours faithfully,	___
6 Dear Diane,	___	12 Kind regards,	___
		13 Best wishes,	___

E Replace the underlined phrases in the email with similar phrases in the box.

> Dear Sir/Madam,   I am fluent in
> I hope to hear from you soon.
> I would like to apply for   Please find attached
> the knowledge and skills I developed there
> Working for   Yours faithfully,

F Work in pairs. What kind of skills, experience and personality would be helpful for this summer job?

Waiters and waitresses wanted (job h384)

Are you looking for part-time work? We need friendly, hard-working people to join our evening table service team at Blue Moon Asian Food Centre. Experience is an advantage, but we will give full training. Attractive wages and free meals. Write with a CV to noi.warumdee@mail.nett.

WRITING

A PLAN You are going to write a covering email to apply for the job in Writing Exercise F. Make notes for a covering email. Use Exercise C to help you.

B WRITE Write your covering email. Use the strategies in the box and Maurice's email to help you.

A Read the product reviews from an online shopping website and match each review (1–3) with a picture (a–c).

a

b

c

1 **Really useful ★★★★★**
I bought this cool little device to help me get fit, and **I'm very** ¹ _pleased_ **with it**. It's comfortable and **I like the colour**. It tells me how many steps I've taken, and how many calories I've burnt each day. It also gives me information about how I slept. **It's very** ² _____ and I find it motivates me to do more exercise than before. **It's made of** rubber, so it's waterproof and also very light. **It was definitely** ³ _____ **the money** and it arrived the day after I ordered it. ⁴ _____ **recommended** for anyone who is interested in health and fitness.

2 **Ouch! ★★★☆☆**
I bought this a few weeks ago to help me exercise. **It was a** ⁵ _____ **price** and it seems to be **well made**. **It was easy to put together** and **came with** a book full of different exercises to try. **The only** ⁶ _____ **is** it is really difficult to use! My stomach muscles aren't very strong and I find most of the exercises in the book impossible. I'm sure with enough practice it will get easier, but for now I have to say I don't look forward to using it. ⁷ _____ **for** those who don't mind the pain!

3 **Save your money ★☆☆☆☆**
My girlfriend bought me these as a birthday present, but **I was very** ⁸ _____ **with them**. Yes, **they look nice** and are comfortable to wear, but there's one big problem. **They are really** ⁹ _____ **quality.** I wore them in the gym once, and after about half an hour, I noticed there was a hole in the side. Obviously these were very **badly** ¹⁰ _____. I sent them back to the website and got a new pair, but after a few more trips to the gym … it happened again! **I don't recommend these** at all. They were **a real** ¹¹ _____ **of money.**

B Read again. Complete the phrases in **bold** with the words in the box.

disappointed	highly	made	~~pleased~~	poor	problem
reasonable	recommended	useful	waste	worth	

C Read again. Which phrases in **bold** describe positive things about the products, which describe negative and which are neutral?

I'm very pleased with it. = positive

I was very disappointed with them. = negative

It's made of … = neutral

D Read the information in the box. Then read the reviews again and number the parts of a review in the correct order (1–4).

> ### Ordering information
>
> Think carefully about the order in which you present information in reviews and other types of factual writing. Organise your ideas into clear and logical paragraphs to make your writing easy for readers to follow.

negative points _____

recommendation (or not) _____

positive points _____

why you bought the product _____

E Work in pairs. Describe one product you have bought recently that you recommend and one that you do not.

WRITING

A **PLAN** Imagine you have bought one of the products below. Make notes on the following questions.

.a pair of running trainers

a fitness game for a games console

a winter sports jacket   a mountain bike

1 What positive points does the product have?

2 What negative points does the product have?

B **WRITE** Write a 100 word review of the product for a shopping website. Explain why you bought it and what positive and negative points it has. Then make a recommendation.

C **REVIEW** Work in groups. Read you classmates' reviews. Which are the best and worst products?

W— using survey report language

A Look at the chart. What does it show? Do any of the findings surprise you?

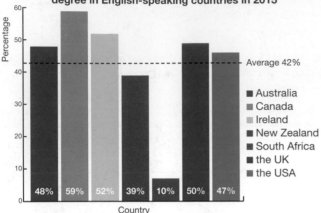

Percentage of population aged 25–34 with a university degree in English-speaking countries in 2015

| 48% | 59% | 52% | 39% | 10% | 50% | 47% |

Average 42%

- ■ Australia
- ■ Canada
- ■ Ireland
- ■ New Zealand
- ■ South Africa
- ■ the UK
- ■ the USA

Country

(c) OECD (2018), Population with tertiary education (indicator).

B Complete the survey report with the correct country.

The survey compares the percentage of people aged 25 to 34 with a university degree in English-speaking countries. According to the survey, an average of 42 per cent of the population of these countries are graduates. [1]_____ has the highest percentage of graduates at 59 per cent. In contrast, [2]_____ has the lowest with just ten per cent of the population having a university degree. The number of graduates in [3]_____ is just over 50 per cent, while in [4]_____ the figure is just under 50 per cent. Similarly, the figure for [5]_____ is 47 per cent, while in [6]_____, 39 per cent of people aged 25 to 34 are graduates.

C Look at the survey report again and complete the words and phrases in the box.

Using survey report language

We can say what the survey is about with:
- *The survey shows ...*
- *The survey [1]_____ ...*
- *According [2]_____ the survey, ...*

We can express differences with:
- *By/In comparison, ...*
- *By/In [3]_____, ...*

We can express similarities with:
- [4]_____, ...
- *Both ...*

We can give data and statistics by using:
- *... has the highest percentage of graduates at 59 per cent.*
- *... an average of 42 per cent of the population ...*
- *... has the lowest with just 7 per cent ...*
- *... the figure for the USA is 47 per cent ...*

Note the different uses of prepositions (*at, of*).

D Complete the sentences with the best words or phrases. Use the strategies in the box to help you.

1 As of 2015 the birth rate in the USA is just under two children per family. _____, in Europe it is around 1.5.

2 _____ the survey, 41 per cent of _____ men and women do sport to keep fit. Thirty per cent say they do sport for social reasons.[1]

3 The survey _____ IQs of brothers and sisters. It _____ that the oldest generally has the highest IQ.

WRITING

A **PREPARE** You are going to write a survey report about World Happiness. Read about the report. What areas of life do you think the survey asks questions about?

> **The World Happiness report** is an annual survey. It collects data from over 150 countries to find out which country has the happiest population. The survey asks people to decide how happy they are with different areas of their life.

B **PLAN** Look at the survey results.
- Decide which of the data you will include.
- Decide how you can compare and contrast the data.
- Use the report in Writing Exercise B to help you.
- Use the information in the *World Happiness* report.
- Use phrases from the Writing skills box.

C **WRITE** Write about 100–120 words. Check your writing for grammar, vocabulary and spelling.

World Happiness report	
Top four countries	**score (out of 10)**
Norway	7.54
Denmark	7.52
Iceland	7.50
Switzerland	7.50
Bottom four countries	**score**
Syria	3.46
Tanzania	3.35
Burundi	2.91
Central African Republic	2.69

Helliwell, J., Layard, R., & Sachs, J. (2017). World Happiness Report 2017, New York: Sustainable Development Solutions Network.

D **DISCUSS** Work in groups. Why do you think the countries in the survey are the happiest in the world?

1 Special Eurobarometer 412 "Sport and physical activity". © European Union, 1995-2017

W— describing and recommending

A Read the film review. Is it positive or negative?
Underline the words and phrases that tell you this.

La La Land is set in modern-day Los Angeles. It stars Emma Stone and Ryan Gosling. It tells the story of a romance between Mia (played by Emma Stone) and Seb (played by Ryan Gosling). She is an actress and he is a jazz pianist. The film is a musical, but it is also a classic love story with some wonderful music and singing and some old-fashioned dancing. At the same time, it is exciting, beautiful and heart-breaking. I found myself completely engaged with the story and with the lives of Mia and Seb. The acting was excellent. Emma Stone and Ryan Gosling were perfect as Mia and Seb. If you like musicals, you'll love this film.

 Share 👍 Like 💬 Comment

Comments:

Stacey99: I agree. Great film. I wasn't expecting that ending, but it's definitely worth seeing.

BillyTom: I liked the ending. I didn't imagine the story would finish that way. It was a nice twist!

DashaV: This film is a work of art, full of colour and life. A modern-day classic.

Rob78: Not my favourite film. But to be fair, I don't like musicals!

B Number the topics in the order they are written about in the review.

The film

___ the plot or story

_1_ where the film is set (location)

___ writer's opinion of the film

___ writer's opinion of the actors

___ writer's recommendation

___ film genre

C Read the comments again. Does each person like or dislike the film? Underline the words and phrases in the comments that tell you this.

D Cover Exercises A, B and C. Complete the missing words in the phrases from the review and comments.

Describing and recommending

1 *La La Land* is s_____ in …

2 It s_____ Emma Stone and Ryan Gosling.

3 It tells the s_____ of …

4 The f_____ is a musical.

5 The a_____ was …

6 It's (definitely) w_____ seeing.

E Write the missing words to complete the review.

The film is ___ ___ ___ in Los Angeles in 1961.
It ___ ___ ___ ___ ___ the true ___ ___ ___ ___ ___ of the author P.L. Travers and film-maker Walt Disney. Disney wants to make a film using one of Travers' books. It ___ ___ ___ ___ Tom Hanks. The ___ ___ ___ ___ ___ is excellent. This film is definitely ___ ___ ___ ___ ___ seeing.

WRITING

A **PREPARE** You are going to write review of a film that you have seen.

B **PLAN** Make notes for each topic in Writing Exercise B.

C **WRITE** Use the review in Exercise A and the strategies in the Writing skills box to help you write your review. Write about 100 words.

D **REVIEW** Work in pairs. Can you find someone in the class who has seen the same film? Read your partner's review and write a comment. Then work with another pair and add comments to their reviews.

W— describing a product

A Read the advice for writing a 'for sale' advert. Complete the advice with the words in the box.

accessories   buyer   condition   details   specifications

The key to a great ad

Attention: The title of the advert needs to get the ¹_____'s attention. Keep it short and simple. Start with the best or key feature of your item. This could be the price, its ²_____ or simply that it is a very popular item. If it has a fixed price, use words like 'only' and 'bargain'.

Description: Your advert needs a detailed description of the item. If needed, include the ³_____ , such as size, height and width. Include any ⁴_____ that it comes with, such as a battery charger. Include pictures to show what condition the item is in.

Action: Encourage the buyer to take action. For example, invite them to contact you with questions or for more ⁵_____. Say how you will post the item and offer free postage if possible.

B Look at the adverts. Do they follow the advice? Find and <u>underline</u> examples of:

- best or key features
- how good the price is
- specification (size or dimensions)
- accessories
- condition
- contacting the seller

digital camera – only £150

The camera is nearly new and hardly used. It comes in the original box and with a case, strap and spare battery. See picture. Please contact me if you have any questions.

Pen and ink drawing – auction

This is an original and signed pen and ink drawing by British illustrator William Miller. It shows a mountain scene in Scotland. The dimensions are 35 cm x 18 cm. The work is in good condition with a few minor marks. Please contact me for further information.

Men's trainers (size 40) – €40

I am selling a pair of trainers. They are size 40 and are yellow with grey stripes. They are in excellent condition with just a few light marks. I am selling them for the bargain price of €40. Free delivery. If you have any questions, just ask.

C Complete the box with words from the adverts.

Describing a product

Introducing the item
- *This is …*
- *I am* ¹_____selling_____ …

Describing its condition, specification and accessories
- *in excellent/good* ²_____ *, nearly* ³_____ *, hardly* ⁴_____
- *It comes in the original* ⁵_____
- *… with (just) a few (light/minor)* ⁶_____
- *It comes with …*
- *The dimensions are …*

Contacting the seller
- *Please contact me if you have any (further)* ⁷_____ *.*
- *Please contact me for further* ⁸_____ */details.*
- *If you have any questions, just* ⁹_____ *.*

D Correct the mistakes and rewrite the sentences from online 'for sale' adverts.

1 The phone comes in the origin box.
_____

2 I sell a Sony Bravia 65XE9005 TV.
_____

3 The camera is near new and is excellent condition.
_____

4 The item in good condition with a few lightly marks.
_____

5 Please contact for further informations and details.
_____

WRITING

A PLAN You are going to write a 'for sale' advert. Choose one of the items in the pictures or chose an item of your own. Invent some details about the condition of the item.

B WRITE Write your advert. Use the Writing skills box, the adverts and the advice to help you. Write 50–75 words.

C DISCUSS Work in groups. Show your advert to your group. Is anyone interested in buying your item?

A Work in groups. Answer the questions.

1 How many school subjects can you think of in one minute?

2 Which were your favourite and least favourite subjects at school, and why?

3 Were/Are you more interested in sciences, arts, languages or humanities (history, geography, etc)?

B Work in pairs. Read Bee's question on an online message board. What recommendation would you make for Bee and why?

Woohaa Answers 🔍

Bee, Thailand: Should I buy a laptop or a tablet?
I'm not sure whether to buy a laptop or a tablet. I need a computer for work, but also for entertainment at home and while I'm travelling. What do you think?

C Now read Dylan's answer and underline any ideas you or your partner said in Exercise B. What other advantages and disadvantages of laptops and tablets does Dylan mention?

Best answer
Dylan, USA
This is not an easy decision, Bee. If you choose the wrong computer, you might regret it. Before you decide, think about size and weight, performance and price.
Most laptops are bigger and heavier than the average tablet. This is partly because they have a normal keyboard. Size and weight may be a problem if you travel a lot or need to carry your computer to work each day.
When it comes to performance, laptops are usually faster and have a bigger memory than tablets. They are also better for people who need to have several apps or programs open at the same time.
On the other hand, the battery in a tablet computer will probably last longer between charges than the one in a laptop.
Of course, your budget is also important. Generally speaking, laptops are more expensive than tablets. If you travel regularly and want to spend less money, I'd recommend a tablet. If you want better performance and a normal keyboard, I'd suggest buying a laptop.
I think you should do some more research online. You could also talk to someone in a computer shop and ask for their opinion. Good luck!

D Read the information in the box. Then find and underline four examples of the structures in the box in Dylan's answer.

Making recommendations

You can tell people what you think they should do using the following language:

- *I think you should* + infinitive without *to*
- *You could* + infinitive without *to*
- *I'd suggest* + noun **or** verb + *-ing* **or** *you* + infinitive without *to*
- *I'd recommend* + noun **or** verb-*ing* **or** *you* + infinitive without *to*

E There is one mistake in each recommendation. Correct the mistakes.

1 I think you should getting a new phone rather than a used one.

2 I'd recommend you checking a used phone carefully before you buy it.

3 You could reading more about different brands online.

4 I'd suggest to buy a used phone because you'll get better performance for your money.

F Work in pairs. Imagine a friend has asked you the following questions. What would you recommend and why? Compare your ideas.

1 Should I travel for six months or get a job straight away when I finish university?

2 What brand of computer do you think I should I buy?

3 Should I study science or languages?

WRITING

A WRITE Read Corey's question on the *Woohaa Answers* website. Write a reply of at least 100 words comparing the two options and making recommendations.

Woohaa Answers 🔍

Corey, Germany: Should I buy a new or used phone?
Should I buy a new mobile phone or a used one? I don't have a lot of money to spend on it, but I'd like the best one I can afford. What do you think?

B REVIEW Work in groups. Read your group's recommendations. In what ways are they similar or different to yours?

Ⓦ— making suggestions and giving advice

A Look at the places in the pictures. Where do you think they are? Read the emails quickly and match them with the pictures. Were your ideas correct?

C Complete the box with words from the emails.

Making suggestions and giving advice

When/If you're in …
I suggest you …
I'd ¹_____ *+ verb + -ing …*
You (really) ²_____ */ ought to / must …*
If I ³_____ *you, I* ⁴_____ *…*
… is a must.
Make ⁵_____ *you …*
It's a good ⁶_____ *to …*

	To: Sam
a	Subject: RE: Any advice?

You really must visit the Joshua Tree National Park when you're in California. It isn't far from Los Angeles and it's really easy to get to by car. It's named after the famous Joshua trees that are found there. It's an amazing desert landscape with huge rocks and boulders everywhere. If I were you, I'd spend at least two days there. You can camp there, but it's a good idea to book in advance.

	To: Carlos
b	Subject: RE: Vietnam tips

In Vietnam, Halong Bay is a must. There are thousands of different-sized islands and rock formations coming out of the sea. It really is an incredible place. According to legend, the bay was formed when an angry dragon destroyed a mountain with its tail. It isn't too far from Hanoi. I'd recommend taking an organised tour from there.

	To: Teresa
c	Subject: RE: Where to go

If you're in the north of England, you really should visit the island of Lindisfarne. It's about a mile from the mainland and you can drive across to it when the tide is out. But when the tide comes in, it becomes a true island. It's a magical place with some beautiful beaches. I suggest you head to the north of the island to get away from the crowds of people. Make sure you check the times of the tides so you know when it's safe to cross.

B Read again and complete the table.

	a	b	c
Name of place			
Location			
Key features			
How to travel there			

D Write the words in the correct order to make sentences.

1 It's / to / a / book the train in advance / idea / good

2 I / in April or May / suggest / go / you

3 I'd / at least two or three days / staying / recommend

4 If / in Krakow, / you're / the Wieliczka Salt Mine / visit / really / you / should

5 When / in Oxford, / you're / make / you / sure / the Natural History Museum / visit

6 If / I'd / you, / were / I / for a few days / hire a car

WRITING

A **PLAN** Imagine a friend is visiting your country or a country you know. You are going to write a short email (50–100 words) to make some suggestions and to give some advice about a place to visit.

B **WRITE** Use the Writing skills box and include information about:

- where it is
- how to get there
- the main features of the place

C **REVIEW** Work in groups. Read each other's emails. Which place would you most like to visit?

A Work in pairs. Read the news story then close your books and retell the story to your partner. What do you think of Brett Sanders's actions?

Texan driver paid speeding ticket with over 22,000 one cent coins.

Brett Sanders was driving at 39 mph in a 30 mph zone when he was stopped by police and was given a $212 fine.

Sanders said the fine was too much and that he wanted to make some kind of complaint. So, he ordered over $212 in one cent coins from the bank and put them into two large buckets. He then went to the payment office and poured the 22,000 coins onto the counter. When he had done this, he immediately walked out of the building. A friend filmed him while he was doing this. He told reporters that after he had done it, he 'felt great'.

According to the payment office, Sanders had actually overpaid by $7.81. They telephoned him to offer a refund, but Sanders was happy to let them keep the change.

Many people have said Sanders's actions were wrong. At the same time, other people think it was a good way to make a point. What do you think?

B Look at the box. Find and <u>underline</u> more examples of the three tenses in the news story.

Writing a story

Tenses

When we tell a story, we usually use three main tenses.

We use the past simple for the main events in the story.

- *So, he ordered over $212 in one cent coins from the bank and put them into two large buckets.*

We use the past continuous for background activities or situations that were in progress when the main events happened.

- *Brett Sanders was driving at 39 mph in a 30 mph zone when he was stopped by police and was given a $212 fine.*

We use the past perfect for events that happened before one of the main events or that happened before the time of the story.

- *When he had done this, he immediately walked out of the building.*

Sequence words

We use sequence words to connect the events and make the sequence clear.

- *Brett Sanders was driving at 39 mph in a 30 mph zone when he was stopped by police ...*
- *So, he ordered over $212 in one cent coins from the bank ...*
- *He then went to the payment office and poured the 22,000 coins onto the counter. When he had done this, he immediately walked out of the building.*
- *A friend filmed him while he was doing this. He told reporters that after he had done it, he 'felt great'.*

C Choose the correct words to complete the news story.

A surfer [1]***was rescued / had been rescued*** yesterday [2]***while / after*** he [3]***was spending / had spent*** 32 hours at sea. It [4]***got / was getting*** dark [5]***when / then*** the helicopter rescue team [6]***spotted / were spotting*** him 13 miles off the coast of Scotland. He [7]***was / had been*** exhausted and thirsty, but he survived as he [8]***wore / was wearing*** a wetsuit and [9]***was / had been*** still on his surfboard.

WRITING

A **PREPARE** Look at the pictures and imagine what the story is. You are going to write a short story using all the pictures. Use this as you first sentence:

A man was arrested yesterday for driving a children's electric car.

B **PLAN** Makes notes and think about the tenses and the sequence words you need to use.

C **WRITE** Write the story (130–150 words). Check what you have written and make any necessary changes.

D **REVIEW** Work in groups. Read some of your classmates' stories. How similar are your stories?

Audioscripts

UNIT 1

Lesson 1.1, Listening, Exercise C

1.1 **P = Paul   I = Isabelle**

P: Hello, and welcome to *Everyday Psychology*. I'm Paul Ross, and with me today is psychologist and expert on relationships, Isabelle Ackerman.

I: Hello, Paul. Hello, listeners.

P: Isabelle, today's topic is meeting new people. Now, we often meet new people at work or in our social lives, but it can be difficult to talk to someone we don't know. I mean, what do you say to a stranger at a party or a new colleague at the office? Is it ok to talk about some topics, but not others? Have you ever met someone new and had no idea what to talk about? Today, you have some advice to help us 'break the ice' and start conversations with new people.

I: Yes, I do. Let's begin with a very simple tip. When you meet someone new, start with a smile. A smile can help us feel more relaxed, but that's easy to forget when you feel nervous.

P: And of course a friendly face is easier to talk to.

I: Yes. A nice way to continue a conversation is to say something positive. You could talk about the place or situation you are in and then ask a question. For example, at a party, try 'Are you having fun?' or 'I love this music! What is your favourite band?' To a new person at work, you can say 'Oh, I'm glad it's lunchtime. How's your first day going?'

P: So no complaining about the boss!

I: Not at first, no. But it is good to ask about other people. For example, in a new group of students, ask 'Do you know our teacher?' or, at a wedding ceremony, 'Did you enjoy the ceremony?' or 'How do you know the happy couple? Were you at school together?' Don't be negative about other people because you don't know who they know.

P: Yes, that could be dangerous.

I: Interests and studies are always good, safe topics to talk about. Questions like 'What kind of music do you like?' or 'Where did you study?' are usually easy to answer. Remember, ask lots of questions and give lots of answers. A successful conversation is like a game of tennis!

P: It takes hours and makes you tired?

I: Very funny. When you feel more relaxed, ask some personal questions. 'Where are you from?', 'Are you married?' and 'Do you have children?' are good examples. But be careful. Don't discuss topics like religion or politics with someone you don't know.

P: Some great tips. Isabelle, thank you very much. That's all for this week. Remember, many great friends meet after a smile and a simple 'hello'. Good luck breaking the ice and meeting new people. Please join us for the next episode of *Everyday Psychology* – we'll be discussing the hot topic …

UNIT 2

Lesson 2.2, Listening, Exercise B

2.2 **P = Presenter   R = Richard**

P: More and more of the world's young people are going home to live with their parents after college or university. Why? And what is it like living at home again as an adult? How do parents feel about the situation? Today, we talk to members of 'the boomerang generation' and their parents about the advantages and disadvantages of living together again. Let's start with Richard …

R: I'm Richard Woodman, from the UK. I'm 25 years old and at the moment, I'm living at home with my mum and dad. I … er … graduated two years ago, but I'm still looking for a permanent job. I love my parents, but we … em … well, they are difficult to live with. We argue about the rules all the time. I'm sleeping in my old room and living with the people who took me to the park when I was little! I know I'm lucky to be here, but it's … you know … it isn't easy.

Lesson 2.2, Listening, Exercise C

2.3 **P = Presenter   R = Richard   G = Gordon   A = Alice   C = Carla**

P: More and more of the world's young people are going home to live with their parents after college or university. Why? And what is it like living at home again as an adult? How do parents feel about the situation? Today, we talk to members of 'The boomerang generation' and their parents about the advantages and disadvantages of living together again. Let's start with Richard …

R: I'm Richard Woodman, from the UK. I'm 25 years old and at the moment, I'm living at home with my mum and dad. I … er … graduated two years ago, but I'm still looking for a permanent job. I love my parents, but we … em … well, they are difficult to live with. We argue about the rules all the time. I'm sleeping in my old room and living with the people who took me to the park when I was little! I know I'm lucky to be here, but it's … you know … it isn't easy.

G: My name is Gordon Woodman. I'm Richard's dad. Of course, Richard's mum and I are, well, we're happy he is staying with us … most of the time. We're his parents and he can always rely on us, but we er … we hope he finds the right job and, well, moves out as soon as possible. I want to make his bedroom into my home office. And his music, it's … well you know, thump, thump, thump all day and night. It drives me crazy! Anyway, we think he needs to be more independent. We love him, but he's unhappy, and he isn't learning about adult life living here with us.

A: Hi, I'm Alice Melo from Portsmouth, in England. I'm 28 years old and I graduated last year. I work as a dentist and, at the moment, I'm living with my parents to save money for my own place. Well, I'm trying to save money anyway, ha ha! I studied in Scotland, but I … er … couldn't find a job there, so, you know, I came back home. More and more of my friends are moving back home. It's great! Mum cooks and does all my washing. She won't take any money from me … I tried, but … er … so I'm not paying any bills. Of course, I help … sometimes … I help with the housework and the garden, I mean, now and again, you know. One day, I will do something special to thank them.

C: I'm Carla Melo, Alice's mum. We're very happy our daughter is home again. She's working hard and she wants to get her own place, but I always tell her she can live here with us forever! She's an adult now, I know, but she's still my baby! This year, my husband is travelling a lot for work, for his job, you know, so I'm very happy Alice is here with me. I don't like being on my own. I can talk to her, and she can save money and enjoy her mum's cooking.

UNIT 3

Lesson 3.2, Listening, Exercise C
3.4 C = Chloe   M = Matt

C: Welcome to this week's *Amazing Adventures* podcast. I'm Chloe Cole, and with me is sailor and survival expert Matt Cabral. This week, the amazing story of the Robertson family and how they survived a month lost at sea in the Pacific Ocean.

In 1970, Dougal and Lyn Robertson and their four children were living on a farm in northern England. One ordinary day, Neil, one of their ten-year-old twins, said he wanted to leave the farm and sail round the world. Most families would probably laugh and say 'don't be silly', but the Robertsons saw the chance for an adventure. They sold their business, bought a boat, and on 27th January 1971, started their journey across the Atlantic. Matt, what do you think of their decision?

M: Incredible. I mean, Dougal was an experienced sailor, but it was still a brave decision. Perhaps not very sensible, but definitely brave!

C: Ha ha, yes. Well, sensible or not, the Robertsons made it across the Atlantic safely in their 13-metre boat, *The Lucette*. But on 15th June 1972, while they were sailing out into the Pacific Ocean, things started to go very wrong.

Their boat was passing the Galapagos Islands when they noticed something large in the water behind them. It was a group of killer whales swimming towards the boat. Douglas, the eldest son, has said that when he saw the whales, he thought they were going to kill and eat the family. Well, the whales hit and sank their boat, but amazingly, the Robertsons all made it onto their small life raft, scared, but alive. I mean, they were very unlucky, weren't they, Matt?

M: Yes, they were. On average, there are only two to three accidents with boats and whales per year. But believe it or not, it wasn't all bad. I mean, firstly, the whales didn't eat them.

C: Ha! That's true.

M: And the life raft and another very small wooden boat survived the accident. And luckily they were carrying some water, some dry bread, biscuits, a bag of onions and some fruit in the life raft.

C: Yes, but after six days, all the food was gone, so they collected rainwater to drink and killed turtles and ate the meat and drank the blood. Then, 17 days after the accident, their life raft failed and they had to move to their wooden boat. It was called *the Ednamair* and was only three metres long. Can you imagine the whole family in that small boat?

M: It sounds like an impossible situation. You have to be strong and stay positive to survive something like this. There was only one dry seat in the boat, so most of the time they were sitting in water. But they didn't give up hope.

C: And finally, 38 days after the accident, a Japanese fishing boat found them and took them to dry land and safely.

M: It's an incredible story of survival.

C: Yes, it is. And now, Douglas Robertson works as an accountant in London, and amazingly, he has said that he actually enjoyed the family's adventure!

UNIT 4

Lesson 4.1, Listening, Exercise B
4.1 S = Sylvia   G = Greg

S: Greggy! Ahhhhhh! It's so nice to see you!

G: Hi, Syl. Give me a hug. It's lovely to see you, too … Do you have to call me Greggy?

S: Ha ha. Yes, and I'm going to introduce you to all my new friends as 'Greggy'. Was the journey OK?

V: Sure, sure. Mum gave me a lift to the station. She sends her love. She misses her darling daughter et cetera, et cetera. She's going to call later.

S: Oh, good. How's Claire? Are you two OK? Still madly in love?

G: Oh, yeah, you know. Lucky girl.

S: Stop it.

G: She wanted to come this weekend, but tomorrow evening she's having dinner with some old friends. They arranged it ages ago.

S: Of course. Never mind. Hopefully she'll make it next time. I've got so many plans for us this weekend! It's such a great city. I can't wait to show you round. Are you hungry?

G: Always.

S: Yep, silly question. Let's go for lunch.

G: Wow, this place is cool.

S: Nice, right? I hang out with my friends here a lot. I think I'm going to bring Mum and Dad here, too … if they ever come and visit!

G: Ha! They will. And then they'll never leave!

S: Ha!

G: So, what are all these plans you've got for us then?

S: Well, when we've finished lunch, I'm going to text Angie and Mark and tell them to come and meet us, and we're going to go for a walk and show you the city centre. Then we're meeting Duncan and Alicia at three o'clock, and I think we're going for a coffee somewhere, but I'm not sure where.

G: Duncan and Alicia?

S: Oh, they're great. You'll like Duncan. He's a bit like you.

G: What, handsome and intelligent?

S: Err … more like he's always thinking about his next meal.

G: I like him already.

S: After that, we're going to the market to look round; it's a beautiful old building, and we're going to do some food shopping because Duncan is making a curry for us all tonight. He's a great cook. Alicia says she and Duncan are going to open a restaurant one day. Anyway, …

G: Sounds great.

S: OK, so then tonight, we're going to the theatre.

G: The theatre?

S: Yes, I've got tickets for a Shakespeare play.

G: What?

S: Ha ha! Only joking. We're seeing a comedy show. One of my friends is filming the show and he got us some free tickets.

G: Phew. That's more like it. What a fantastic day you have planned, Syl! I can't wait.

S: And that's just today. Wait until you hear about tomorrow … In the morning, we're …

G: Er, Syl, hang on. Did you hear that?

S: What?

G: Listen!

S: What? Is it the music?

G: No … no … it's … I think … yes, it's the sound of my empty stomach. Are we getting something to eat, or what?

S: Pfffft. You and your stomach. Pass me a menu …

UNIT 5

G: Good morning. You must be Barry. I'm Gemma.

B: Oh mmmm hmmfff … sorry. I'm just finishing my sandwich!

G: That's OK … Egg sandwich, is it?

B: Er … Yes, egg. Sorry. My favourite. Nice to meet you, Emma.

G: It's Gemma.

B: Pardon?

G: It's Gemma, not Emma.

B: Sorry! What a terrible start.

G: Please don't worry, Barry. Gemma. Lockwood. Base One IT Services. I work in Human Resources. Sorry we're a bit delayed today. Have you been here long?

B: Actually, I've been here since 9 am.

G: You've been here for … three hours?

B: Yes, well, I didn't want to be late. That's why I was hungry.

G: OK … well … er … good! Come in and have a seat.

B: Thanks.

G: So, Barry, we are looking for people to work at our head office in the customer services team. First, could you tell me a little about yourself?

B: Ha ha. OK. Well, I'm Barry. I'm er … 23 years old. Single, male, blonde hair. Rather nervous in interviews … ha. I er … I'm one metre tall, I have a cat called Yoda and I love … er … egg sandwiches, ha ha, and … erm … computers and … wait, did I just say one metre tall? Ha ha sorry. Er … I'm one metre seventy tall, and I …

G: Er … Barry, perhaps we could focus on your work experience. You work for a telemarketing company at the moment, is that right? How long have you worked there?

B: Er, well, I left my old job in June … and now it's … well, I … I've worked at the call centre for six weeks. Have you read my CV? I did send one. I mean, I wrote everything there, so …

G: Er … yes, but … tell me more. For example, why do you want to change jobs and work for Base One?

B: Oh, well, that's easy; I hate my job at the call centre! I sit on the phone all day long asking people questions and nobody wants to talk to me. People get really angry and sometimes, well, they put the phone down.

G: I … see. Er … So, what do you know about Base One?

B: About what? OH! Yes … well … I'm … I think it's … could you repeat the question, please?

G: Er … well … OK. What do you know about Base One IT Services?

B: Erm, well Base One is a … great IT company, with … great services … and the office here is … erm … really cool. And, you seem very nice, and I …

G: Barry, ahem! Teamwork is very important for us here at Base One. Can you tell me about a time when you worked as part of a team?

B: Erm, you mean a real example?

G: Er, yes.

B: Let me think … err, I … erm, actually … err …

G: Erm … OK. It says on your CV that you enjoy skydiving. Wow! How long have you been interested in that?

B: Oh, well. I've liked skydiving since I was a teenager. It just looks so exciting! I've always wanted to try it.

G: So you haven't actually tried skydiving?

B: Well, I really want to.

G: And French poetry?

B: What?

G: Your CV says you enjoy French poetry.

B: Does it? Oh yes! That's right. Of course, French poetry – love it.

G: Er, Barry, I, er, I think we've finished for today.

B: Oh, great – that was quick.

G: Yes, er … do you er … do you have any questions?

B: Erm … No! No, I don't!

G: OK, so thanks again and … please don't call us … we … er, we'll contact you. Thank you, Barry.

B: No, thank YOU, Emma.

UNIT 6

🔊 **Lesson 6.1, Listening, Exercise C**

6.1 **P = Pippa   DS = Doctor Singh   M = Michael**
DT = Doctor Tremblay   L = Lia

P: G'day, Australia! Pippa Chan on chatfmmelbourne.nett. Today, we are talking about health myths.

Half an hour on the internet leaves most people pretty confused about what's good for their health and what isn't. You know, one article says 'you drink too much coffee, but you don't drink enough water', then the next says coffee is good for you, but too much water is dangerous! Confusing? Very!

I mean, let's say you are one of the many people who goes through life feeling tired a lot of the time. If you look online, you'll find one expert that says 'you don't sleep enough' and another that says 'you sleep too much'. Ha! And if you can't sleep? Oh, it's because you go to bed too early. No, no, no it's because you don't go to bed early enough! And of course EVERYthing makes you fat.

So how do we know what to believe? Well, we've been down to Melbourne City Hospital to ask some medical professionals about the reality behind some common health myths. Let's hear from the experts …

DS: Hi. I'm Dr Singh and I work at Melbourne City Hospital. My myth concerns how much water we need to drink. Most people have probably heard that not drinking enough water can cause headaches. And they are right – that isn't a myth. But many of us have probably also heard that we need to drink eight glasses of water per day to stay healthy – well, that isn't exactly true. The eight glasses, or around two litres, includes all liquids: tea, coffee, juice, etcetera – plus the water you get from food, which is around one fifth of your daily total. So how much water should we drink? Well, my advice is drink when you are thirsty and you'll be OK.

M: Hi, my name is Michael. I'm a nurse here in Melbourne. Many people believe that eating fatty food makes them fat, but in fact, that isn't the whole truth. Eating more calories than you need makes you fat. Yes, it's true that fat has lots of calories, but so do carbohydrates and sugars. It isn't actually too much fat that makes you fat, it's too many calories. Some fat is necessary, so you can still enjoy your burger as part of a balanced diet. And to burn those extra calories? Get up off that sofa and get moving!

DT: Hi, I'm Dr Tremblay from Canada. The Australian winter is here and so are colds and flu. You remember Grandma's advice … 'Hat! Scarf! Keep warm, or you'll catch a cold.' Well, Australia isn't as cold as Canada, but it is sensible to make sure you're warm enough. However, the truth is that cold weather doesn't cause colds and flu. They are caused by viruses. You are more likely to catch a cold inside, where there are lots of people. And remember, if you have a cold and are suffering with a headache, a cough or a sore throat, get plenty of rest, drink warm drinks – unless you have a temperature – and make sure you are getting enough vitamins. Don't take antibiotics! They don't kill viruses and they won't help a cold.

L: Hi, I'm Lia. I'm a medical student from London and I want to talk about eggs! Some people believe that you shouldn't eat more than one or two eggs a week. This is probably because of old advice. In the past, the warning was always 'too many eggs are bad for your heart', but we now know that an egg or two per day doesn't increase the risk of heart disease in healthy people. Egg-cellent news for egg lovers – Egg-xactly what they wanted to hear! Ha ha – sorry!

P: Wow! Thank you to all our egg-sperts. Interesting stuff! We'll be back with music from Enrique Egg-lesias after the break.

UNIT 7

🔊 **Lesson 7.3, Listening, Exercise C**

7.4 **S = Shauna**

S: Welcome to *Great Minds*. I'm Shauna Andrews, and today we're talking about William James Sidis. You have possibly never heard of him. But he is perhaps one of the most intelligent people who ever lived. He had an IQ of between 250 and 300.

He was born in the United States in 1898, and grew up in New York. His parents, who were originally from Ukraine, were doctors and were both highly intelligent.

They wanted to give their son the best possible chance in life. So, his mother gave up her job and taught him at home. He didn't go to school. And they brought him up to have a 'love of knowledge'.

As a result, Sidis was reading and writing at 18 months, and enjoyed reading the *New York Times* newspaper. He wrote several books and newspaper articles before he was four and, by the time he was eight, he spoke seven languages. He also made up his own language, which he called 'Vendergood'. At 11, he went to university to study maths – to Harvard University, actually. And in fact, he had previously given a maths lecture there when he was nine. Sidis became front page news and news reporters followed him everywhere at the university. He became known as a child prodigy all over the country.

Sidis graduated from Harvard University with a degree in mathematics at age 16. He then joined Rice University as a teacher of maths. However, he found teaching difficult, especially because of his age. After only eight months, he left Rice University and went back to Harvard, this time to study law.

While studying law, he became more and more interested in the political and social issues of the day. And as a result, he dropped out of university before he finished his degree. This was a big turning point in his life. Soon after, in 1918, he was arrested while he was taking part in an anti-war demonstration. He received an 18-month prison sentence. However, he didn't go to prison and instead he spent a year in hospital. It was actually the hospital where his parents worked.

After this, Sidis tried to stay out of the public eye. He moved from city to city around America and he had a number of simple low-paid jobs. He became more and more lonely and finally, he fell out with his parents and lost contact with them. The newspapers printed stories about how the child prodigy had failed as an adult.

After his death in 1944, many people questioned his high IQ and many of his other childhood achievements. Despite this, Sidis has been the subject of a number of books and academic studies and he is still one of the world's greatest child prodigies.

UNIT 8

 Lesson 8.1, Listening, Exercise C
8.2 **L = Lizzie   S = Suzy**

L: Welcome to *Music matters* with me, Lizzie Reid. Our taste in music says a lot about who we are. But why do we have different tastes in music? To answer this question, we are joined by Professor Suzy Harrison, an expert in the psychology of music. Welcome, Suzy.

S: Hello, thank you.

L: So, why do some people, say, prefer rock music or blues or jazz, while other people prefer pop or rap music?

S: Well, there are three main points which might explain our taste in music. The first is the music we grew up with. We don't choose this music ourselves, of course. But as a child, the music that we hear at home is familiar and comforting. Later in life, these same sounds bring back these feelings and this gives us pleasure. So, when we start to discover music by ourselves, it is influenced by what we listened to when we were growing up.

L: So, you're saying our first musical influence is our parents and our brothers and sisters?

S: Yes, that's right – particularly, our older brothers and sisters. Secondly, music brings people together. It creates an atmosphere and mood that people can share. So the second point is that we listen to certain types of music to help us form or join social groups. We want to be with people similar to ourselves. In contrast, for other people, musical taste is a way to make themselves different from other people. It's a way to be an individual. If you listen to music that others don't like, people will see you differently.

L: Yes, and I suppose it's true that we are generally attracted to people with similar music tastes to our own.

S: Yes, that's generally the case. And the third point is about how we feel when we listen to the music. Music can help to create a mood! For example, when you want to study, you might listen to something in the background, something without words – classical music, for example. And when you're preparing for a night out, you might want to energise yourself and play something loud

and full of energy – maybe some rock or pop or reggae music. At other times, you might play the same sad song over and over again. Because of the internet, finding music is very quick and easy for our different moods. Interestingly, studies have shown that because of this easy access to different kinds of music, people today like a much wider range of music styles compared to previous generations.

L: I see. So, our individual taste in music is a combination of three things: the music we grew up with, the need to fit in with other people and finally, to match our different moods?

S: Yes, that's right. Of course, one thing may be stronger than the others. But, yes, over time it is most likely a combination of these things which influence our music choices.

L: Very interesting, Professor Harrison. Thank you for speaking to us today.

S: You're welcome.

 Lesson 8.3, Listening, Exercise C
8.7 **A:** … Well, I'd say the main difference between films and books is how they tell the story and how we connect with it.

B: Yes, I agree. Books allow the reader to use their imagination. We can visualise the story and the people and the places in our own way. With films, on the other hand, we see what the director and the actors want us to see. There's much less possibility for us to use our own imagination.

A: I agree. And another important difference is that with books, the story generally moves more slowly and goes into more detail. With a film, though, the whole story needs to start and finish in 90 minutes. So, in a book, we have more time to get to know the characters and to understand them. I think this makes the experience more personal and engaging.

B: Well, yes, I see what you mean – a book can be more engaging, but at the same time, a film can be much more exciting and gripping than a book. It can use sounds and images and dialogue all at the same time. We use our different senses. And for many people, this is more entertaining than reading a book. Music can also make the film more interesting and memorable.

A: That's true. I think another important difference is that with a book, the chapters provide natural breaks in the story. This gives us time to think about what we have read. A film doesn't give us this opportunity.

B: Yeah, and also, of course, watching a film is usually a social experience. We generally watch a film with other people and then talk about it and share our opinions. But reading a book is more individual and personal. I think that's a really important difference.

A: Yes, I agree that reading is a less sociable activity. Although, book clubs are very popular these days. I guess that's a similar social experience.

B: And one more thing is that people usually say that the book is better than the film. Compared to the book, people often say they are disappointed by the film – especially if they have read the book first. However, I think in many cases people actually prefer the film.

A: Interesting. That's something that we can …

🔊 Lesson 8.3, Listening, Exercise E
8.8

1 Books allow the reader to use their imagination. With films, on the other hand, we see what the director and the actors want us to see.

2 With books, the story generally moves more slowly. With a film, though, the whole story needs to start and finish in 90 minutes.

3 We generally watch a film with other people … But reading a book is more individual and personal.

4 Reading is a less sociable activity. Although, book clubs are very popular these days.

5 People often say they are disappointed by the film. However, in many cases people actually prefer the film.

🔊 Lesson 8.3, Vocabulary, Exercise B
8.9

1 It was totally engaging and the acting was amazing.

2 I was, well, a bit bored by the end. It isn't very memorable, I'm afraid.

3 You won't be disappointed. The singing was incredible.

4 It's really gripping. And it's quite moving and sad, too.

UNIT 9

🔊 Lesson 9.2, Listening, Exercise B
9.3

Today's lecture is about philanthropy. Philanthropy, as you know, is the act of giving away a large amount of money which is used to benefit society.

There are many famous and not so famous people who have given away large amounts of money. Two of the 20th century's most famous philanthropists are John D Rockefeller and Andrew Carnegie. Rockefeller of course made his money from oil and Carnegie from the steel industry. Rockefeller gave away about $540 million before his death in 1937, and Carnegie gave away about $350 million. This was about 90 per cent of his wealth. And today there are many celebrities who have given money to charity. For example, the TV personality Oprah Winfrey has so far given away around half a billion dollars.

But perhaps today's most well-known philanthropists are Bill Gates and his wife Melinda, and Warren Buffett. Their main aim is to improve global health and to end poverty. And between them, they have already given away tens of billions of dollars. In 2010, they also created the Giving Pledge. The Giving Pledge asks …

🔊 Lesson 9.2, Listening, Exercise D
9.4

But perhaps today's most well-known philanthropists are Bill Gates and his wife Melinda, and Warren Buffett. Their main aim is to improve global health and to end poverty. And between them, they have already given away tens of billions of dollars. In 2010, they also created the Giving Pledge. The Giving Pledge asks the world's richest people to give away

at least half of their wealth in their lifetime. In its first ten years, many people agreed to this, including Facebook's Mark Zuckerberg, Virgin boss Richard Branson and Ann Gloag, who started the international transport group Stagecoach.

However, not everyone agrees that the Giving Pledge is a good thing, and some people have decided not to join. So, let's now look at five modern-day philanthropists that you may or may not have heard of.

First, Carlos Slim. Slim is a Mexican businessman and is one of the world's richest men. He made his money in telecommunications and is worth around $80 billion. He has so far given away about $8 billion. However, he has not joined the Giving Pledge because he disagrees with the approach of Bill Gates and Warren Buffet. Instead, he believes that education and jobs are the best way to end poverty.

Next, we have Sara Blakely, an American businesswoman. She recently became the world's youngest self-made female billionaire, and she was also the first woman to join the Giving Pledge. Her philanthropy focuses mainly on women and girls' education and career possibilities. She believes that if there are more women in powerful positions, this will make the world a better place.

Li Ka-shing is a Hong Kong businessman and has promised to give away a third of his $30 billion fortune. His aim is to promote education and health, but mainly in China. He has not joined the Giving Pledge. This is because he wishes to keep control of how and when he gives his money away.

Billionaire Meg Whitman was the president of eBay for ten years. She has said that she would refuse if she was invited to join the Giving Pledge. Instead, she has her own charity that focuses on the environment and education.

And finally, Azim Premji. Premji is one of India's richest people. He has joined the Giving Pledge and has already given away a quarter of his wealth. Premji's aim is to improve Indian school education and he has also set up a university which promotes educational thinking.

So, what do you think? Is the Giving Pledge a good thing? And what about philanthropy in general? What are the pros and the cons of this …

UNIT 10

🔊 Lesson 10.1, Listening, Exercise A
10.1

1: I travel and fly a lot for work, and this device means my bag is a lot lighter than it used to be. I can honestly say it's the best gadget I've ever bought. Before I got it, I always used to carry three or four heavy novels with me, but now I can fit hundreds into my coat pocket. I got the cheapest one, but the battery lasts for a long time and it has a dictionary. You can check words so much more quickly than in a paper dictionary. You just touch the word you don't know and it shows you the meaning.

2: This is definitely the most useful piece of technology I own. I don't enjoy driving in new cities or foreign countries, but I can find my way so much more easily than in the past thanks to this clever device. Obviously, it was more expensive than an old-fashioned paper map, but I don't regret buying it. My wife and I don't argue about which way to go anymore! It's very reliable – it never makes mistakes and even tells you when there is traffic or a speed camera.

3: This has to be the greatest invention of the 21st century! I take it everywhere with me and it is just the right size to fit in my bag. They are getting cheaper and cheaper – mine cost less than a lot of phones do these days. I don't have many apps on it, and most of the time, I just use it to go online or watch videos – the screen is so much bigger than on my phone. The best thing about it is that it starts so quickly. It's much faster and more convenient than my old laptop. The worst thing about it is that I now spend even more time online!

4: Every Saturday morning, I go to the city park and meet other … err … fans. We spend a lot of time talking about our favourite 'toys', as my girlfriend calls them, and arguing about which is the best, or which turns the most quickly, or a thousand other things! And of course we fly and race them. Mine is a bit heavier than some of them because it has a camera, but I can take pictures and films from the air. And of course, they are not just for fun – they have many possible uses. You know, delivering packages, helping the police, taking pictures for scientific research and so on.

UNIT 11

🔊 **Lesson 11.1, Listening, Exercise B**

11.3 **P = Presenter   M = Mike**

P: Welcome to this week's edition of the *Travel Show*. Today, we are joined by travel writer Mike Harold. A year ago, Mike decided to visit the Seven Natural Wonders of the World. Last week, he finally achieved his aim. Mike, tell us a little bit about the seven natural wonders.

M: Well, the Seven Natural Wonders of the World was the idea of the Seven Natural Wonders organisation. The organisation was created to promote and to protect the natural wonders of the world. Not just these seven, but many others as well.

P: So, how did they choose the seven places?

M: The decision was based on three main things. The places were chosen according to how unique the place is, how important it is and, finally, its pure natural beauty.

P: And why did you decide to visit them?

M: Well, I've always loved travelling and I like a challenge! As a travel writer, I thought this was an interesting thing to do professionally.

P: OK, so, what are the seven natural wonders?

M: First, I visited the Great Barrier Reef. The reef is 2600 km long and is located off the north-eastern coast of Australia. It's made of over 400 different kinds of coral and is the largest and most colourful coral reef in the world. It really was amazing.

After that, I went to the Grand Canyon, in the USA. It was chosen as a natural wonder because of its enormous size and incredible scenery. The canyon was created by the Colorado River, which you can see at the very bottom. It's the most popular of the seven natural wonders and is visited by over five million people a year.

The next place was the most difficult to get to, as it's located in the Himalayan mountain range.

P: Ahh, this has to be Mount Everest!

M: Yes, the highest place on Earth. I didn't go to the top, but I went to the base camp, which is at about 5000 metres. The views were unbelievable.

P: I can imagine. And where did you go next?

M: My fourth natural wonder was Victoria Falls. This, of course, is the famous waterfall on the Zambezi River in southern Africa. It is actually on the border of two countries, Zambia and Zimbabwe. The waterfall is almost two kilometres wide and over 100 metres high. It really was an incredible sight.

For numbers five and six, I travelled to Central and South America. The first is perhaps the least well known. It's the Paricutin volcano in Mexico.

P: Yes, I must admit, I've never heard of this.

M: Well, it was only formed in 1943, so it's quite new! It was also the first time modern science saw the creation of a volcano – and that's why it's a natural wonder. I was able to climb the volcano and walk around the crater and look inside. I then went to South America to see a more familiar 'wonder' – the bay and natural harbour of Rio de Janeiro in Brazil. The bay includes several islands and is surrounded by beautiful beaches and spectacular mountains with some fantastic views.

P: And I understand for the final natural wonder, you had some good luck.

M: Yes, I did. The final natural wonder I saw was the northern lights, or Aurora Borealis. I went to Iceland to see them. You can only see them at certain times of the year. And yes, I was very lucky. It really was amazing. And the perfect way to finish my challenge.

P: That sounds amazing! Thanks for sharing your journey with us.

UNIT 12

🔊 **Lesson 12.3, Listening, Exercise C**

12.4 **K = Kerry   A = Alex**

K: Hi, Alex, over here!

A: Hey, Kerry, long time no see! Isn't this amazing?!

K: What's going on? It's so busy!

A: YES! She did it.

K: Did what? What is this?

A: Well, it's an ad campaign for trainers. If you run past the ad, past the billboard, … if you run fast enough, you win a pair of trainers. It's clever, isn't it?

K: Oh, yeah. That's really cool. And yes, a really clever idea. What brand is it for? I can't see a logo or anything.

A: It's for Reebok, I think. Yes, look, there's the Reebok logo.

K: And what's 'fast enough'? Does it say how fast you have to run?

A: I'm not sure, but everyone seems to be going pretty quickly. Look, watch this guy … Go on. Go on! … Ah, no. He didn't do it.

K: You should have a go, Alex. Go on. Win yourself some new trainers. You're a fast runner, aren't you?

A: Actually, I'm not so sure I am, to be honest. I think I'll just watch.

K: We were talking about advertising in a class at university last week. Have you seen that one for vacuum cleaners? That's another clever one.

A: I'm not sure. What is it?

K: Well, they made a video of cars going through a tunnel. They then added a billboard to the background which showed a huge vacuum cleaner so that it looked like the cars were sucked into the vacuum cleaner.

A: Ah, I think I have seen that, actually.

K: And when they put the video online, people didn't know if it was real or just a video. It created a lot of interest and discussion. It was a very successful ad.

A: Ah, I see. I thought it was a real billboard.

K: No, it's just a video. They did it because they didn't have enough money for an actual billboard campaign.

A: Ah, that's really clever. Really original. And simple.

K: Yes, that's what we were talking about in the class last week – what makes a good ad. And it's exactly that in my opinion – something simple and original.

A: Yeah, and something with a clear message, something you can connect with. And a catchy slogan you can easily remember, you know, like McDonald's 'I'm lovin' it'.

K: Yeah, but I think the most important thing is that it catches your eye and gets your attention in the first place. Like this Reebok one.

A: Yeah, I agree. You know what, I think I might have a go at it. Shall I?

K: Yes, go for it. You can do it. Alex, Alex, Alex …

Macmillan Education
4 Crinan Street
London N1 9XW
A division of Springer Nature Limited

Companies and representatives throughout the world

Language Hub Pre-Intermediate Student's Book ISBN 978-1-380-01695-9
Language Hub Pre-Intermediate Student's Book with Student's App
ISBN 978-1-380-01690-4

Text, Design and Illustration © Springer Nature Limited 2019
Written by Daniel Brayshaw and Jon Hird.
With thanks to Edward Price and Carol Goodwright for additional authoring and to
Signature Manuscripts for the Grammar Hub pages.

The authors have asserted their right to be identified as the authors of this work in
accordance with the Copyright, Designs and Patents Act 1988.

The right of Sue Kay and Vaughan Jones to be identified as authors of the Speaking Pages
in this work has been asserted by them in accordance with the Copyright, Designs and
Patents Act 1988.

First published 2019

All rights reserved. No part of this publication may be reproduced, stored in a retrieval
system, or transmitted in any form or by any means, electronic, mechanical, photocopying,
recording, or otherwise, without the prior written permission of the publishers.

Designed by emc design ltd
Illustrated by Peter Lubach, Rasmus Juul, Rose Frith represented by Lemonade Illustration
Cover design by Restless
Cover image by Getty Images/Linghe Zhao
Picture research by Emily Taylor and Victoria Gaunt
Café Hub videos produced by Creative Listening.
Café Hub video scripts written by James and Luke Vyner.

Authors' acknowledgements

Daniel Brayshaw would like to thank the whole team for their invaluable support. Also, a
special thanks to Sue Kay and Vaughan Jones for all their advice and guidance, and to my
wife, Lucyna Brayshaw, for everything. Last but not least to Flash, our dog, for insisting I
take regular breaks from the desk. Good boy.

Jon Hird would like to thank the Macmillan Editorial team for their input, ideas and hard
work in shaping the content of the book.

The authors and publishers would like to thank the following for permission to reproduce
their photographs:

Alamy p150(2-band), Action Plus Sports Images p148(4), AF archive p76(5), Ian Allenden
p161, Alvey & Towers Picture Library p29(tr), Claudio Baldini p70(c), Axel Bueckert p69(3),
the box studio p155(c), Roger Cracknell 01/classic p160, Cultura p42(ken), 158, Cultura
Creative (RF) p82, John Davidson Photos p151(6), Deymos Photo p163(c), Stephen Dorey/
Bygone Images p166(bcl), Gioia Emidi p151(10.1-6), Jürgen Fälchle p96, GeoPic p22,
Photo Stock/National Geographic Creative p71, Givaga p69(7), Ted Horowitz p150(5),
Incamerastock p13(cl), jvphoto p52(9), itdarbs p169, Natallia Khlapushyna p69(8), Metta
image p69(2), Minden Pictures p104(t), NakoPhotography p42(bret), Losevsky Pavel
p150(1-band), Photo 12 p76(6), robertharding pp102(7), 150(7), Alexandre Rotenberg
p12(r), Unknown p84(tr), Michiel Vaartjes p147(4), Alex Witt p101; **Anastassia Elias** p74(d);
Bananastock p69 (background); **Banksy**, London, 2004 p75(d); **BrandX** p146(3); **Corbis**
pp36(tl), 53(1),102(3); **Bridgeman Images** Little Dancer, Aged 14, viewed from the back
(polychrome bronze, satin ribbon & wood) (see also 100777), Degas, Edgar (1834-1917)/
Private Collection/Photo © Christie's Images p75(a), Guitar on a Chair (oil on canvas), Gris,
Juan (1887-1927)/Private Collection/Photo © BEBA/AISA p150(4); Mona Lisa, c.1503-6 (oil
on panel), Vinci, Leonardo da (1452-1519) / Louvre, Paris, France p150(3); **Fancy** p56(1);
Getty Images pp17(a), 28-29(background), 42(lena), 47, 48-49(background), 52(3), 52(5),
52(10), 70(a,b),146(2, 4,5,f,g,h), 147(1,2), 152(bmr), 151(1), p152(bmr), AFP/Timothy A
Clary p51, AFP/John Macdougall p34(tl), AFP/Justin Tallis p44, Age footstock p13(bl),
16(clocks), Ajr images p42(helen), alexxl66 p166(bl), Daniel Allan p99(background),
Altrendo p17(d), Jacob Ammentorp Lund p33, Sally Anscombe pp17(c), 61, Archive
Photos p66(cr), ARB p66(tr), Raul Arboleda p66(cl), AYImages p163(cl), Baiterek Media
pp36(b), 37(b), 148(l), Jonny Baker p18(b), Scott Barbour p56(tl), Thomas Barwick p55(tl),
jez_bennett p105(e), Bettmann p84(l), p150(6), Katarzyna Bialasiewicz p52(7), Blend Images
pp14, 146(e), Tyler Boley p111, bopav p89(scarf), Hervé Bois/EyeEm p81, Suphawinee
Boonpeng p52(br), Caiaimage/Paul Bradbury p162(l), Adrienne Bresnahan p39(cr), Peter
Cade p114(t), iStockphoto/caimacanul p89(jeans), Colin Carter Photography p105(b),
Sandra Clegg p79(b), EyeEm/Pinghung Chen p69(c), Petar Chernaev p34(tr), China Photos
p41, Chombosan p35, L. Cohen/WireImage p152(t), The Print Collector/Print Collector
p150(1), Aurora Creative p148(8), Cultura pp56(5), 148(8), 152(bcr), Jim Cumming p105(d),
Jake Curtis p32, DaveLongMedia p147(7), Caiaimage/Robert Daly p153(l), DeAgostini
p102(5), Sofie Delauw p15, iStockphoto/demidoffaleks p89(jacket), domin_domin
p163(bl), David Doubilet p102(6), DNY59 p58(br), Dorling Kindersley p28(cl), Karin Dreyer
p59(toothache),E+ p148(2), iStockphoto/Eshma p163(br), FatCamera p163(cr), filadendron
p151(a), Antonio de Moraes Barros Filho P62(d), Fizkes p59(bad back), FotografiaBasica
p58-59(background), Franckreporter pp19, 18-19(background), fstop123 p39(br),
Mitchell Funk p148(7), www.galerie-ef.de p78(b), Katherine Gaines p151(4), Vladimir
Godnik p59(headache), Vincent van Gogh p75(c), Bill Greenblatt/AFP p66(b), GretaMarie
p48(b), grinvalds p112, Haag & Kropp p49(br), Izabela Habur p36(tcr), 65, iStockphoto
Thinkstock Images/halfbinz p151(7), istockphoto/StHelena p77, Hero Images pp2, 54(br),
72(background), Rolf Hicker p25(bl), Hindustan Times p55(bl), Blend Images/Ronnie
Kaufman/Larry Hirshowitz p151(e), Stephan Hoeck p154(r), Andrew Hounslea p52(bl),

Andrew Howe p89(background), icreative p89(shirt), The Image Bank pp42(t), 56(6), 148(6),
Image Source pp52(8), 146(1), Emma Innocenti p114(b), Chase Jarvis p148(1), iStockphoto
Thinkstock Images/johny007pan p118(background), Jokic p162(r), Mark Keelan p168(l),
Dorling Kindersley p89(skirt), Thomas Koidhis p102(1), Kozorog p36(tcl), Nicole Kucera
p102(4), Alexander Kuguchin p26(inset), Jason Langley p52(bcl), Liquidlibrary p86(t),
simonlong p151(2), Loop Images p31, Lumina Images p89(bl), MariusFM77 p56(2), Dawid
Markiewicz p62(f), Michael Marquand p59(br), Scott Masterton p168(m), Maurusone
p98(b), Maximilian Stock Ltd p52(bcr), Ian McKinnell p113, Mervana p30(travel icons),
Stuart Miller p146(g), Monkeybusinessimages p4(cr), Sabrina Bekeschus Monteiro/EyeEm
p108(background), Dean Mouhtaropoulos p54(t), Naumoid p147(6), Steve De Neef
p105(f), Nikada p13(cm), Michael Ochs Archives p62(o), OJO Images pp52(4), 59(stomache
ache), 152(br), iStockphoto/Thinkstock Images/Edu_Oliveros p69(4), Andrew Olney
p16(inset), Omgimages p146(d), James O'Neil p168(r), PeopleImages p64, Prasit photo p93,
oneinchpunch p83, Rudy Orozco P8(croissants), Pobytov p109(background), Perspectives
p1, Getty/PhotoDisc pp98(bcr), 166(cml), Zoltan Polgar p56(3), Martin Poole p151(c),
Prasit photo p167, Querbeet p147(3), Ranplett p38-39(background), Alex Raths p17(b),
Jack Reynolds p105(a), RG-vc p166(cr), Nicholas Roberts/AFP p84(br), Paul
Rojas p102(2), Kirill Rudenko p153(r), iStockphoto/scanrail p166(cmr), Daniel Schoenen
/LOOK-foto pp62(b), 63(b), Science Photo Library p8-9(background), Davide Seddio
p151(2), shayes17 p109(b), Jordan Siemens p21, Ariel Skelley p155(bl), skynesher p91,
SIphotography p53(2), spooh p151(5), Daniel Smith p151(f), by sonmez p118(b), SolStock
p92, James Steidl p147(5), kaisphoto p89(t-shirt), George Stroud p66(tr), studiocasper
p166(cl), Santi Sukarnjanaprai p103, Superstock p150(2), Sundown100 p26-27(b), Svetikd
p36(tr), Tarzhanova p89(dress), B. Tanaka p11, Tetra Images pp95, 151(b), Thinkstock
Images/Jupiterimages p150(8), Tom And Steve p52(6), Shomos Uddin p8(bl), Lise Ulrich
Fine Art Photography p105(c), Universal History Archive/UIG p75(b), Umbertoleporini
p12(l), Universal Images Group pp59(sore toe), 62(a), Betsie Van der Meer pp7, 148(3),
Vkuslandia p56(4), Wavebreakmedia p151(10.1-2), Fabian Wentzel p43, Westend61 pp46(b),
p151(10.1-5), Barry Willis p155(br), iStockphoto/Thinkstock Images/Steven Wynn p66(tl),
XiXinXing p146(h) Carol Yepes p151(d); **IMAGE 100** p40; **Image Source** p52(tl,tcl), 146(c);
Mihaela Noroc p4-5; **Mayer** McCann Erickson Slovakia p116(tr,cr,br); **Nature Picture
Library** Ingo Arndt p104(b); **Photodisc** p146(b); **Rex/Shutterstock** p165, David Boily
p86(b), Universal History Archive p76(2), Rob Latour/Variety p84(br), IMAS/JENNIFER
LAVERS HANDOUT/EPA p106(t,b), Lucasfilm/Bad Robot/Walt Disney Studios/Kobal p76(1),
Peter Schneider/Epa p157(tr); **Robertson Family Archive** pp24(bl,br), 25(br); **Robin Nilssen**,
Boon Photography. Creative Agency: Animal p116(tl,cl,bl); **Shutterstock**/Cubolabo p69(1),
Yulia Glam p62(e), Mark & Anna Wilson p152(bmr); **Solent News & Photo Agency** Stanislav
Aristov p74(c); **STOCKBYTE** p151(3); **Thinkstock** pp52(tr),146(a),148(5); **Scott Wade** p74(b);
Stockphoto Bulgac p155(b); **Max Zorn** p74(a); **123RF** Elnur Amikishiyev p62(c), Mile
Atanasov p163(a,b), Tyler Olson p151(10.1-4), Baiba Opule p69(5), Andriy Popov p151(10.1-
1), p154(l), Irina Roibu p69(6), Stockfotocz p151(10.1-3).

Commissioned photographs in the Café Hubs by Creative Listening.

The authors and publishers are grateful for permission to reprint the following copyright
material:

p36 Helliwell, J., Layard, R., & Sachs, J. (2016). World Happiness Report 2016. New York:
Sustainable Development Solutions Network. p42 Extract from 'One in five children just
want to be rich when they grow up' by Keith Perry. Originally published in The Telegraph,
5 August 2014. © Telegraph Media Group Limited 2014. Reprinted with permission of The
Telegraph. p106 Eriksen M, Lebreton LCM, Carson HS, Thiel M, Moore CJ, Borerro JC, et al.
(2014) Plastic Pollution in the World's Oceans: More than 5 Trillion Plastic Pieces Weighing
over 250,000 Tons Afloat at Sea. PLoS ONE 9(12): e111913. https://doi.org/10.1371/journal.
pone.0111913. p106 Extract from '38 million pieces of plastic waste found on uninhabited
South Pacific island' by Elle Hunt. Originally published in The Guardian, 15 May 2017.
© Copyright Guardian News & Media Ltd 2018. Reprinted with permission of The Guardian.
p107 Extract from 'Marine Conservation Society' © Marine Conservation Society (MCS)
2017. Reprinted with permission of Marine Conservation Society. p106 Significant
anthropogenic debris on remote island, Jennifer L. Lavers, Alexander L. Bond. Proceedings
of the National Academy of Sciences Jun 2017, 114 (23) 6052-6055; DOI: 10.1073/
pnas.1619818114. p112 Extract from 'Here is Facebook's guide to fake news' by Aatif
Sulleyman. Originally published in The Independent, 9 May 2017. © Independent Digital
News and Media Ltd 2017. Reprinted with permission of The Independent. p114 Extract
from 'How binge-watching has changed TV forever' by Sarah Rainey. Originally published
in The Telegraph, 22 January 2015. © Telegraph Media Group Limited 2015. Reprinted
with permission of The Telegraph. p164 Helliwell, J., Layard, R., & Sachs, J. (2017). World
Happiness Report 2017, New York: Sustainable Development Solutions Network.

These materials may contain links for third party websites. We have no control over, and
are not responsible for, the contents of such third party websites. Please use care when
accessing them.

The inclusion of any specific companies, commercial products, trade names or otherwise,
does not constitute or imply its endorsement or recommendation by Springer Nature
Limited.

Printed and bound in Dubai

2023 2022 2021 2020 2019
10 9 8 7 6 5 4 3 2 1